Haunted Texas Vacations

The Complete Ghostly Guide

Text and photography by
Lisa Farwell

Illustrations by
John Scott

Foreword by
Dennis William Hauck

WESTCLIFFE PUBLISHERS

www.westcliffepublishers.com

International Standard Book Number: 1-56579-383-8

Text, photographs, and illustrations copyright: Lisa Farwell, 2000. All rights reserved.

Editor: Kelly Anton
Design and Production: Craig Keyzer and Carol Pando

Published by:
Westcliffe Publishers, Inc.
P.O. Box 1261
Englewood, CO 80150
www.westcliffepublishers.com

Printed by: Mountain West Printing Ltd.

Library of Congress Cataloging-in-Publication Data:
Farwell, Lisa, 1966-
    Haunted Texas vacations : the complete ghostly guide / text and photography by Lisa
  Farwell ; illustrations by John Scott ; foreword by Dennis William Hauck.
      p. cm.
    Includes bibliographical references and index.
    ISBN 1-56579-383-8
      1. Ghosts--Texas. 2. Haunted places--Texas. I. Title.

BF1472.U6 F375 2000
133.1'09764--dc21   00-040429

For more information about other fine books and calendars from Westcliffe Publishers, please contact your local bookstore, call us at 1-800-523-3692, write for our free color catalog, or visit us on the Web at **www.westcliffepublishers.com**.

Please Note: The author and publisher disclaim any liability for shock, heart attack, injury, or damage caused by the sighting of any ghosts or spirits mentioned in this book.

ACKNOWLEDGMENTS

Writing this book has been one of the most wonderful learning experiences of my life. It would not have been possible without the love and support of my family and friends, who listened endlessly to my ghost stories and pretended that they had heard them only once.

I thank my mother, Gayle Farwell, and my late father, Tom Farwell, who taught me to love books, traveling, and exploring the unknown. Thank you to my sister and best friend, Lara Farwell-Griffith, and my brother-in-law, Darrell Griffith, who believed in me throughout this long process and love Halloween and "things that go bump in the night" as much as I do.

Photo by Lara Farwell-Griffith

I'm grateful to all my friends who provided endless encouragement, especially Pamela Gursoy, Robin Scott, Dawn Adair, and Michael Begeman, who gave me the strength and inspiration to follow my dream. Marsha Walker and Jill Humphreys nurtured me and helped me focus. Thanks to Susan Tormollen, who understood the demands of my writing schedule and allowed me to work around it. Thanks also to Tomi Hotarinen, who provided emotional support during the last crucial months of finishing this book.

I'm indebted to John Scott for contributing his wonderful illustrations and for being such an enthusiastic work partner. Veteran ghost hunters and writers Dennis William Hauck and Docia Schultz Williams provided valuable, reliable research and advice. Linda Doyle and Jenna Samelson with Westcliffe Publishers believed in this book and took the time to mentor me through an unfamiliar process.

The members of the Capital City Ghost Research Society gave their time and trusted opinions. Richard Foster's research assistance was invaluable and helped bring many of these ghost tales to light. Many thanks to Jeanine Plumer, Pat Roeling, Jeff Johnson, and Martin Leal as well.

Lastly, thanks to the dozens of helpful folks I met on my haunted vacations who retold their ghost stories in a sincere and candid manner—especially Jodi Breckenridge, Carol Meissner, Ernesto Malacara, Vernon Randle, Randy Woods, and Edward Weissbard.

Lisa Farwell
Austin, Texas
May 4, 2000

TABLE OF CONTENTS

FOREWORD

I first met Lisa Farwell in 1998. Ghost researcher Richard Foster, who supplied many of the cases presented in my book, *The National Directory of Haunted Places*, invited me to speak before Austin's Capital City Ghost Research Society about my investigations into the paranormal. Lisa was president of the organization, and I was impressed by her intensity and intelligence from the moment I met her. Her interest and belief in paranormal phenomena was obvious, yet she had the ability to step back and keep her objectivity, using her keen observation and deductive abilities to cut through the nonessential details and get to the heart of the matter. These are traits I much admire. How difficult it would be for anyone to put anything over on this paranormal investigator! Sifting through all the hoaxes, mistaken identities, and just plain wishful thinking is the hardest part of this job, but Lisa has that special combination of intellect, intuition, and frankness that makes it look easy.

The meeting took place in the main conference room at the haunted Driskill Hotel in downtown Austin. The ghost of the Driskill is said to be the flirtatious spirit of a Texas man who is still attracted to pretty women. Many female guests have been harassed by his poltergeist, which likes to play jokes by hiding personal belongings in weird places or scattering belongings all over the room. Johnette Napolitano, robust vocalist for the rock band Concrete Blonde, encountered the playful spirit when the group stayed at the Driskill during a Texas tour. The ghost kept rearranging things in Napolitano's room and she became a believer in Driskill's nonpaying guest. The singer later spoke about her experiences in an MTV interview and wrote a ballad called the "Ghost of a Texas Ladies Man."

However, he is not the only ghost of the Driskill. Long-time employee Arthur Cicchese took us on a tour of the building and related many of his own strange experiences at the Driskill. He also pointed out other areas of the old hotel, such as the basement and ballroom, which seem to have ghostly activity. One of the elevators in particular has the habit of making unsolicited trips to the top floor, which, incidentally, is where our Texas ladies' man liked to entertain his guests. But the highlight of the Driskill that night was Lisa Farwell's open and forthright presence. Always connected to the attitudes and feelings of everyone around her, she knew how to direct the group's energies toward something positive and truthful.

You can find that same gently guiding presence in Lisa's writing, too. You'll find her special combination of intellect, intuition, and frankness in every one of the cases presented in this book. She has combed the great state of Texas for its best ghost cases and brings them together in one volume. From the Louisiana border to El Paso, from the Gulf of Mexico to the Amarillo grasslands, the real hauntings of the Lone Star State are all here. These are all actual places, and she provides directions, addresses, and phone numbers of people to contact once you arrive. Lisa puts the paranormal happenings in true perspective by providing a short history of the area, including its traumas and triumphs. She even includes some "less spooky" things to do in each area, so you can at least get a flavor for the place, even if you don't encounter any of its spectral residents.

Moreover, Lisa captures the moods and ambience of these haunted spots. I've always believed there is a deep-lying connection between human consciousness and paranormal events. The attitudes of people and their unspoken connection to a location can elicit the unseen forces there. Indian shamans knew this, and we can feel it at their sacred sites to this day. Lisa knows how to capture this spirit of place. I have seen other haunted guidebooks describe East Texas as the earliest settled area, full of living history that is bound to generate a few ghosts. Compare that typically touristy approach with that of Lisa Farwell's:

> *The Piney Woods region of East Texas is filled with darkened forests where nature lovers can walk ankle-deep through decaying pine needles beside still lakes. Towering trees dripping with Spanish moss block out the sun and create all sorts of wonderfully hidden nooks and crannies where the spirits of long-dead Caddo Indians roam. Native East Texans speak with soft drawls, love the spicy food inspired by their Cajun neighbors' cuisine, and hold generations-old beliefs in the ghosts that inhabit their forests, towns, and homes.*

Need I say more?

—Dennis William Hauck

INTRODUCTION

Have you ever bumped into a ghost on your way to the bathroom? Ever had a romantic candlelight dinner with a friendly specter? How about spending an evening camped out in a secluded cemetery waiting for a lonely, hoarse sigh to register on your tape recorder?

If you answered "yes" or maybe "no, but I sure would like to" to any or all of the above questions, this book may just become one of your most-treasured, dog-eared tomes. *Haunted Texas Vacations: The Complete Ghostly Guide* is intended for those with a healthy and lighthearted interest in all things supernatural. Staying in a haunted hotel, only to awaken in the middle of the night to an icy chill that sweeps into the room and settles next to you is admittedly not for everyone. But those of us who love a good ghost story—and perhaps even fancy ourselves as ghost hunters—welcome these experiences with just the mildest of shivers.

People love to experience haunted houses because they can be in the presence of something otherworldly, possibly even participate in a paranormal experience, and then return to the familiarity of home. One researcher described a visit to a haunted house as similar to visiting a zoo—you can see the tiger, but you know it won't jump into your backseat and come home with you. Your next vacation can be a journey of paranormal possibilities. I invite you to experience the unknown in the most haunted cities in Texas.

—Lisa Farwell

HOW TO USE THIS BOOK

I wrote *Haunted Texas Vacations: The Complete Ghostly Guide* because I love taking haunted vacations and want to share some of these wonderful, sometimes scary places with fellow travelers and ghost enthusiasts. Visiting the locations listed in this book will increase your likelihood of having a paranormal experience in some of the most historically interesting places in Texas.

This guide includes a variety of haunted vacation destinations, some in big cities, others in small towns or the countryside. The six geographical regions of the state are represented: West Texas and the Panhandle, the endless North Texas prairie, the piney woods of East Texas, the windswept Gulf Coast, the rolling hill country of Central Texas, and the lonely plains of South Texas. At the beginning of each regional section, there is a map showing the locations of the haunted places in that region of Texas. You will also find the names of the towns listed in alphabetical order in the Haunted Locations box at the beginning of each section.

Whether you want to spend a weekend close to home hunting ghosts or a week in a far-away city experiencing the paranormal, this book has a vacation destination just for you. Ghosts love to frequent old hotels and houses, saloons, theaters, cemeteries, churches, missions, forts, battlefields, and even schools. These are all places that act as "storehouses" for past emotional energy, positive and negative, from the many people who have lived and died there. *Haunted Texas Vacations* chronicles more than 150 locations and their respective ghosts. You can spend every moment of your trip exposing yourself to potential paranormal manifestations by staying in haunted hotels and bed-and-breakfast inns and eating in haunted restaurants and taverns, as well as touring haunted museums and historical landmarks or taking local "ghost tours." In this way, you'll make yourself available to catch a glimpse of one of these sometimes bold, sometimes elusive spirits in their place of residence. All haunts are divided into the following categories and marked by icons:

Haunted Hotels
The paranormal potential in these old hotels runs high.

Spooky Sidelines
The haunted Lone Star State has ghost tours in several towns.

Bed & Breakfasts with a Boo
Once family estates, these bed-and-breakfasts include a possible paranormal prankster.

Less Spooky Things To Do
For those who desire a little less excitement during their vacation, other Texas treasures are listed.

Restaurant Revenants
A delightful gastronomic—and possibly, supernatural—experience awaits you at these restaurants.

Elusive Boos
These locations are rumored ghost hangouts.

Spirited Buildings and Houses
Now housing public offices, museums, schools, and theaters, many of these structures have witnessed memorable triumphs and tragedies.

Ghost Clubs
Regional ghost clubs are listed, along with contact information.

Ghostly Missions and Churches
These places of reverence harbor many dark mysteries of the past.

Most Haunted Location
The dapper skeleton announces each region's most haunted location.

Frightening Forts and Battlegrounds
Negative energy abounds in these locations of past violence.

 The "shiver scale" distinguishes the locations with historically high paranormal manifestations. The range is from one shiver, representing minimal haunting activity, to five shivers, representing a location having so many specters that you'd be hard-pressed not to trip over one or two while on your haunted Texas vacation!

Ghosts of the Great Outdoors
Ghosts can be attached to their place of death or burial rather than the buildings they occupied in life.

WHAT IS A GHOST?

Is there life after death? This is perhaps humankind's oldest question and most sought-after answer. We are intrigued by the idea of seeing a ghost for several reasons. For some it is confirmation of life after death. Often a culture's belief in spirits is the basis for its religious beliefs. For thrill-seekers, a ghost sighting produces an adrenaline rush equivalent to that of skydiving or bungee jumping. For others it is a glimpse into an unknown world that cannot be explained by traditional science.

Premier ghost hunter Dr. Hans Holzer characterizes three phenomena that occur when a person dies under traumatic, tragic circumstances. The first is the most common form of passing: The transition from the physical human being to spirit being happens without difficulty and without the need to stay on Earth. The individual accepts death and moves on.

The second phenomenon occurs with ghosts—those individuals who don't realize they've died or refuse to accept their deaths and remain "hung up" in the physical world, unable to participate or function as living people. Often, they were victims in life and have unfinished business here on Earth. Ghosts remind us of the errors we are capable of committing and the traps we can lay for ourselves in life that may haunt us in death.

The light beams streaking around this private Texas cemetery were invisible to the naked eye when this photograph was taken.

Some ghosts stick around because they don't want to leave a beloved house they once owned, a painting they don't want to part with, or a loved one who is grieving. Dr. Holzer calls this type "stay behind" ghosts, who choose to stay in a familiar place where they felt comfortable in life. Reasons such as these and many more can tie a ghost to the Earth for varying lengths of time, some haunting the same location for hundreds or thousands of years and others appearing once or twice and moving on.

Most ghosts are rather shy and make infrequent

The ghostly mist hovering around this haunted church's rooftop was captured with a digital camera.

appearances, preferring to pace darkened hallways and whisper in empty rooms. Others are quite mischievous, raising a ruckus in the attic and hiding car keys from the living. Some spirits return regularly on the anniversary and to the location of their deaths.

The third phenomenon, called a psychic imprint, is very much like a photograph or film of an actual event that replays again and again throughout time. Imprints are lifeless and do not represent an actual presence at the time of observation. Some paranormal researchers theorize that certain weather and atmospheric conditions, such as humidity and barometric pressure, can influence chances of witnessing a "replay." This is interesting support for the stereotypical notion of ghosts' fondness for roaming on "dark and stormy nights." Our moon's phases also seem to affect the probability of a sighting, with increased supernatural activity occurring during the full moon.

Throughout the ghostly accounts in this guide, I refer to two types of spiritual energy manifestations captured in photographs called "orbs" and "vortices." An orb is the basic energy pattern of the spirit world and is the most commonly photographed phenomenon. Orbs show up on film as glowing, bubble-like shapes. Many researchers believe these orbs to be the life force—or energy—that survives the death of the physical body. Ghost hunters theorize that vortices consist of dozens of orbs working together as one force. This phenomenon shows up in photographs as columns of light or a swirling collection of orbs.

Sightings are rare but tantalizing and depend on each individual's psychic sensitivity. Ten percent of the population claims to have seen a ghost. An eerie glowing light in an abandoned building, a whiff of rose-scented perfume, a murmured word—these are the things we wait hours in the dark to experience. When you hear the floor creak or catch the glimpse of something out of the corner of your eye (most ghosts appear for 15 seconds or less), remember that others have passed this way before and we are not alone.

GHOST HUNTING

 Every good ghost hunter knows that successful ghost hunting is a combination of being in the right place at the right time, a little bit of patience, and a whole lot of luck. This book will increase your chances of being in the right place. The rest is up to you. Follow these tips to improve your chances of catching a ghost in the act:

Distract yourself. Instead of straining your eyes in a darkened hotel room, read a book. By doing so, you're taking your mind off your surroundings and increasing your chances of seeing a ghost. Some scientists think that only by removing yourself from the real world can you open yourself up to paranormal experiences.

Don't think about ghosts. Almost everyone who has ever seen a ghost has reported that the encounter happened unexpectedly. The key is to distract your mind from what's happening around you so you can see the ghost who may be there.

Go to bed. One-fourth of all people who see ghosts see them immediately after they awaken. Consequently, the largest percentage of ghost sightings takes place while a person is in bed.

Trust your instincts. If you sense that someone or something is behind you or on the other side of a door, don't ignore that sensation. Feeling that you're not alone in an empty room or a general sense of uneasiness may indicate a spirit's presence.

Use all your senses. Drops in temperature often precede a ghostly appearance. If your hair suddenly stands on end, you may be in the presence of something paranormal. Lights and ceiling fans may turn on and off—phantoms often affect the electricity in a haunted building. Scents associated with the deceased in life, such as cigar smoke or lilac perfume, can herald the approach of an otherworldly visitor.

Spend some time in the bathroom. Ghosts love water. They have been known to turn water faucets in sinks and showers on and off and flush toilets. Throughout the pages of this book, you will find many such water-loving wraiths.

Feel lucky. Most people understandably report that a healthy fear of the unknown accompanied their paranormal experience. This is a natural reaction to a ghost sighting. Glimpsing a ghost should also be an exciting and exhilarating experience. It will remain with you for life and will be a favorite topic at dinner parties. If and when you do see something unexplainably otherworldly, feel fortunate. Remember—ghosts were people too.

A GHOST HUNTER'S TOOL KIT

Along with the sunscreen, travel sewing kit, road maps—and of course, *Haunted Texas Vacations: The Complete Ghostly Guide*—you may want to pack a ghost hunter's tool kit to take with you on your haunted vacation. These tools will help you document and scientifically record your paranormal experiences while on the road.

Cameras: A 35mm manual-focus camera loaded with high-speed film (Kodak's Gold Max works well) for shooting in low light. Bring a second camera loaded with infrared color film or infrared black-and-white film. To shoot with infrared film, you need to follow a special technique, and it can get a bit tricky. With the color film, you'll need to purchase a #12 yellow gel filter to screw on over your lens. Use a #25 red gel filter when shooting black-and-white film. You must load your infrared film in total darkness and place a piece of black electrician's tape over the small window on the back of most cameras. You can find the film, supplies, and advice on shooting with infrared film at a professional camera supply store. You will need to take your infrared film to a professional lab for processing.

In addition, many ghost chasers swear by the results they've achieved using digital cameras to record ghostly images. Using a couple of different types of cameras is always a good idea and presents especially compelling evidence when you capture the same anomaly on two different types of film.

Compass: A compass for specifying directions and to keep you from getting lost in dark cemeteries.

Electromagnetic Field Meter: An electromagnetic field (EMF) meter for tracking ghosts by measuring their electromagnetic fields. New research in this area has provided dramatic results. Dave Oester, president of the International Ghost Hunters Society (IGHS), says, "Many ghost researchers have reported magnetic fields as anomalous energy fields associated with paranormal activity, such as cold spots, sensations of electrostatic energy discharges, and anomalous images captured on film."

It seems that all ghosts will generate a magnetic field that surrounds them while they are in this physical domain. This distortion of the EMF field is physically detectable with a magnetic field meter.

You can purchase EMF meters from the International Ghost Hunters Society by contacting the Society at www.ghostweb.com; 541-548-4418; or Dave Oester, IGHS, 12885 SW North Rim Road, Crooked River Ranch, OR 97760.

Lights: Flashlight, lanterns, and candles—bring at least two of each in case one fails, and don't forget kerosene, matches, and plenty of extra batteries. Batteries can fail and cold drafts can cause candles to extinguish, usually just when you need them the most.

Paper and Pen: Paper and pen for taking good notes while the experience is still fresh in your mind. You can complete your ghost report the next day while referring to your notes from the night before. Graph paper might come in handy for mapping out the haunted location. In Appendix I you'll find a "Ghost Investigative Report" to copy and bring along with you to record your paranormal investigations.

Tape Measure: A tape measure or ruler so you can accurately record location dimensions and distances on your "Ghost Investigative Report."

Tape Recorder: A tape recorder with an external microphone and music-quality cassette tapes. This tool will help you capture on tape ghostly sounds called electronic voice phenomena or EVP. You may not hear anything during your investigation, yet capture otherworldly sounds on your tape recorder. EVP usually consists of incomplete sentences and has a harsh, whispering quality.

Thermometer: A thermometer to record the drop in temperature that often occurs when spirits are present. For a "high-tech" ghost-hunting tool, check out the infrared thermal scanner. This sophisticated tool aids in tracking anomalous "cold spots," which can be 25 to 60 degrees colder than the surrounding ambient air temperature. The scanner uses infrared technology to measure the surface temperature of material without touching it. You can find the infrared thermal scanner on the IGHS (Ghostweb) website (www.ghostweb.com/index.html).

Now that you're all packed and ready to go, I hope your vacation is filled with icy drafts, hairs standing on end, and feelings of not being alone in your room late at night.

Happy ghost hunting!

REGIONAL MAP OF TEXAS

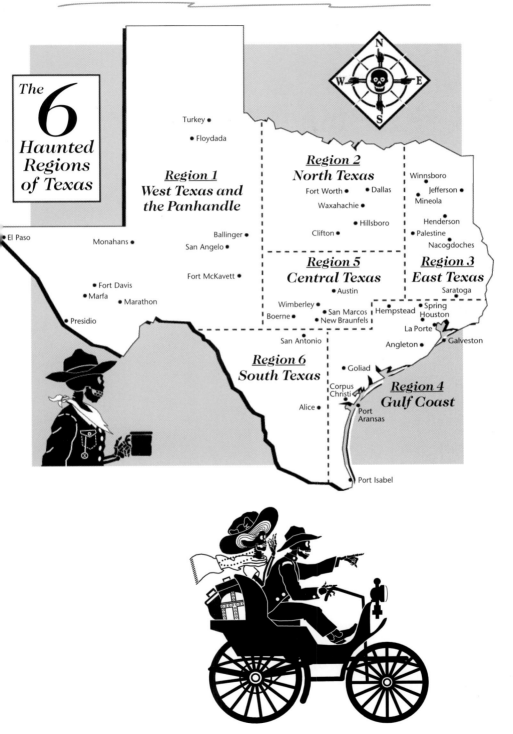

The **6** Haunted Regions of Texas

Region 1
West Texas and the Panhandle

Region 2
North Texas

Region 3
East Texas

Region 4
Gulf Coast

Region 5
Central Texas

Region 6
South Texas

Turkey
Floydada

El Paso
Monahans
Ballinger
San Angelo
Fort McKavett
Fort Davis
Marfa
Marathon
Presidio

Fort Worth
Dallas
Waxahachie
Hillsboro
Clifton

Winnsboro
Jefferson
Mineola
Henderson
Palestine
Nacogdoches
Saratoga

Austin
Wimberley
Boerne
San Marcos
New Braunfels
Hempstead
Spring
Houston
La Porte
Galveston
Angleton

San Antonio

Goliad
Corpus Christi
Alice
Port Aransas

Port Isabel

Region 1

Ghosts of Wild West Texas & the Panhandle

West Texas and the Panhandle have more than their fair share of empty highways that seem to stretch endlessly. Tumbleweeds, roadrunners, and, some say, spirits, frequent these lonesome roads in the form of the oldest and most famous ghost lights in the world at Marfa. Spectral soldiers live among the ruins of deserted forts that dot the landscape. This is a harsh land. The men and women who tamed this desolate area of the state, when the Comanche and Apache Indian tribes still roamed its windy plains, craggy mesas, and desert valleys, were some tough characters. Likewise, their ghosts are definitely not the shy, shrinking violet types!

From the historic streets of El Paso, the largest city in West Texas and the most haunted city in this region, to the spirits who haunt the beautifully appointed hostelry, the Gage Hotel in Marathon, the ghosts of the wild, Wild West provide interesting investigation opportunities galore.

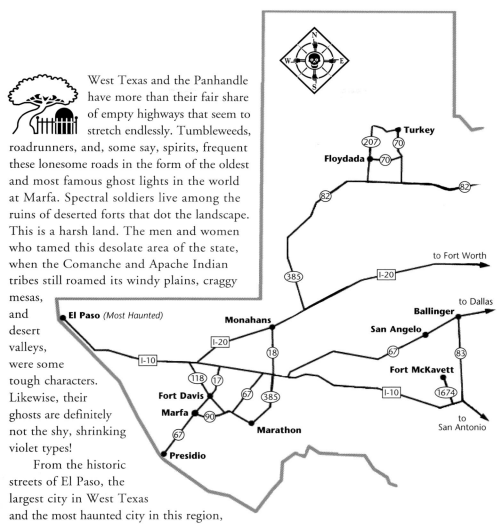

HAUNTED LOCATIONS

Ballinger's Boos

Ballinger is located east of San Angelo at the junction of Highways 83 and 67. Established in 1886 as Hutchins City, Ballinger is the present seat of Runnels County and is primarily an agricultural community.

RESTAURANT REVENANTS

Texas Grill 👐😟😟👐

700 Hutchins Ave., Ballinger, TX 76821 • 915-365-3314

Description and History

The Texas Grill is an old-fashioned café located right in the middle of town on the main drag. It occupies a building constructed in 1901, and was originally a saloon. The onset of Prohibition closed the bar in 1913. It was used as a department store for a time and was converted into a restaurant in 1954. Larry and Joyce Sikes have leased the building and operated the Texas Grill since 1989. The

A true ladies' man—er, ghost—"Norton" inhabits the Texas Grill.

Texas Grill is open Sunday through Wednesday from 5 a.m.-11 p.m. and serves delicious American and Mexican favorites such as hamburgers and enchiladas.

Ghostly Visitations

The restaurant is a famous local haunt and several television stations and newspapers in the area have done stories about the ghost called "Norton," who inhabits the Texas Grill.

Paranormal activity occurs on a regular

Most Haunted Areas:
The upper floor, kitchen, hallway leading to the restrooms, and the back dining room

basis at the old café. Employees and patrons have seen flying forks and levitating tortilla chip baskets. The owners have been in the front dining room after closing and heard the refrigerator doors repeatedly opening and closing—obviously, this ghost is hungry! Joyce has heard someone walking around upstairs above the ladies restroom at 5 a.m. when she was alone in the restaurant. During a Christmas party in the back dining room, many group photos were taken. Norton showed up in a couple as a white, misty figure wearing a broad-brimmed hat.

Most of the activity occurs along a long, dark hallway leading to the men's and ladies' rooms. Many have seen dark shadows passing down the hallway with no explanation. The strong smell of a man's cologne lingers in the hallway long after closing. Once, a pretty, young employee was pinched on the behind while walking down this hallway to the ladies' room. Norton sure does have a way with the ladies!

After a waitress's three-year-old grandson saw a man in this hallway and a diner reported he'd been following a man down the hall to the bathroom when he disappeared into thin air, the Sikes' daughter consulted a psychic about the entity inhabiting their restaurant. The psychic claimed the male spirit haunting the Texas Grill was running from the law. Prior to 1901, he was living in a shack on the land where the Texas Grill stands today. Authorities discovered his hideout and shot him in cold blood. Paranormal research tells us this is the perfect prelude to a haunting. Ever since, Norton has been pacing and pinching his nights away at the Texas Grill!

 ## Less Spooky Things To Do In Ballinger

Water lovers should plan a trip to beautiful **Lake Ivie**, only 20 miles southeast of Ballinger on FM 1929, just east of Highway 83. **The Cross**, commissioned by Jim and Doris Studer, attracts thousands every year. The monument stands 100 feet tall and weighs 50 tons. Doris Studer commissioned it to show her thanks for all the blessings bestowed upon the couple since moving to Ballinger from Florida in 1988. Booklovers will enjoy a visit to the **Carnegie Library**, which became a Texas Landmark in 1962. Completed in 1911, the building is one of 34 libraries funded by Andrew Carnegie. The **Santa Fe Depot** was built in 1911 by the A, T, & SF Railroad and was renovated in 1983. Today the depot houses the city offices and the Ballinger Chamber of Commerce. On the last weekend of April, Ballinger hosts the **Texas State Festival of Ethnic Cultures and Arts & Crafts Show**, which is held on the largest landscaped courthouse lawn in Texas. The festival features the **Colorado River Bike Fest**, a large parade, ethnic-food booths, handmade arts and crafts from 100 artists, live entertainment, and a dance with local bands on Saturday night.

For more information on Ballinger, contact:
Ballinger Chamber of Commerce
7th Railroad Ave., Ballinger, TX 76821
915-365-2333 • 915-365-5611
www.ballingertx.org

Western Wraiths of El Paso

Most Haunted City in West Texas

El Paso is located in the extreme western tip of Texas on I-10. The name El Paso is a shortened version of *El Paso del Rio del Norte*, meaning "the pass of the north," the name given to the pristine river valley by conquistador Don Juan de Oñate more than four centuries ago. There is virtually no recorded history of the El Paso/Juarez area before the arrival of Spanish missionaries in the late 1500s. Indians lived in the valley along the Rio Grande for hundreds of years due to the presence of the Rio Grande River and the natural pass through the surrounding mountains.

El Paso has seen the westward expansion of pioneer America, the coming of the railroads to the western frontier, the days of outlaws and gunslingers, Indian wars and Indian peace, and the births of the U.S. Cavalry and the Texas Rangers. In 1873, El Paso became a city —a brazen city that soon entered the rambunctious era from 1881 to 1887 known as the Wild West. El Paso certainly hosted its fair share of marauding gunfighters, dangerous cattle rustlers, and rowdy saloons—all in all, a perfect setting for ensuring the presence of ghosts!

HAUNTED HOTELS

Camino Real Hotel 👻👻👻

101 S. El Paso St., El Paso, TX 79901 • 915-534-3000

Description and History

Built in 1912, the Camino Real is El Paso's most historic and luxurious downtown hotel and is listed on the National Historical Register. The hotel has hosted such diverse guests as Pancho Villa and President Taft. Its most stunning feature is the original Tiffany glass dome that crowns the lobby. The Camino Real is the only 4-Diamond hotel and restaurant in the El Paso area and offers ghost hunters 359 elegantly appointed rooms and suites. Amenities include a health club, outdoor swimming pool, four restaurants and bars, nonsmoking rooms, and 24-hour room service. For more information about the hotel, visit the website at www.caminoreal.com/elpaso/default_i.htm.

Ghostly Visitations

The Camino Real Hotel is said to house a sad spirit in its dark basement. Security guards and cleaning staff have spotted a lady in a white gown with a melancholy expression wandering the floor's dark recesses.

> **Most Haunted Area:**
> *The basement*

SPIRITED BUILDINGS AND HOUSES

El Paso High School 👶👶👶

800 E. Schuster Ave., El Paso, TX 79902 • 915-533-6851

Description and History

El Paso High School is the oldest operating high school in El Paso. It sits on a mountainside at the foot of the Franklin Mountains, overlooking the central portion of the city and its boundary with Mexico. Designed as a classic revival building by Trost and Trost architects, the high school was completed in 1916. The brick and terra-cotta building is reminiscent of Greek and Roman architecture.

Ghostly Visitations

Around town, El Paso High School is known as a haunted site. Over the years, many school staff members and students have heard the sounds of a seemingly large group of people talking and laughing when no one was in the building.

> **Most Haunted Areas:**
> *The auditorium and fourth floor classroom*

Returning to the school after an out-of-town track meet, a coach and his team heard the sounds of a large crowd cheering and applauding coming from the school's auditorium. There was just one problem—it was 3 o'clock in the morning! When they opened the large doors to the auditorium, the curious athletes found an empty, dark room. As soon as they closed the doors, the cheers and clapping resumed. Exhausted and puzzled, the team decided to call it a night.

Some of the staff working late at night have heard footsteps and rustling feet. In addition to the auditory manifestations, shadowy figures have been seen walking the dim hallways.

El Paso Ghost Research investigators Edward Weissbard and Heidi Crabtree interviewed an El Paso High teacher who sometimes hears a scream near one of the windows of her fourth-floor classroom. Rumor has it that a young woman jumped out of this window to her death in the 1930s.

The El Paso Ghost Research team held an investigation of the building in October 1999, but recorded no unusual results. Not to worry. Everybody—even ghosts—needs a break from school now and then!

The Magoffin Home 👶👶

1120 Magoffin Ave., El Paso, TX 79901 • 915-533-5147

Description and History

East of downtown El Paso and south of I-10, the Magoffin Home is located in Magoffin State Historical Park, just east of the intersection of Octavia Street and Magoffin Avenue. Pioneer Joseph Magoffin constructed the Magoffin Home for his large family in 1875.

Magoffin family members may still wander their ancestral home in death.

The 19-room adobe home is built of sun-dried brick and is a prime example of Territorial-style architecture, a building style developed in the Southwest during the mid-1800s.

Joseph Magoffin was very active in civic and political affairs during the turbulent period that saw El Paso emerge from a raw frontier town into a bustling commercial center. Magoffin's public offices included Justice of the Peace, County Judge, and Federal Customs Inspector-Collector for the Port of El Paso. He was elected mayor of the city four times: 1881, 1883, 1897, and 1899. During his tenure in city government, virtually all the utility companies were started, the first schools and hospitals were built, and the fire department was established. As a result of Magoffin's high social standing, his home became the social center of El Paso for many years. The Magoffins threw elaborate dinner parties, receptions, dances, and concerts inside their beautiful home.

In 1976, the City of El Paso and the State of Texas jointly purchased the Magoffin Home. Since the home's purchase, the Texas Parks and Wildlife Department has operated the site. Docent-guided tours provide information on the three generations of Magoffins that occupied the home. The Magoffin Home is open from 9 a.m.-4 p.m. seven days a week. The home is closed on Thanksgiving, Christmas, and New Year's days. There is a tour fee (group rates are available).

In addition to the guided tours of the home, the Casa Magoffin Companeros (Friends of the Magoffin Home) host several annual events at the home, including a Victorian Tea in May and a Holiday Tea and Reception in December. With respect for the social tradition, portions of the home are available for receptions, dinners, and special events. The Casa Magoffin Companeros also manages the park gift shop, which specializes in books on local and regional topics. Call 915-533-5147 for more information or visit the website at www.tpwd.state.tx.us/park/magoffin/magoffin.htm.

Ghostly Visitations

Many visitors and staff members have reported seeing transparent figures walking through rooms of the old house. Footsteps are often heard without a traceable source. Are

these the spirits of deceased Magoffin family members who refuse to leave their beloved home? The most frequently reported paranormal event is an old chair rocking all by itself in the living room of the adobe.

The intrepid El Paso Ghost Research team detected the undeniable scent of roses throughout the Magoffin home during an investigation. A former family member was known to have loved and worn rose petal perfume during her lifetime. Perhaps she is one of the souls who wanders the hallways of this beautiful historic home.

 **Less Spooky Things To Do In El Paso**

While on our side of the border, check out a couple of El Paso's 15 museums, including the **Fort Bliss Museum**, which is a reproduction of the Magoffinsville Post from 1854 to 1868. The **El Paso History Museum** displays the colorful history of Indians, conquistadors, vaqueros, cowboys, and cavalrymen who settled the Wild West. The family-oriented **El Paso Art Museum** features film and video programs, lectures, gallery talks, concerts and performances, workshops, and storytelling sessions. Take in the beautiful local scenery with a visit to the **Wilderness Park Museum**. A mile-long nature trail offers breathtaking views of the mountains and valleys. You'll find three of the country's oldest missions on the **Mission Trail. Missions Ysleta, Socorro**, and **Presidio Chapel San Elceario** are located just 15 minutes east of downtown El Paso. **Concordia Cemetery**, located just northwest of the intersection of I-10 and Highway 54, was started in 1856. By the 1880s, the graveyard had become the main burial site for El Paso. A section of the cemetery served as El Paso's "Boot Hill," where towns used to bury outlaws who were killed in gunfights or were hanged. This is where the infamous gunfighter John Wesley Harding is buried. Just across the border from **Juarez, Mexico**, El Paso is "at the corner of Texas and Old Mexico." A visit to Mexico brings the flavor of another country into your vacation. Juarez is known for its great bargains, authentic Mexican food, and the traditional art of bullfighting. You can purchase tickets and arrange transportation from El Paso at **Papa's Cantina**. Within a day's drive you'll find the reputedly haunted **Davis Mountains, Monahans Sandhills, Big Bend National Park, Fort Leaton State Historical Park**, and the **Fort Davis National Historic Site**. The **Carlsbad Caverns National Park** and **McDonald Observatory** are also within easy driving distance.

Floydada's Paranormal Population

Established in 1890 as Floyd City, Floydada is located 50 miles to the northeast of Lubbock on Highway 651. The town was originally named after an early Texas hero, Dolphin Floyd, who died defending Texas at the battle of the Alamo. When the post office denied the town a permit because it was the second Floyd City in Texas, local rancher T.W. Price suggested the name "Floydada," a combination of the town's name and his mother's name, Ada. Today, Floydada is the county seat of Floyd County and the "pumpkin capital of the United States."

HAUNTED HOTELS

The Historic Lamplighter Inn 😀😀😀

102 S. 5th St., Floydada, TX 79235-2702 • 806-983-3035

Description and History

A state historic landmark, the Lamplighter Inn has served the needs of the South Plains since 1912, playing host to such dignitaries as Governor "Pappy" O'Daniel, as well as to the participants in traveling medicine shows. A night at the historic hotel is an inexpensive treat. Offering travelers a trip back in time, the 18 rooms showcase the decor of past decades, from precolonization through the 1950s, 1960s, and 1970s.

Three generations of the Daily family operated the hotel until the early 1990s, when it was purchased by Evelyn Branch and her daughter, Roxanna Cummings. Nine rooms are available with private baths. Smoking is not allowed on the premises, but pets are permitted in carry kennels. The owners accept American Express, personal checks, and traveler's checks. Your stay includes a delicious breakfast, and ghost hunters passing through Floydada can stop into the Lamplighter Inn for a wonderful lunch every day of the week.

Ghostly Visitations

Evelyn and Roxanna believe at least two ghosts—a male and a female—reside at the Lamplighter. Both spirits announce their presence with their favorite cologne, with the

> **Most Haunted Areas:**
> *The staircase, dining room, and several upstairs guest rooms*

woman wearing the sweet scent of magnolias and the gentleman preferring Old Spice. Overnight guests tell the owners that they've felt the woman's presence and smelled her perfume in their rooms at night.

Once a bit of a skeptic, Evelyn changed her mind when she began catching a glimpse of a man's feet and trouser-clad legs dashing up the stairs. Others have spotted this strange apparition and followed it upstairs only to find an empty hallway.

The figure of a woman dressed in the style of the 1930s or 1940s has been seen staring out an upstairs guest room window. Witnesses have seen the window shade in this room go up and down without the aid of *human* hands.

Evelyn has also seen the very distinct figure of a woman dressed in purple walking through the empty dining room. The woman literally vanished into thin air without an explanation of who she might be or what she was doing in the hotel.

In her book *Best Tales of Texas Ghosts*, Docia Williams provides an excerpt from a letter Roxanna Cummings wrote to her: "After our last large group left a couple of weeks ago… after everyone had left we cleaned up the hotel and straightened up. The next morning (this was when there were no guests at all!) we awoke to find a table set in the dining room, not for breakfast, but for lunch, complete with china, napkins, cups, glasses, and silverware. No explanation. By the way, it was set up for two."

Another strange occurrence took place when a set of new curtains was installed in a guest room. The drapes were hung on sturdy rods and well secured to the window frame. The owners were stunned when they later entered the empty room and found the curtains neatly arranged on the floor, still on their rods and without any wrinkles. When employees were questioned, they could offer no explanation.

At least two deaths took place in the old hotel. A man caught in the middle of an illicit tryst with another man's wife ended up murdering the jealous husband. Mr. Cornelius, an elderly gentleman who lived at the hotel for many years, also died on the premises.

Do the ghostly feet and legs belong to one of these poor souls? Who is the woman in the purple dress, and is she the same woman who wears the magnolia perfume? An overnight stay at the Lamplighter just may answer these questions for you.

 ## Less Spooky Things To Do In Floydada

The **Floyd County Museum**, located just north of the courthouse, features period furnishings and a collection of photographs of early settlers and ranchers.

For more information on Floydada, contact:
Floydada Chamber of Commerce
114 W. Virginia St., Floydada, TX 79235
806-983-3434

Woeful Souls of Fort Davis

Fort Davis is located on Highway 17. If you're coming from the north, take I-10; if from the south, take US Route 67/90.

FRIGHTENING FORTS AND BATTLEGROUNDS

Fort Davis National Historic Site 👻

P.O. Box 1456, Highways 17 and 118, Fort Davis, TX 79734 • 915-426-3224

Description and History

Fort Davis is located just a mile or so from downtown, along Highways 17 and 118, at the foot of Sleeping Lion Mountain and Hospital Canyon. It was a key military post in West Texas from 1854 to 1891. Soldiers from Fort Davis assisted in opening the area to settlement and protected travelers and merchants from Indian attacks along the San Antonio-El Paso Road. Fort Davis is regarded as one of the best-preserved forts in the Southwest.

A lonely spirit named "Alice" haunts the Fort Davis compound.

Thousands of tourists travel back to the days of the Wild West by visiting Fort Davis every year. Three hiking trails start at Fort Davis, with two linking to the hiking trail at Davis Mountains State Park. Fort Davis is open May 27 through September 2 from 8 a.m.-6 p.m. and from 9 a.m.-5 p.m. the rest of the year. The fort is closed on Christmas Day. Admission is $2 per person or $4 per carload. For more information on Fort Davis, visit the website at www.nps.gov/foda/.

Ghostly Visitations

The lonely ghost haunting Fort Davis has been reported wandering these grounds since Civil War days. She is thought to be Alice Walpole, a young Alabama beauty who disappeared from the fort during a Confederate troop occupation during the war.

> **Most Haunted Area:**
> *The grounds surrounding the old fort*

Legend asserts that Alice was picking white roses along the banks of Limpia Creek when Apache Indians abducted her. Her ghost showed up a few days later, possibly because her body was never located for proper burial. The fearful nature of her untimely death, and the fact that her body was never recovered, make up the necessary ingredients for a long-term haunting. The sweet scent of roses often announces her appearance and, to this day, out-of-season white roses are sometimes found within the Fort Davis compound without explanation.

Less Spooky Things To Do In Fort Davis

The focal point for outdoor recreation in the Fort Davis area is **Davis Mountains State Park**, offering outdoor recreation enthusiasts 2,700 acres of beautiful scenery just 4 miles north of Fort Davis on Texas 118. With 1,000 feet of elevation change within the park boundaries, it is certainly among the most scenic parks in Texas. The park offers visitors a variety of camping options, from hookups for recreational vehicles to primitive campsites, several miles of hiking trails, and an interpretive center. The **McDonald Observatory**, operated by the University of Texas at Austin, houses three large telescopes, hosts visiting astronomers from around the world, and fascinates more than 130,000 tourists every year. The observatory's evening **Star Parties** present a rare opportunity to learn from a resident astronomer about stars, planets, passing satellites, and other interesting astral features under one of the darkest skies in North America. Bring a jacket—the evening mountain air is cool. Less than 20 miles from Fort Davis, you can view the ghostly **Marfa Lights**.

> *For more information on Fort Davis, contact:*
> Fort Davis Chamber of Commerce
> Box 378, Fort Davis, TX 79734
> 1-800-524-3015 • 915-426-3015
> www.fortdavis.com/

Fort McKavett's Phantoms

Fort McKavett is a rural community located west of Menard on FM 864, just south of Highway 190. It occupies the site of an old frontier Army fort founded in the mid-1800s to provide protection for settlers from marauding Indians.

FRIGHTENING FORTS AND BATTLEGROUNDS

Fort McKavett State Historical Park 👐👐

P.O. Box 867, Fort McKavett, TX 76841 • 915-396-2358

Description and History

To visit Fort McKavett, take Highway 190 west of Menard for 17 miles, then go south on FM 864 for 6 miles to the park. Fort McKavett was established on the San Saba River in 1852. Originally known as Camp San Saba, the old fort was later renamed for Captain

A dead sergeant commands the grounds of Fort McKavett.

Henry McKavett, a hero killed during the Mexican War. One of six forts instituted to provide military protection for the West Texas frontier settlers from Indian attacks, the fort was first abandoned during the Civil War but later reoccupied by the military in 1868.

By 1876, the fort had stone barracks for eight infantry companies, an officers' quarters, a hospital, guardhouse, magazine, bakery, post office, large headquarters building, storehouses, and stables. After 1874, when a major and brutal Army offensive against the Indians produced several significant victories and decreased the threat of violence against settlers, the importance of this fort declined. The fort was abandoned for good in 1883, but a few civilian residents remained until the early 1970s.

When the site became a historical landmark, extensive restoration of the ruins began. Fort McKavett offers visitors interpretive exhibits in the original hospital, historical photos, dioramas, and more than 200 artifacts discovered during the restoration process. The fort is open daily from 8 a.m.-5 p.m. The daily entrance fee, which includes special rates for students, ranges from $.50-$5 for those 13 and older; children 12 and under are admitted free of charge. (Proof of enrollment is required for students over 18.) For more information on Fort McKavett, visit the website at www.tpwd.state.tx.us/park/fortmcka/fortmcka.htm.

For Texas State Park information, call 800-792-1112 (select 3 and 3). For reservations, call the Central Reservation Center at 512-389-8900 from 9 a.m.-8 p.m. Monday through Friday and 9 a.m.-12 p.m. Saturday.

Ghostly Visitations

One winter morning several years ago, park superintendent David Bischofhausen was in his office in the fort's old hospital when he heard someone wearing heavy boots walking back and

forth along the porch. Knowing he was alone in the park, he walked outside to investigate, but found nothing out of the ordinary. When he returned to his office, the heavy footsteps resumed their steady pace along the porch floorboards.

On another occasion, Bischofhausen was working at his home near the park when he heard "a voice like a first sergeant talking to his troops." The voice sounded distant and seemed to originate from the direction of the park. Curious, Bischofhausen walked towards the parade grounds of the fort and heard the voice grow louder as he drew closer. As soon as the superintendent approached the grounds, the voice faded. Satisfied there was nothing to see, Bischofhausen began the walk back to his house—and was accompanied by the angry voice of the "first sergeant" the entire way.

Marathon Tumbleweeds & Spirits

Marathon is located on Highway 90 at the junction with Highway 385. In 1882, Albion Shepard, a former sea captain turned engineer for the Southern Pacific Railroad, named the town after Marathon in Greece, because of the wild, mountainous terrain found in both locations.

Today, Marathon is tiny, with a population of 800 souls (not including the dead ones). Literally in the middle of nowhere, this is the perfect place to "set a spell" before continuing your ghost hunting in West Texas.

 **HAUNTED HOTELS**

Gage Hotel 😧😧😧

102 W. Highway 90, Marathon, TX 79842 • 800-884-GAGE

Description and History

Alfred Gage built the Gage Hotel to serve as a combination home and ranch head-quarters for his 500,000-acre spread near Marathon. Henry Trost, a famous architect in America at the beginning of the twentieth century, designed the lovely building.

The Gage Hotel opened to the public in 1927, but unfortunately was not enjoyed by its owner in this capacity for very long. Alfred Gage died in 1928. It seems that Gage has returned to enjoy his hotel in death.

The 37 guest accommodations (29 with private bathrooms) at the Gage Hotel range from inexpensive to expensive. All are decorated with Mexican primitive, Spanish colonial, and regional ranch period furnishings and artifacts. Guests may relax in the courtyard, rocking in chairs under large shade trees, or get out of the West Texas heat with a swim in the large pool. The Gage Hotel's restaurant is known far and wide for its delicious Southwestern-influenced dishes with a sophisticated touch. The hotel does not allow smoking or pets, but children are welcome. The Gage Hotel accepts cash, traveler's checks, American Express, Discover, MasterCard, and Visa. For more information, call 915-386-4205.

Ghostly Visitations

The first specter to haunt the Gage Hotel is former owner Alfred Gage. Gage materialized behind an employee working late one night in the basement and told the startled worker, "I do not want you in my hotel any longer." After another encounter with

> **Most Haunted Areas:**
> *The basement, Rooms 10 and 25, and the courtyard by the swimming pool*

Gage's ghost in the basement two weeks later, the frightened young man left the hotel, never to return.

Room 10 is home to an art-loving apparition. Guests and staff members have heard mysterious music and the soft voice of a woman reciting poetry waft out of the empty room. Guests staying in this room have reported being awakened in the night by a light tap on the arm from an unseen hand.

Located in the Los Portales unit of the hotel, Room 25 has its own resident wraith. A misty figure of a young woman in her early 30s awoke a gentleman sleeping in this room by tugging on his arm. The groggy guest watched the hazy woman for a few seconds before she disappeared.

One evening around 10 p.m., a grounds maintenance man saw perhaps this same ghost near a Coke machine in this area. A transparent young woman in her 30s with short brown hair, she was wearing a white blouse and dark blue skirt. The figure walked by the stunned man towards the courtyard where the swimming pool is located and slowly melted away.

Just who is the woman who haunts the Gage? A trip out west to this beautiful, historic hotel may be the only way to find out for sure.

 **Less Spooky Things To Do In Marathon**

Fine art enthusiasts will love a tour of the **Chisos Gallery** on Highway 90 in downtown Marathon. The gallery features Texan and southwestern art. Marathon is the last stop for most campers heading toward the beautiful, haunted **Big Bend National Park**, with the park's northern entrance located where Highway 385 reaches its end, 40 miles south of Marathon.

> *For more information on Marathon, contact:*
> Marathon Chamber of Commerce
> W. Highway 90, Marathon TX 79842
> 915-386-4516

Mysterious Marfa Lights

Marfa, located 26 miles west of Alpine on Route 67/90, originated as a water stop on the Galveston, Harrisburg, and San Antonio Railroad. In 1883, the wife of a railroad executive named this town for a character in Dostoyevsky's *The Brothers Karamozov*. Marfa is now a trading point for many large ranches located throughout the surrounding Davis Mountains.

GHOSTS OF THE GREAT OUTDOORS

Marfa Lights 😀😀😀

Ghostly Visitations

The favorite viewing site for the Marfa Lights is on Highway 90, 9 miles east of Marfa. The first recorded sighting of the Marfa Lights took place in the 1880s, with a report from a cowboy named Robert Ellison. Considered the most famous ghost lights in Texas and the United States, the unexplained phenomenon has received world-wide attention and attracted researchers from several countries, all trying to solve the mystery of the "Marfa Lights."

The lights may appear as one sphere that divides into balls of many colors. Sometimes they appear elongated, then snap back to their original spherical shape. The ghost lights have been seen flitting about the Davis Mountains as well on the desert flats east of Marfa. Some witnesses claim that if you flash your car's headlights at them, they come in for a closer look. Recently, a motorist traveling on US Highway 90 claimed that one of the lights entered his speeding car through an open window and stayed in his vehicle for 2 miles before exiting.

Explanations such as gases, natural phosphorescence, or static electricity have never been proven. Members of the Houston Association for Scientific Thinking (HAST) investigated the Marfa Lights on three successive nights and admitted that the lights are indeed entrancing and even mildly mystical. Their report closes with the following statement: "A reminder that caution must be taken. Because what we saw three nights in Marfa did not go out of the bounds of the ordinary does not mean that the extraordinary has never occurred in this place."

White settlers attributed the lights to the lanterns of a family who got lost and died in the wilderness in the 1850s. Some say the lights are phantom Indian campfires or the spirits of dead Apache Indians who roamed this arid land long ago. Others swear the lights are the souls of miners trapped in a cave-in during the last century.

Less Spooky Things To Do In Marfa

Plentiful deer and antelope attract hunters from all over. Soaring is popular and sailplanes can be seen over Marfa, winging gracefully above the mesas and peaks of the West Texas desert.

> *For more information on Marfa, contact:*
> Marfa Chamber of Commerce
> 200 S. Abbot, Marfa TX 79843
> 915-729-4942

Sandy Spirits of Monahans

Monahans is located southwest of Odessa on Highway 20. Evidence of human occupation in this area dates as far back as 12,000 years ago. More than 400 years ago, Spanish explorers were the first Europeans to report the vast hills of sand.

Indians used the dunes as a temporary campground and meeting place until the 1880s, when the Texas and Pacific Railroad selected the area for a water stop between the Pecos River and the town of Big Spring. The town of Monahans was established in 1881 to serve this purpose and became the county seat of Ward County. In the late 1920s, oil production began in the area commonly known as the Permian Basin. Today, the town is a financial and marketing center for the more than 800 square miles of surrounding cattle and oil country.

SPIRITED BUILDINGS AND HOUSES

Monahans Sandhills State Park 😊😊😊

P.O. Box 1738, Monahans, TX 79756 • 915-943-2092

Description and History

Monahans Sandhills State Park consists of 3,840 acres of sand dunes—some as high as 70 feet—that once proved a formidable obstacle to pioneer travelers and wagon trains. Indian tribes knew the territory better and frequently camped here because fresh water lies beneath the sands, game was abundant, and acorns and mesquite beans were available for grinding with stone tools into a tasty paste.

The area boasts one of the largest oak forests in the nation, stretching across 40,000 acres of arid land, but it is not apparent. The

These sandy dunes comprise Monahans Sandhills State Park.

forest is hard to see because the mature Harvard Oak trees seldom reach more than 3 feet tall, yet they send roots down as far as 90 feet to maintain the miniature surface growth.

A private group, the Sealy-Smith Foundation, leased the land from Texas in 1956 (through 2056) and opened it to the public as Monahans Sandhills State Park in 1957. To reach the park, travel I-20 and exit at Mile Marker #86 to Park Road 41. Monahans Sandhills State Park has a modern museum and interpretive center with picnicking, camping, and sand surfing available to visitors. The daily entrance fee, which includes special rates for students, ranges from $.50-$5 for those 13 and older; children 12 and under are admitted free of charge. (Proof of enrollment is required for students over 18.) For more information on Monahans Sandhills State Park, call 915-943-2092 or visit the website at www.tpwd.state.tx.us/park/monahans/monahans.htm.

For Texas State Park information, call 800-792-1112 (select 3 and 3). For reservations, call the Central Reservation Center at 512-389-8900 from 9 a.m.-8 p.m. Monday through Friday and 9 a.m.-noon on Saturday.

Ghostly Visitations

Staff members at Monahans Sandhill State Park report hearing mysterious footsteps in the visitors' center building. Employees have heard doors that

> **Most Haunted Area:**
> *The visitors' center building*

were already closed slam, have seen sliding shadows from their peripheral vision, and have heard the sounds of heavy objects falling in empty rooms. Careful investigations have failed to provide explanations.

A new employee, learning of these phenomena, was skeptical until the day she was alone in the office and heard the terrified screams of a woman just outside the building. With her heart racing, she ran outside to help, but found no one. The panic-stricken shrieks continued as the shaken employee frantically searched the grounds around the building. The screams eventually subsided and the former skeptic never found the source of the frightened cries.

According to legend, the visitors' center at Monahans Sandhills State Park is built on the site of a nineteenth-century Comanche burial ground. In 1967, two boys digging near the building unearthed a skeleton, lending credence to the ghost story.

 **Less Spooky Things To Do In Monahans**

The **Million Barrel Museum** was constructed in 1928 as an oil-storage facility, but the huge tank was eventually abandoned due to leakage. Converted to a museum in 1987, the relocated and restored **Holman House**, which once served as a hotel at the end of Monahans-Fort Stockton Stage Line in the early twentieth century, is open to visitors, as is the first **Ward County Jailhouse**. You can also check out a display of antique oil field equipment. The **Million Barrel Museum** is open daily and is located on US Highway 80, 1.5 miles east of the city. The old military installation that is now the **Pyote Museum and Rattlesnake Bomber Base** was home to the 19th (B-17) Bomber Group during World War II. The Pyote Museum and Rattlesnake Bomber Base is in a county park that offers picnicking, swimming, a three-hole golf course, tennis, and overnight camping. The museum is located on I-20 just 15 miles west of Monahans.

Presidio's Poltergeists

Presidio is located on the banks of the Rio Grande River, 18 miles south of Shafter in southern Presidio County at the junction of FM 170 and Highway 67. The countryside surrounding Presidio is the oldest continuously cultivated region in the United States. Farmers have worked this land since 1500 B.C.

By 1400 A.D., Indians lived throughout the area in small settlements that the Spaniard would later call *pueblos*. The first Spaniards came to present-day Presidio in 1535 when Álvar Núñez Cabeza de Vaca and his three companions stopped at the largest Indian pueblo and placed a cross on the mountainside establishing the village of *La Junta de las Cruces*. On December 10, 1582, Antonio de Espejo and his company arrived at the site and renamed the village *San Juan Evangelista*. By 1681, the small settlement was known as *La Junta de los Ríos*, or "the Junction of the Rivers," because two rivers, the *Río Conchos* and the *Río Grande*, join at the site.

In 1830, the name of the area around Presidio was changed from *La Junta de los Rios* to *Presidio del Norte*, which was eventually shortened to today's Presidio. During the Mexican Revolution, General Pancho Villa often used Presidio's neighboring town (just across the Texas/Mexico border), Ojinaga, as his headquarters for operations, and visited Presidio on numerous occasions.

White settlers came to Presidio in 1848 following the Mexican War. The handful of Anglo settlers who came to the region assimilated into the Hispanic population; their descendants are primarily Spanish speakers today. A post office was established at Presidio in 1868, and the first public school was opened in 1887. In 1930, the Kansas City, Mexico and Orient Railway reached Presidio and the town incorporated.

FRIGHTENING FORTS AND BATTLEGROUNDS

Fort Leaton State Historical Park 👹👹

P.O. Box 2439, Presidio, TX 79845 • 915-229-3613

Description and History

A former scalp hunter for the Mexican government, Ben Leaton moved to the banks of the Rio Grande in 1848 and built the massive fortress known as Fort Leaton. The park is located 4 miles southeast of Presidio on the River Road to Big Bend (FM 170)—along one of the most scenic highway routes in the Southwest. Leaton died in 1851, leaving his widow alone in the wilds of West Texas. She remarried a local customs agent named Edward Hall and the couple made their home in the adobe fort.

When the Halls fell on hard times, Edward borrowed a large sum of money from Leaton's old partner and friend, John Burgess, using the fort as collateral. Hall failed to repay the money and Burgess foreclosed on the fort. Hall refused to leave and paid a very high price for this refusal: Burgess allegedly had Hall murdered in the fortress. Following Hall's death, the Burgess family assumed ownership of the fort and moved in lock, stock, and barrel.

Soon after moving in, Burgess converted the room in which Hall had been brutally murdered into a chapel. Many wondered if Burgess's actions were the result of a guilty conscience or a ghostly demand for retribution coming from beyond the grave. Bill Leaton, Ben Leaton's son and Edward Hall's stepson, eventually killed John Burgess (his stepfather's murderer) in 1875. The Burgess family abandoned the fort in 1926. Due to the amount of bloodshed and violence these adobe walls have witnessed over the years, Fort Leaton is the perfect home for the group of ghouls who have come to reside here.

Fort Leaton is open to the public seven days a week from 8 a.m.-4:30 p.m.; the fort is closed Christmas Day. The park offers guided tours for a fee. Bus tours for Big Bend Ranch State Park depart from Fort Leaton the first Saturday of every month. The park includes historic ruins, restored rooms, interpretive exhibits, shaded picnic grounds, and a Texas State Park Store. The daily entrance fee, which includes special rates for students, ranges from $.50-$5 for those 13 and older; children 12 and under are admitted free of charge. (Proof of enrollment is required for students over 18.) For more information on the Fort Leaton State Historical Park, visit the website at www.tpwd.state.tx.us/park/fortleat/fortleat.htm.

For Texas State Park information, call 800-792-1112 (select 3 and 3). For reservations, call the Central Reservation Center at 512-389-8900 from 9 a.m.-8 p.m. Monday through Friday and 9 a.m.-12 p.m. Saturday.

Ghostly Visitations

When Fort Leaton stood empty during the 1920s, its rooms served as temporary shelter for many homeless families. Recently, an elderly couple visited the fort and relayed a spooky tale to Superintendent Luis Armerdariz. More than 60 years ago, the newly married couple moved into the old fort. They soon realized they were not alone. After retiring for the night, the couple would be startled awake by the sounds of dishes crashing to the floor and breaking. Jumping up to check for intruders, the couple found no evidence of broken dishes and no explanation to account for the persistent nocturnal tumult. After experiencing this unsettling activity for several nights in a row, the couple fled the old fort for quieter quarters elsewhere.

Rumors of Ben Leaton's gold buried under the fort circulated for years throughout the community. As a result, treasure hunters searched in vain, digging a huge hole in the process. When the Texas Parks and Wildlife Department purchased Fort Leaton in 1968, the first order of business was to hire a team of workers to clean the pit of collected garbage and fill it in. The job was halfway completed when the group quit en masse one day. Two men claimed that while they worked, something tried to drag them into the pit. The frightened locals left the fort and never returned, not even for their paychecks.

Workers in the area often report seeing an old woman sitting in a rocking chair in the fort's kitchen. Could this apparition be Mrs. Hall or Mrs. Burgess watching over her beloved home? Witnesses have reported the shadowy figure of a man fitting Edward Hall's description standing in the chapel room where he was murdered long ago. Does he realize that he's dead?

Staff and visitors have heard a rattling noise in the granary that sounds like a group of riders removing the harnesses from their trusty horses. One legend speaks of a horseman caught in a sudden thunderstorm near Fort Leaton around the turn of the century. Spooked by an abrupt stroke of lightening, the horse bolted with the rider's foot caught in the stirrup. The doomed man was dragged along behind the horse, slammed into a boulder, and beheaded. Talk persists of a headless horseman in a flowing black cape riding a white horse around the compound of the fort.

Less Spooky Things To Do In Presidio

Shopping always seems to revive your "spirits" and gives serious ghost hunters a much-needed break from their paranormal endeavors. Try the **D7 Cowboy Company** and **Whistle Stop Sandwich Shop**, located right at the intersection of Business 67 and O'Reilly. They have a huge collection of fun and interesting items to keep the entire family entertained. Visit Mexico! **Ojinaga** is just across the bridge from Presidio. The two towns were once one and the same until the river that ran through town was deemed an international border dividing the United States and Mexico. Ojinaga is truly an unspoiled border town—walk through its streets to experience the sights and sounds of interior Mexico. While experiencing Ojinaga, stop into **Fausto's Art Gallery,** which specializes in original works of art as well as collectibles and souvenirs. Visitors see the work of Luis Roman, the acclaimed folk artist honored at the prestigious Smithsonian Institute's Folkways Festival for his participation in Fausto's retablo revival. For nature lovers, this beautiful area of Texas offers majestic scenery to accompany your hiking, mountain biking, bird watching, river rafting, camping, and fishing. Our largest national park, **Big Bend National Park**, covers more than 800,000 acres of incredible desert and is visited by 350,000 tourists each year. Or visit **Peguis Canyon**, just 25 miles from Ojinaga; this is far and away the most spectacular sight in the entire Big Bend region.

> *For more information on Presidio, contact:*
> Presidio Chamber of Commerce
> Highway 67, Presidio, TX 79845
> 915-229-3199
> http://presidiotex.com/index.html

Spooks of San Angelo

San Angelo is located southwest of Abilene at the junction of Highways 87 and 277. The lawless village of Santa Angela grew up around Fort Concho, established by the United States Army to protect settlers from Indian attacks. As the village grew into a community, it became a trade center for the many farmers and ranchers who settled in the area.

By 1889, the Indians had moved westward and the soldiers followed, abandoning Fort Concho. However, with the economic base of agriculture and trade, the community (later renamed San Angelo) has continued to grow and move into the twenty-first century.

FRIGHTENING FORTS AND BATTLEGROUNDS

Fort Concho National Historic Landmark 👹👹👹👹

630 S. Oakes, San Angelo, TX 76903 • 915-481-2646

Description and History

Fort Concho, founded in 1867 at the junction of the North and Middle Concho Rivers, protected frontier settlements and transportation routes in this area until 1889. Famous military commanders, such as William "Pecos Bill" Shafter, served here. A number of cavalry and infantry units, including all four regiments of the Buffalo Soldiers, were stationed at the post. Fort Concho is the most well-preserved survivor of the Indian Wars era, which lasted from 1866 to 1891.

Fort Concho is owned and operated by the City of San Angelo. Fort Concho National Historic Landmark includes 23 original and restored fort structures, including the headquarters building, soldiers' barracks, chapel/schoolhouse, and post hospital. Living history demonstrations are held at Fort Concho, with soldiers in authentic dress conducting exercises on the parade grounds, and other events are held at the fort throughout the year, including Frontier Day in June and Christmas at Old Fort Concho in December. The museum is open from 10 a.m.-5 p.m. Tuesday through Saturday and from 1 p.m.-5 p.m. Sunday. Admission is $2 for adults, $1.50 for military and senior citizens, and $1.25 for students. For more information, call 915-481-2646 or visit the website at www.fortconcho.com/.

Ghostly Visitations

For years, park employees have told tales of ghostly footsteps heard echoing through the old soldiers' barracks and of the presence of a shadowy apparition. Unaccountable lights have been seen zooming around inside the headquarters building late at night. The post hospital is home to long-dead camp surgeon, Captain William Notson, who just can't seem to leave his former workplace. The spirits of a group of transients murdered at this old fort in the 1890s are also said to have set up camp in the museum library.

> **Most Haunted Areas:**
> *The headquarters building, soldiers' barracks, officers' quarters, post hospital, and museum library*

Less Spooky Things To Do In San Angelo

Visitors will enjoy a stroll along **Concho Avenue**, the first street in Santa Angela. Whether browsing through antique malls or designer fashion stores, visiting a working saddle maker, having lunch at a sidewalk café or tearoom, or enjoying music at the watering hole, you will have a wonderful time. Relive history at **Miss Hattie's Bordello Museum**, the "Best Little Bordello Museum in Texas," where gentleman were served by Miss Hattie's girls for 50 years before the Texas Rangers closed her down. The museum is furnished much as it was during its heyday, providing its many visitors a look at the past. The **Concho River**, named for the mussels that produce the unique pink Concho Pearl, is a true city treasure. San Angelo's downtown **River Beautification Project** features beautiful gardens, a river walk-plaza area, 14 water features, turn-of-the-century lighting, a 4-mile jogging/walking trail, a nine-hole golf course, a miniature golf course, and an amusement park.

For more information on San Angelo, contact:
San Angelo Chamber of Commerce
500 Rio Concho Dr., San Angelo, TX 76903
800-375-1206
www.sanangelo.org/tourindex.html

Turkey's Invisible Cowboy

The town of Turkey, which is 126 miles northeast of Lubbock on Highway 86, got its name from the hundreds of wild turkeys roosting along the banks of a small creek running through the area. Originally called Turkey Roost, the post office shortened the name to just plain Turkey, and the name stuck. The town was incorporated in 1920 and the railroad came to the community in 1927. During this year the entire town, as it exists today, was built.

Catch 40 winks with the ghost of a Texas cowboy in the Hotel Turkey.

HAUNTED HOTELS

Hotel Turkey ☺☺☺

Third and Alexander, Turkey, TX 79261 • 800-657-7110

Description and History

The Hotel Turkey opened its doors November 11, 1927, to provide warm beds and hot meals for the traveling salesmen that came from Dallas and Fort Worth. The hotel has been in continuous operation since the day it opened.

A stay at the Hotel Turkey is an inexpensive treat with its 14 rooms, 10 of which have private bathrooms complete with claw-foot tubs. An overnight stay at the Turkey includes a full breakfast the next morning. Smoking is not allowed on the premises, but pets are permitted. Innkeepers Gary and Suzie Johnson accept American Express, MasterCard, Visa, personal checks, and traveler's checks. Call 806-423-1151 for more information.

Ghostly Visitations

When former owners Scott and Jane Johnson purchased the hotel, a lady told them, "All the rooms are locked because someone keeps getting upstairs somehow and sleeps in a bed." Evidently, the woman wasn't aware that locked doors mean little to ghosts!

> **Most Haunted Area:**
> *Room 20*

On her first stormy night in the hotel, Jane heard the bell ring at the front desk. Surprised that someone would be out on such a night, Jane walked down to the lobby. Finding no one, she returned to her work upstairs and didn't think anymore about the mysterious bell until the next morning when she walked into Room 20. On the bedspread was the clear outline of a body from the night before—legs crossed at the ankles, hands placed under the head with the elbows sticking out and the impressions of boot heels!

Over time, Jane surmised that the hotel's nocturnal visitor was simply a long-dead cowboy coming in from the elements for a good night's rest in a warm bed. She began to expect him on bad weather nights, when he came with regularity, always announcing himself with a ring of the front desk bell.

Less Spooky Things To Do In Turkey

Country music lovers should plan to visit the **Bob Wills Museum**. The museum honors the man known as the "King of Western Swing," who was raised on a farm just north of town. The first weekend in April every year is dedicated to Wills's music during the **Bob Wills Country Music Festival**.

Elusive Boos of West Texas & the Panhandle

 West Texas is an enormous and somewhat desolate part of our great state. The longest part of most road trips outside of Texas is the actual "getting out of Texas" part. Nowhere is this fact more evident than while you're driving through the West Texas desert. The terrain is startlingly beautiful and cruel at the same time. Maybe because of this, the number of ghost hunters and documented hauntings in West Texas is relatively small compared to the rest of the state. I encourage you to make a trek into this wild part of Texas and see if you can rustle up any spooks and specters along the way!

Delores Mountains Outside of Alpine

In *The National Directory of Haunted Places*, author Dennis William Hauck reports that these mountains are named for the heartbroken ghost roaming here. Delores and her sweetheart, a sheepherder, lit fires in the hills to communicate their love for each over great distances. After her lover was killed by Apaches, Delores continued to light the fires to express her love for her slain suitor and apparently she's still at it.

Bruja Canyon, Big Bend National Park

The Spanish word *bruja* means "witch," and many believe this canyon is truly bewitched. Ghost lights, the apparition of a silent *hombre* wearing a sombrero, and photography equipment failures are reported.

Los Chisos Mountains, Big Bend National Park

The name Los Chisos means "the ghosts" in English and this seems to be no coincidence. Several spooks are said to frequent these peaks, including the phantom Apache Chief Alstate, a sobbing Indian maiden, and a bull named "Murderer."

Terlingua Abaja, Big Bend National Park

This crumbling ghost town exudes a certain eeriness that can only mean one thing the presence of paranormal participants.

Panhandle Plains Museum, Canyon

2401 Fourth Ave., Canyon, TX 79015 • 806-651-2244

The museum is located on the campus of Texas A&M University, West Texas. A spirit wearing a lavender calico dress has been seen standing near a turn-of-the-century, horse-drawn Army ambulance. Her name is believed to be "Sarah Jane."

El Paso Public Library, El Paso

501 N. Oregon St., El Paso, TX 79901 • 915-543-5433

A Civil War soldier haunts the basement of the library. The El Paso Ghost Research team is conducting ongoing investigations of the building.

Plaza Theater, El Paso

More than one spirit is said to haunt this historic theater. The ghost of a woman murdered by her jealous husband, whose house once stood on this site, comes back to tend her garden. Another spirit is believed to be that of a man who died from a heart attack on the mezzanine level of the theater. The Plaza Theater is currently undergoing restoration and is closed to the public.

Hamilton Hotel, Laredo

1219 Matamoros St., #512, Laredo, TX 78040 • 956-722-3836

Employees have reported lights going on and off and equipment that misplaces itself. A priest is rumored to have been pushed from an upper-floor window to his death. Does he roam the halls of this historic hotel in downtown Laredo?

Landmark Hotel, Sterling City

Currently, this building stands empty. The owners may turn it into a bed-and-breakfast inn or café in the future. Unexplained footsteps and the sounds of breaking china and clanking pots and pans have been heard in this former restaurant and hotel.

Badlands Hotel, Terlingua

Hc 70 Box 400, Terlingua, TX 79852 • 915-424-3451

The old stone building that serves as the accounting office for this hotel has a terrible history behind its haunting. Two murders have taken place here. The first occurred when a man beat his pregnant wife with an iron pipe until she died, spraying the small room with her blood and bits of brain. The second involved the murder of a park ranger. Staff members refuse to enter the building due to strange noises and negative energy.

Oil Fields Around Wink

The unlikely specter of a Russian cossack haunts the oil fields around Wink. Rumor has it that the cossack's treasure is still buried on the prairie he's searching. The late, famous rock and roll star Roy Orbison saw the ghost on a dirt road east of town in 1950.

Ghost Clubs of West Texas & the Panhandle

 Even though ghost clubs are as scarce as Yankees in this part of Texas, the lone club operating out of West Texas is an active one.

El Paso Ghost Research

5701 Squires Ct., El Paso, TX 79924 • 915-751-8420

Edward Weissbard and Heidi Crabtree were very helpful in providing information on El Paso for this book, and they conduct regular investigations in the El Paso area. For more information, visit the website at http://members.delphi.com/epgr/index.html.

Region 2

Ghosts of the Endless North Texas Prairie

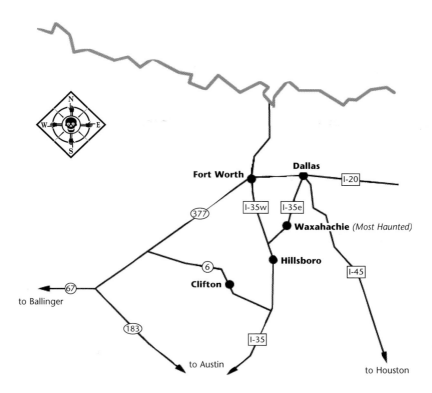

 The plains may be endless, but North Texas boasts an endless variety of activities to keep travelers very busy indeed. Some of the state's most famous ghosts "live" in this part of Texas, including the wet wraith, known as the "Lady of the Lake," that wanders the shores of Dallas's White Rock Lake, and the trio of spirits who inhabit the Catfish Plantation in Waxahachie, the most haunted town in North Texas.

Rough-and-tumble personalities founded the boomtowns of Dallas and Fort Worth, instilling a mode of living that is truly "larger than life." The view of Texas most "foreigners" have comes from the characters who inhabit North Texas—from the rich socialite with a diamond on every finger and "big hair" to the cowboy driving a loaded $40,000 truck, complete with gun rack and SMU sticker in the back window. With these characters and this reputation, it makes sense that the ghosts in this area follow suit as some of the most interesting in the state!

Clifton's Mysterious Church

Clifton is located in the Bosque Valley in east-central Texas, 28 miles northwest of Waco on Highway 6 at the junction of County Road 219.

GHOSTLY MISSIONS AND CHURCHES

St. Olaf Lutheran Church 👁️👁️

RR 2 Box 1730, Cranfills Gap, TX 76637 • 254-597-2738

Description and History

This historic Lutheran church is located in Cranfills Gap, near Norse, 16 miles west of Clifton. Built in 1886, it was abandoned in 1917 when another church was constructed closer to town. The church is an austere, white-plastered rock building with a modest bell tower.

Ghostly Visitations

According to late ghost-story teller Ed Syers, in his classic book, *Ghost Stories of Texas*, a group of Fort Worth photographers came to St. Olaf's to include the church's

> **Most Haunted Area:**
> *The entire church*

image in a collection of historic buildings. While touring the deserted building, all three heard indistinct, muffled, arguing voices coming from below the little balcony. Intrigued by the experience, the group returned to the church with a *Fort Worth Star Telegram* reporter, Jon McConal, in tow. During their tour of the little church, six people heard the garbled voices that Jon McConal described "as though passing through a wall or a blanket of time." A Dallas parapsychologist offered a simple explanation for the unintelligible voices—they were speaking Norwegian!

Less Spooky Things To Do In Clifton

The **Bosque Memorial Museum** contains Texas mineral and fossil collections, guns, coins, model ships, pioneer kitchen equipment, farm tools, and Indian artifacts. The **Norse Settlement** near Clifton is considered the capital of Norwegian communities in Texas. During the 1850s, Cleng Peerson ("the father of Norse immigration to America") and fellow pioneer Ole Canuteson brought groups to this area to set up homesteads. Norwegian descendants across the United States revere Peerson's grave, located in the churchyard of Our Savior's Lutheran Church in Norse. The **Texas Safari Wildlife Park** offers visitors more than 850 acres of beautiful landscapes and exotic creatures from all over the world. **Lake Whitney State Park** is about 27 miles to the northeast of Clifton. Visitors can enjoy camping, boating, picnicking, swimming, and fishing there.

Dead Denizens of Dallas

Dallas is located east of Fort Worth on I-35. A Tennessee lawyer and entrepreneur, John Neely Bryan, founded Dallas in 1841. Bryan believed the endless prairie, the Trinity River, and the friendly American Indian population provided the perfect ingredients for developing a successful trading post and town. The site was the easiest place to cross the Trinity and was near where the planned Preston Trail would link North and South Texas. Bryan laid claim to 640 acres and sketched out a town, designating a courthouse square and 20 streets. Bryan's log cabin, the first structure built in Dallas, can be seen standing in the Dallas County Historical Plaza at Market, Elm, Commerce, and Houston Streets. Bryan, an alcoholic, spent his last days in the State Lunatic Asylum and died September 8, 1877.

Over the years, the young town grew with the introduction of the railroad in the 1870s, Southern Methodist University in 1915, and the Dallas Love Field Airport in 1927. In 1930, C.M. "Dad" Joiner struck oil 100 miles east of Dallas. With the discovery and development of the East Texas Oil Field (the largest petroleum deposit on earth at the time), Dallas became a center of oil-related activity. Although Dallas has never had a working oil well, the city's role as the financial and technical center for much of the state's drilling industry has proven invaluable. Commerce and industry have followed suit, adding to the city's success and progress. Home to the country's most famous upscale department store, Neiman-Marcus, and the world's largest international airport, Dallas has come a long way in a short time!

RESTAURANT REVENANTS

Snuffer's Bar and Grill 👻👻👻

3526 Greenville Ave., Dallas, TX 75206 • 972-661-9911

Description and History

Snuffer's Bar and Grill is located on Lower Greenville Avenue. This is a true "joint," attracting crowds of burger-lovers and college students from all over the city. Snuffer's famous (and delicious) chili cheese fries are definitely not to be missed!

One of Dallas's favorite eateries, Snuffer's Bar and Grill is home to a mysterious revenant.

Ghostly Visitations

Weird manifestations have transpired in this burger joint since it opened in 1978. Pat Snuffer and his employees have found a sure-fire way to experience their otherworldly patron: All they have to do is mention a past haunting incident and wait a few days. Following a discussion of the Snuffer's ghost, employees get cold chills, hear their names called three times, and feel a hand on their shoulders. After-hours, glassware and ashtrays in empty rooms move from 6 to 8 feet away from their original locations, and are later found out of place by confused employees. The Snuffer's resident spook has not been identified.

> **Most Haunted Area:**
> *The original south side of the restaurant*

SPIRITED BUILDINGS AND HOUSES

The DeGolyer Estate 👻👻

8525 Garland Rd., Dallas, TX 75218 • 214-327-8263

Description and History

The Dallas Arboretum and Botanical Gardens features 66 acres of flowers, display gardens, and rolling lawns on the shores of haunted White Rock Lake. The DeGolyer Estate is located on the Arboretum and Botanical Gardens grounds. It is a 21,000-square-foot mansion once owned by millionaire oilman, Everette DeGolyer. The 1930s-era home was patterned after a Mexican hacienda.

The grounds of the Dallas Arboretum and Botanical Gardens are open daily from 10 a.m.-6 p.m., except on Thursday, when the grounds are open until 8 p.m. During the winter months, closing hours move to 5 p.m. The grounds are closed on Thanksgiving, Christmas, and New Year's days. Admission is $6 for adults, $3 for children 6-12, and children 5 and under are admitted free of charge. Parking is $3 per car and the grounds are accessible to people with disabilities.

Ghostly Visitations

While working as a tour guide to earn graduation credits, a high school student named Beverly Bailey had a brush with the paranormal forces residing inside the DeGolyer mansion.

> **Most Haunted Area:**
> *The parlor where the piano is located*

One summer evening, after closing around 9 p.m., she reentered to retrieve her keys and heard a strange noise coming from the parlor. Bailey turned on the floor lamp in the living room and found the piano open as if ready to be played. A photograph of Everette DeGolyer, usually sitting on the piano, had been moved to another table in the room. The young guide was certain the room had not appeared like this at 5:30 that afternoon when she helped close the museum for the evening. Bailey took a few determined steps into the room, intending to close the piano and replace the photo, but she had the overwhelming feeling she was intruding and left quickly.

Other docents have reported feelings of being watched and objects moving about on their own. Just who is haunting the DeGolyer Estate is a mystery. A visit to this lovely historic home could provide you with the necessary clues to solve this case of the paranormal parlor and provide answers as to who is residing here.

 # Lizard Lounge 😵😵😵
2424 Swiss Ave., Dallas, TX 75204 • 214-826-4768

Description and History

The Lizard Lounge nightclub is located in a historic Victorian section of Dallas. The restored warehouse once housed the Grand Crystal Palace Theatre. The Lizard Lounge is open every night and has a cover charge.

Ghostly Visitations

According to Dallas lore, several spirits inhabit this old theater. These lost souls are described as workers who lost their lives in the building when it was used as a warehouse. One is known as the "man in black," a gentleman dressed in a black turn-of-

> **Most Haunted Areas:**
> *The second floor dressing room, and the balcony level near the north grand stair*

the-century suit, complete with a black cape and hat, who stalks the old audience area.

Molly Louise Shepard, an actress in the theater several years ago, had many encounters with the ghosts of the Grand Crystal Palace. Most of Shepard's experiences transpired in the second floor dressing room. Upon entering the room alone, all the light bulbs surrounding the vanity exploded and plunged the creepy room into total darkness. Shepard took her first of many runs into the kitchen, only to be chided by the Mexican cook as "la gringa es loco en la cabeza" (the girl is crazy in the head!).

Shepard's next encounter in the dressing room involved the unexplained melting of the stainless steel face of an iron. Leaving the iron on the "cotton" setting while rehearsing a song downstairs, Shepard returned 15 minutes later to get her costume ready for her performance and found the iron sitting in a puddle of melted steel. Last, a near miss convinced Shepard that she was confronting a "mean-spirited spirit" haunting this area

of the theater. While she was sitting at the dressing room table, an unplugged blow dryer flew across the room, barely missing her head.

I wonder what the ghosts think of the building's new incarnation as a popular nightclub? Hopefully, they enjoy loud music.

Dance the night away with the specters who inhabit the Lizard Lounge nightclub.

Majestic Theatre 👶👶👶
1925 Elm St., Suite 300, Dallas, TX 75201 • 214-880-0137

Description and History

The Majestic Theatre is located between Highway 75 and the Dallas County Historical Plaza. The historic Majestic Theatre opened in 1921 to rave reviews. Since then, the theater has been renovated and restored, surpassing its former glory with a state-of-the-art stage, sound, and lighting equipment, and sight-line seats for the best views. The 1,589-seat theater hosts local and touring dance, theater, and music companies. The nineteenth-century baroque building is listed as a City of Dallas Landmark, a Texas Historical

Perpetually hungry, the Majestic's paranormal squatter loves to cook breakfast.

Landmark, and is on the National Register of Historic Places. Call for hours, admission, and prices, as these change along with the plays.

Ghostly Visitations

In her *Dallas Morning News* article titled "Favorite Haunts," Catherine Cuellar relates the story of the ghost who haunts this favorite Dallas landmark. As we've seen time and again, ghosts love old theaters, and who better to haunt

> **Most Haunted Areas:**
> *Throughout the entire building*

the beautiful old Majestic Theatre than the late theater mogul Karl Hoblitzelle? Hoblitzelle is described by the Majestic's Office of Cultural Affairs staff as being "great" and "our best friend." A portrait of Hoblitzelle hanging in a fifth-floor conference room shows him wearing a white suit, dark tie, and slacks. His eyes seem to follow people regardless of where they stand in the room.

Program coordinator Ronnie Jesse has seen telephone lines light up as though they are in use, even when he's alone in the office at night. Guards have witnessed backdrops being slowly lowered to the stage when they are alone in the old theater—backdrops that must be lowered by a hand crank. After calling out several names into the darkness, the guards crank the backdrops back up and continue with their rounds, knowing it's just Hoblitzelle trying to attract attention.

One early Saturday morning, former managing director Celia Barshop was working alone in the building. While going about her tasks, she smelled the unmistakable aroma of breakfast cooking. Determined to pinpoint the origin of the smell, she walked through the office area to the commercial kitchen on the second floor, but there was no smell. On the way back to her office, Barshop stopped to check the bolted theater doors in the main lobby and smelled what she describes as a Sunday brunch.

Rushing back to the kitchen, Barshop felt she wasn't alone. Someone else was there with her. She pushed through the kitchen's swinging door and jammed a wooden wedge under it to hold it open. After looking in empty trash cans, ovens, and refrigerators, and touching the stone-cold stove ranges to see if anyone had been cooking, a very perplexed Barshop thought, "You're tired, go back to your office." When she turned, the kitchen door that she had wedged open was closed.

"I said, 'Enjoy your meal. Please don't cause me any harm. I won't bother you,'" she said, still spooked by the memory of that strange morning. "I'm sure there's some logical explanation, but I believe in ghosts," Ms. Barshop said. Maybe the logical explanation is that Hoblitzelle was hungry and made himself a ghostly brunch to enjoy on a Saturday morning.

Millermore House 👶👶👶
1717 Gano St., Dallas, TX 75215 • 214-421-5141

Description and History

The Millermore House is located in Old City Park in South Dallas. Old City Park is a remarkable outdoor museum and home to some of the oldest structures in North Texas, including the haunted Millermore House. The park's 37 restored historic homes, buildings, and shops in the museum village provide a step back to the 1800s.

Why is "Minerva," the ghost who haunts the Millermore House, so angry?

William Miller Brown began building the mansion in 1855 for his second wife, Minerva Barnes Miller, but she died a year later. Completed in 1861, the Millermore House sheltered members of the Miller family until 1960. In 1963, the house was disassembled and stored in a warehouse. Six years later, it was rebuilt near the springs of a former Indian campground in South Dallas, now known as Old City Park.

The Old City Park grounds are open from dawn to sunset every day. You can take an hour-and-a-half guided tour of the grounds Tuesday through Saturday from 10 a.m.-4 p.m., and Sunday from noon-4 p.m. Tour admission is $12 for a family, $5 for adults, and $3 for children 3-12. Call 214-421-5141 for details.

Ghostly Visitations

In an article that appeared in the *Dallas Morning News* on Halloween in 1999, Catherine Cuellar tells of the hauntings at the Millermore Home. Employees, volunteers, and visitors have reported strange sensations while standing in the upstairs rooms, including the original nursery and master bedroom. All witnesses

> **Most Haunted Areas:**
> *The nursery and master bedroom*

sense a presence they cannot see. Curator Hal Simon has observed two crows pecking at the windows of the nursery and master bedroom, but not on other windows in the house. One recent first-time visitor to Millermore grew so fearful during his tour of the upstairs rooms that he asked to leave his group and wait outside rather than continue.

Volunteers decorating the front balcony during the winter holidays have reported seeing in their peripheral vision something moving between the nursery and master bedroom. Witnesses feel the presence is a woman—an angry woman at that!

Deborah Lister, office administrator at Old City Park, says she has seen an agitated female spirit looking out of the master bedroom window. Looking at the glass, "you see someone standing with her hands together, in a dress and the dress is light-colored. You can follow it up and make out details of the dress, and if you come up you run into where the face is," Lister said. "Almost everyone I can point it out to can see the hands in front of the dress in the bottom center pane. It's pretty recent that that manifestation has happened."

The disturbed figure of the woman appears in the same clothes Minerva Barnes Miller wore in an old daguerreotype Simon found in the house. Why "Minerva" is haunting her old home and what has happened to anger her so is anyone's guess.

 **GHOSTS OF THE GREAT OUTDOORS**

White Rock Lake 👻👻

830 E. Lawther Dr., Dallas, TX 75218 • 214-670-8281

Description and History

White Rock Lake is located only minutes from downtown to the east. This true Dallas treasure features a scenic park with approximately 9 miles of leisure hike-and-bike trails and excellent fishing, sailing, and various leisure activities.

Ghostly Visitations

Some say the beautiful young woman whose spirit roams the shores of White Rock Lake wears the fringes and bangles of the Roaring Twenties. Others say she sports the taffeta hoop skirt of a southern belle. All witnesses agree the dress is white and dripping wet. This "Lady of the Lake" is Dallas's most famous ghost, and definitely the most glamorous.

In his book *Ghost Stories of Texas*, late writer Ed Syers quotes Mark J. McCarthy when describing the origin of this ghost: "In the 1920s, an excursion boat operated on the Lake. One warm summer night, perfect for a moonlit ride, a young couple attended a formal party on the boat. An argument between the lovers ensued—possibly alcohol-induced—and the woman left the boat, jumped into her date's car, and sped off into the dark night. The poorly maintained road around the lake twisted and turned, and the distraught woman lost control of the car where Lawther Road runs into Garland Road. The car careened into the lake and she drowned."

The dead beauty in white returns to the scene of her demise regularly. Reports of motorists giving the distressed girl a lift (only to have her disappear from their passenger seats on the way to her home) have circulated throughout Dallas for several decades.

Several shocked witnesses said she left an expensive wrap, complete with a 1920s-era Neiman-Marcus label, in the car. According to Syers, some of McCarthy's friends were driving along the lake and saw a ghost. They recognized the apparition as the "Lady of the Lake" and did not stop to assist her. Owners of homes along Garland Road that face the lake have received a late-night visitor who rings the doorbell and asks to borrow the telephone—only to have her disappear from their front porches without a trace.

The late Frank X. Tolbert, who worked as a columnist for the *Dallas Morning News* for many years, described another version of the legend of the phantom of White Rock Lake. While driving around the lake on a quiet night, a couple noticed a sad figure in a beautiful white gown standing by the side of the road. Concerned, they stopped to give her a lift. The girl in white was soaking wet and told the couple that she was separated from her boyfriend and was searching for him. The good Samaritans offered her a ride home, but along the way the girl disappeared from the back seat of the car, leaving a wet spot where she was sitting.

The disturbed couple drove to the address the shivering girl gave them and were horrified to hear from the man who answered the door that his beautiful daughter drowned in the lake several years before. Every year on the anniversary of her death, she returns to the lakeshore and asks an unsuspecting motorist to drive her home.

One of the scariest reports of the ghost appeared in a 1987 *Dallas Times Herald* article by Lorraine Iannello. Iannello interviewed a mother and daughter, Phyllis Thompson and Sue Ann Ashman, who had a frightening encounter with the female phantom. The two were sitting on one of the boat docks at night when they spotted a white object floating in the lake. The women heard a blood-curdling scream and saw the white object roll over onto its back. The object turned out to be a body; it stared at the horror-stricken women through big, hollow sockets where the eyes should have been. Then, just as quickly, the terrifying sight disappeared. I do love ghost hunting, but stories like this one make me think twice about going out to White Rock Lake alone on a dark, starless night!

Less Spooky Things To Do In Dallas

Conspiracy theorists will enjoy visiting **The Conspiracy Museum** with exhibits describing theories on numerous political figures, including John F. Kennedy, Robert Kennedy, and Abraham Lincoln. The source of the granddaddy of all conspiracy theories, the assassination of JFK in **Dealy Plaza**, is memorialized and analyzed at the **John F. Kennedy Memorial** in the **Dallas County Historic Plaza** and in the **The Sixth Floor (JFK) Museum**, an educational exhibit and memorial to the life, death, and legacy of President Kennedy. The display is on the sixth floor of the former Texas School Book Depository, the site from which the shots that killed President Kennedy were allegedly fired. Visitors will enjoy a trip to the **West End Historic District**, the city's most unique restaurant, retail, and nightlife district, offering hungry ghost hunters a wide variety of international cuisine and eclectic entertainment options. This area is chock full of historically preserved buildings and a colorful street life featuring old-fashioned street vendors as well as sidewalk cafés where ghost buffs can have a cup of coffee and plan their next investigation.

Fair Park is located two miles east of downtown Dallas on I-30. Each October, Fair Park hosts the **State Fair of Texas**, which originated in 1886. The **Cotton Bowl, Science Place, Dallas Aquarium, Museum of Natural History**, and other exhibit buildings are located here. For music lovers, **Deep Ellum**, a former industrial area just east of downtown (including Elm, Main, and Commerce Streets), now houses much of Dallas's creative and artistic talent in nightclubs, galleries, shops, and restaurants. Dallas has many historically interesting (and haunted) cemeteries. The reportedly haunted **Freedman Cemetery**, north of downtown and bounded on the east by Central Expressway, is a pre–Civil War African-American burial ground. When plans to widen the highway were announced in 1989, the community intervened and successfully preserved the state and local historic landmark. Famous gangsters Bonnie and Clyde, both from Dallas, are buried here. Clyde Barrow's grave is located at the **Western Heights Cemetery** and Bonnie Parker is buried at **Crown Hill Cemetery**.

> *For more information on Dallas, contact:*
> **Dallas Convention and Visitors Bureau**
> 1201 Elm St., Suite 2000, Dallas, TX 75270
> 214-571-1000
> www.dallascvb.com

Fort Worth Phantoms

Fort Worth is located in northeastern Texas at the junction of I-20 and I-35. In 1849, Major Ripley Arnold and a troop of soldiers built Fort Worth to protect settlers homesteading in North Texas from Indian attacks. By 1853, the frontier had moved west. The fort was abandoned and the remaining buildings became the town of Fort Worth.

Fort Worth became a frequent stop for cattlemen who herded cattle on the open range and drove them north for a huge profit. By 1866, the city was a major rest stop for wranglers along the Chisholm Trail, earning its nickname "Cowtown." The city began to prosper in the cattle business and Fort Worth became the second largest livestock market in America. Between 1902 and 1912, 16 million cattle passed through the stockyards. Today, Fort Worth retains the spirit that earned it the nickname Cowtown, and has cultivated its softer, more sophisticated side, which has a burgeoning arts community.

BED & BREAKFASTS WITH A BOO!

Miss Molly's Bed & Breakfast Inn 👻👻👻👻

109–1/2 W. Exchange Ave., Fort Worth, TX 76106 • 800-99-MOLLY
Note: *At press time, Miss Molly's was changing ownership. Call for current information.*

Description and History

In 1910, the building that houses Miss Molly's, located in the North Stockyards, was a proper boarding house for visitors, traveling salesmen, and cattle buyers who came to the stockyards in droves. In the 1920s, a respectable woman named Amelia Elsner ran another rooming house here.

When "Miss Josie" King took over, everything changed. Miss Josie opened a bordello called the Gayette Hotel, and her girls serviced cowboys and businessmen in the nine rooms of the sporting house.

Several invisible visitors still frequent this old bordello, now Miss Molly's Bed and Breakfast Inn.

After the Gayette Hotel closed, the building was used as an art gallery before Mark and Susan Hancock purchased it. Today, Miss Molly's Bed & Breakfast Inn is the perfect base from which to truly experience the Fort Worth Stockyards and step back into the rowdy days of Cowtown's colorful past.

Most of the rooms at Miss Molly's are available for under $100 a night, with the exception of Miss Josie's room, which goes for closer to $200 per night. Seven of the eight rooms reflect the original décor, including lace curtains, iron beds, antique quilts, and oak furniture. The bathrooms, which are down the hall from the guest rooms, contain iron tubs, pull-chain toilets, and pedestal sinks. Miss Josie's room, the madam's quarters, possesses an elegant Victorian decor and private bathroom.

Breakfast is served in the parlor beneath the stained glass skylight—the perfect spot to enjoy coffee, tea, juice, fresh fruit, and hearty specialty breads while reading the paper or visiting with other guests. For more information on Miss Molly's Bed and Breakfast Inn, call 800-99-MOLLY or 817-626-1522.

Ghostly Visitations

A local journalist staying the night in the Cowboy Room was awakened by a lovely blond woman standing at the foot of his bed. A night in the Cattlemen's Room provided another gentlemen with an unexpected nocturnal visitor, albeit not as attractive as the blond in the Cowboy

Most Haunted Areas:
The Cowboy Room, Cattlemen's Room, and kitchen

Room. In the light coming from the transom over the door, the Englishman saw the prim and proper figure of an elderly woman standing at the foot of his bed. The Hancocks believe this could be the spirit of Miss Amelia Elsner, who ran a respectable rooming house here in the 1920s.

And a visiting psychic sensed an overwhelming female presence in the kitchen, next door to Miss Josie's former room. It seems the old building is still being used as a boarding house—for spirits this time around!

SPIRITED BUILDINGS AND HOUSES

Barber's Bookstore 👻👻👻
215 W. 8th St., Fort Worth, TX 76102 • 817-335-5469

Description and History
Located just off Highway 30 near General Worth Square, the old building, constructed in 1908, was once a walk-up hotel. Brian Perkins has owned Barber's Bookstore, a popular Fort Worth landmark, since 1955. The bookstore sells used and rare books and keeps regular business hours. The store is closed on Sunday.

Ghostly Visitations
Perkins believes that three entities call Barber's Bookstore home. The first ghost Perkins refers to as the "Sunday spirit," a quiet soul who loves to browse through books while Perkins

> **Most Haunted Area:**
> *The upstairs*

is restocking or catching up on paperwork. Perkins can hear pages turning quite clearly in the still store and is happy for the company on these peaceful days.

He has also heard unaccountable noises and seen shadows when alone in the store. One morning after hearing someone walking around upstairs, he set the alarm, walked down the street, and called his son for assistance. Sure there was a burglar in the store, he asked his son to bring a gun. The alarm never sounded and the father and son searched the entire store without discovering anyone or finding an explanation.

While working alone, Perkins and his son have heard someone (or something) run up the stairs. Early one morning, while enjoying the quiet solitude of the empty building, Perkins's son heard heavy footsteps approaching from outside the open door. He looked up just in time to see the figure of a man wearing bluejeans and a T-shirt pass by the open doorway. He jumped up, grabbed his gun, and searched the entire building, never finding the guy in the T-shirt. He believes the man he saw was definitely a ghost!

Log Cabin Village 👻👻👻
2100 Log Cabin Village Lane, Fort Worth, TX 76109 • 817-926-5881

Description and History
The haunted cabin, now part of the Log Cabin Village, was the home of Harry Foster, his wife Martha, and their five children in the late 1830s or early 1840s. Foster built the cabin close to the cotton-producing town of Calvert, near the present site of Texas Christian University and Forest Park. After the death of Foster's wife in 1870, a woman thought to have worked as a housekeeper for the aging Mr. Foster, a Mrs. Jane Holt, lived with the elderly man and his children in the cabin.

In the early 1970s, the two-story, 55-foot-long house was disassembled and brought to Fort Worth for exhibition. The Log Cabin Village is a re-creation of pioneer life in frontier Texas during the 1880s, with tours of authentic log cabins and demonstrations of the activities of early settlers. Call 817-926-5881 for hours and admission.

Ghostly Visitations

The staff at the Log Cabin Village has had numerous encounters with a female spirit they believe to be either Martha Foster, or more likely, Jane Holt. The spirit's presence is

accompanied by the scent of lilacs, a sudden drop in temperature, and a static charge in the air (perfect for measuring with an electromagnetic field meter).

A team of parapsychologists called the corner upstairs bedroom a paranormal hot spot, validating what employees have felt for years to be true. Many witnesses have seen the apparition of a woman between 30 and 40 years old with long dark hair in the house. She is wearing a long black skirt and a high-collared mauve blouse with wide-shouldered leg o' mutton sleeves. In the 1800s, Texas pioneer women commonly wore this type of outfit. Most of the time, she appears to visitors on the upper floor, but has been known to venture down the stairs at least twice.

Visitors to the cabin were so frightened by these surprise visits that the city closed the upper floors of the cabin to the public and turned them into staff offices. The book *Phantoms of the Plains* by Docia Williams quotes Bettie Regester, the museum's historical curator until 1994. According to Regester, while she was working there, "I wouldn't have thought of her for months, but then I'd have to go up into the attic for something, and at the base of the stairs I would suddenly feel her presence. I knew she was up there, waiting for me. Three times it happened, and each time I just couldn't do it. I turned around and didn't continue up the stairs." You can hardly blame her!

Thistle Hill Historic Home 👻👻👻

1509 Pennsylvania Ave., Fort Worth, TX 76104 • 817-336-1212

Description and History

Built in 1903, Thistle Hill was one of many mansions on Quality Hill, most of which have been torn down over the years. The National Register of Historic Places describes Thistle Hill as "one of the few remaining examples of Georgian Revival architecture in the Southwest," making the home as important for its architecture as for its history—and its plentiful paranormal population.

During the guided tour of Thistle Hill, you will hear family anecdotes, learn local history, and discover information about the house and furnishings.

Several investigators have experienced strange occurrences inside the historic Thistle Hill mansion.

To visit the mansion, travel I-35 to the Rosedale Street exit and make a left on South Henderson Street followed by a right onto Pennsylvania Avenue. Call 817-336-1212 for hours of operation and admission.

Ghostly Visitations

This huge mansion is home to an entire gang of ghosts. Reports are plentiful of a woman in white appearing period- ically on the grand staircase; of a man with a handlebar mustache, wearing tennis togs and looking down from the top of the stairs; and of mysterious music coming from the sealed-off third-floor ballroom.

> **Most Haunted Areas:**
> *The ballroom and the staircase*

A group of ghost hunters including Andy Grieser, who writes for the *Star-Telegram*, spent an eventful night at the historic home and were not disappointed. In his article "The Haunting of Thistle Hill," Grieser reports that a rocking chair covered in heavy plastic in the grand ballroom was found uncovered and moved at least three times during the investigation. Two team members heard a deep voice coming from the veranda outside the ballroom saying, "What the hell?"

Andy reports that on a previous visit to the mansion, an envelope of newspaper clippings and a flashlight left on a downstairs table disappeared, only to turn up later in the billiards room. Something strange is definitely going on inside the grand Thistle Hill Historic Home. One of my best friends is getting married in the house soon. I plan to bring a wedding gift and my electromagnetic field meter, just in case!

 # Less Spooky Things To Do In Fort Worth

Experience the legend of the Old West in the **Stockyards National Historic District**. Walk along covered boardwalks while listening to troubadours. Attend a thrilling rodeo or cattle auction at the **Cowtown Coliseum**. Learn the two-step in the "world's largest honky- tonk," **Billy Bob's Texas**, and satisfy your hunger with a Texas-size steak. Downtown Fort Worth has **Sundance Square**, a variety of restaurants, art galleries, boutiques, theaters, and night spots. Jazz lovers *must* spend an evening at **Caravan of Dreams**, Fort Worth's best jazz club. Only two miles from downtown, the **Fort Worth Cultural District** is surpassed in size only by its counterparts in New York City and Washington, D.C. Two well-known art museums are must-sees—the **Amon Carter Museum**, featuring works by Western artists and major nineteenth- and early twentieth-century American artists; and the **Kimbell Art Museum**, recognized as "America's best small museum" for its world-renowned collection. The largest science and history museum in the Southwest, the **Fort Worth Museum of Science and History**, features an Omni theater and plane- tarium shows. Visit the **Fort Worth Zoo**, one of the top five zoos in America. Its nat- ural habitat exhibits bring you face-to-face with the animals.

> *For more information on Fort Worth, contact:*
> Fort Worth Convention and Visitors Bureau
> Water Gardens Plaza, 100 E. 15th St., Suite 400
> Fort Worth, TX 76102
> 800-433-5747 • 817-336-8791
> www.fortworth.com/index1.html

Haunted Hillsboro

Hillsboro is located just off I-35 between Waco and Fort Worth. In the last quarter of the nineteenth century, when cotton was king and ruled this part of Texas, Hillsboro was born. Centrally located in the heart of the Lone Star State, Hillsboro is known as the "Antique Capital of I-35" and boasts more than 200 antique shops in the downtown area. Residents are proud of Hillsboro's roots: More than 250 Hillsboro homes are listed on the National Register of Historic Places, including the haunted Tarlton House Bed and Breakfast of 1895.

 ## BED & BREAKFASTS WITH A BOO!

Tarlton House Bed and Breakfast of 1895 👶👶👶

211 N. Pleasant, Hillsboro, TX 76645 • 800-823-7216

Description and History

A prominent Hillsboro attorney named Green Duke Tarlton built the Tarlton House in 1895 for his growing family. Located just off the main square downtown, the home is the largest in Hillsboro, measuring more than 7,000 square feet. Of the Tarltons' seven children, one was born in the house and four lived to adulthood. In 1907, Mrs. Tarlton died of unknown causes. To the dismay of his children, Tarlton remarried

A hanging started the haunting of the Tarlton House.

fairly quickly. Because his children hated his second wife, Tarlton built his new bride a pretty yellow house next door.

During the Great Depression, the Tarltons lost everything—except for the grand house on North Pleasant. In 1931, the second Mrs. Tarlton passed away from pneumonia. The newspaper obituary states that Green Duke Tarlton died on the same day from undisclosed causes. After staying overnight as guests, current owners Pat and Bill Lovelace bought the large Victorian house.

The Tarlton House Bed and Breakfast of 1895 is listed on the National and Texas State Registers of Historical Places. Accommodations include eight rooms with private baths. Each room is individually climate-controlled and has its own TV. Pat Lovelace offers fun-filled Murder Mystery Weekends and relaxing Pamper Package Spa Weekends—

be sure to call for information, 254-582-7216, or visit the website at www.triab.com/tarlton. You can make reservations in advance with check, money order, cash, or credit card (American Express, MasterCard, or Visa). A night at the Tarlton House is an inexpensive treat with special rates for the weekday traveler. All rates are quoted at double occupancy with a $10 charge for additional persons in the room. The cancellation policy requires 72 hours advance notice; special groups and packages require more notice. Smoking and pets are prohibited, and restrictions may apply to children under 12. The staff serves coffee and juice at 8 a.m. and a full breakfast at 9 a.m.

Ghostly Visitations

Hillsboro legend holds that 70 years ago, Tarlton left his dead second wife in her little yellow house, walked next door into his beloved home, and climbed the stairs to the dark attic, where he hanged himself from a sturdy beam. Pat Lovelace

> **Most Haunted Areas:**
> *The Floral Suite, the Gables Suite bathroom, Abby's Attic, and the Tower Suite*

believes the shade that walks the third floor of her beautiful Victorian home is indeed Green Duke Tarlton. By all accounts, Tarlton loved his house and it seems sensible that he would choose to stay in the home where he raised his family and spent his final destitute days after losing his fortune.

Green Duke Tarlton still mourns for his wife in their home.

For years, citizens of Hillsboro thought of the Tarlton House as haunted. Several long-time residents told Pat that they habitually cross to the other side of the street rather than walk by the old home. This reputation saved the building from vandals during the years it stood vacant. As a result, many treasures, such as the seven original coal-burning fireplaces rimmed in imported Italian tiles, remain intact.

The most commonly reported occurrence in the third-floor guest rooms is the "sinking" of the beds' mattresses as if someone has just sat down. Pat experienced this phenomenon once while kneeling on the bed in Abby's Attic to adjust the air conditioning. She felt the depression and thought her cat, Sadie, had jumped up on the bed. Looking down, Pat saw an empty bed. A quick check downstairs confirmed that Sadie and the Lovelace's other cat, Steely Dan, were secured in the kitchen.

Maria, former housekeeper and current masseuse for Pat's Pamper Package Spa Weekends, claims she saw Tarlton while making the bed in the Tower Suite. He was crouched over with his hands on his knees, studying Maria from the hallway, and appeared very real and solid.

On the sweltering June afternoon that I toured the third floor with Pat, I found myself covered with goosebumps and having difficulty adjusting the pressure in my ears. Pat apologized for the heat upstairs, explaining that the third floor air conditioning units had not been turned on due to the lack of guests that day. Although I was sweating, every hair on my arms and legs was standing on end.

The supernatural antics are not confined to the third floor. Another guest felt an ice cube drop from an unseen hand into her glass of iced tea while she was standing in the dining room. Pat has experienced a small storage door in the Gables Suite bathroom opening on its own. Another visitor, spending the night in the Floral Room, reported overhearing a conversation between a man and woman in her room, but she couldn't make out what was being said. Pat wonders if this was perhaps a conversation between Tarlton and his first or second wife.

Pat also said the ghost is particularly active when teenagers are in the house. Recently, 13 teens stayed overnight and experienced several different camera malfunctions in the dining room. Pat theorizes that the spirits of Tarlton House are attracted to and make use of the bountiful energy of adolescents. Many ghost researchers believe in "paranormal parasites," or entities relying on *living* energy to aid in manifesting their activities in the physical world.

Less Spooky Things To Do In Hillsboro

Visit the renovated **Hill County Courthouse**, the **Texas Heritage Museum**, the **MKT Depot**, and the **Cell Block Museum**, where Elvis spent an event-filled evening in jail for a drunk and disorderly charge. For those of you who delight in a good deal, there's the **Hillsboro Outlet Center**, with more than 100 designer-quality shops offering selections at discount prices. Outdoor lovers will like the nearby **Lake Aquilla** and **Lake Whitney**, where visitors enjoy camping, fishing, boating, and water sports. Hillsboro sponsors monthly activities year-round. From the **Confederate History Symposium** in April to the **Heritage League Tour of Homes** in December, there is something for everyone on Hillsboro's annual calendar.

For more information on Hillsboro, contact:
Hillsboro Chamber of Commerce
Convention and Visitors Bureau
P.O. Box 358, Hillsboro, TX 76645
800-HILLSBORO • 254-582-2481
www.hillsboro.net/chamber

Waxahachie Revenants

Most Haunted Town in North Texas

Waxahachie is located 40 miles south of Dallas on I-35. A tour brochure for Waxahachie urges travelers to "Listen…for a moment, you can hear the carriages on stone streets and the creaking of rockers on verandas made of pine." Waxahachie, home to more than 20 percent of all Texas buildings listed on the National Register of Historic Places, is known as "Gingerbread City." More than 20,000 visitors flock to the town annually to admire the Victorian, Greek Revival, Carpenter Gothic, and Queen Anne homes presiding over tree-lined streets.

BED & BREAKFASTS WITH A BOO!

The BonnyNook Bed and Breakfast Inn 👻

414 W. Main St., Waxahachie, TX 75165 • 800-486-5936

Description and History

The BonnyNook Bed and Breakfast Inn, formerly known as the Brown/West home, was built between 1887 and 1894, on Main, otherwise known as Highway 287. The Victorian is located in the West End Historical District, just two short blocks from the town square and the historic Waxahachie courthouse. The BonnyNook is documented in the National Register of Historic Places and recognized by Historic Waxahachie.

A tragic explosion set the stage for the haunting of the BonnyNook Inn.

Nathan Brown, a Waxahachie merchant, purchased the land in 1887 to build this beautiful Gingerbread home. He later sold the property to W.T. Hunt, who, after one year, sold the home to Dr. W.F. West, a prominent doctor.

In the late 1890s, Dr. and Mrs. West moved into the house with their son and Mrs. West's sister. During the early 1900s, they added a kitchen that included a heavy iron stove. Tragically, the stove was defective and blew up, killing Mrs. West with flying pieces of metal and nearly burning the house to the ground. Just three months later, Dr. West married the late Mrs. West's sister, and not waiting the normal one-to-two-year mourning period, caused quite a bit of controversy.

In 1914, Mary Wyatt bought the home and converted it into a boarding house. The home remained in her family until 1979, when

Dean Cory, a famous cellist with the Fort Worth Symphony, bought it. Vaughn and Bonnie Franks purchased the property in 1983 and began renovations for the first bed-and-breakfast inn in Waxahachie. The BonnyNook Inn opened for business in 1989.

The BonnyNook Inn has six guest rooms, all furnished in antiques of different periods. Two rooms have king-size beds with Jacuzzis. All have private baths, tables and easy chairs, books, fresh flowers, and snack trays.

An overnight stay at the BonnyNook Inn is inexpensive. The inn caters to business meetings, card parties, weddings, and other group activities. The room rates include complimentary refreshments and a full breakfast.

The B'Nook Dining Salon is open to guests as well as the public and offers "Haute Texas Nouveau Victorian Cuisine," including such delicious possibilities as beef BonnyNook (sirloin encased in a pastry shell), Cajun chicken, fish with marinara sauce, breast of turkey with oyster sauce, and a vegetarian mushroom medley. Entrées include an appetizer, soup, salad, sorbet, vegetable, and dessert, all for a *prix fixe* of $45 per person. Make reservations by noon the day of your dinner. If making reservations for four or more, make your request 24 hours in advance. For more information, call 972-938-7207 or visit the website at www.hat.org.

Ghostly Visitations

The Franks believe their ghost is the first Mrs. West, who was tragically killed in the kitchen explosion a hundred years ago. Mrs. West's shade inhabits the Morrow Room and

> **Most Haunted Area:**
> *The Morrow Room*

rarely ventures into other parts of the house. When the Franks moved into the Gingerbread house in 1983, this room had been closed for more than 70 years. The roof had collapsed and major repair work was required to make the room safe and habitable once again.

Bonnie Franks has experienced Mrs. West's benign presence in the Morrow Room; she communicates with the spirit, receiving positive and negative feedback from Mrs. West regarding changes made to the home. Guests in the Morrow Room have reported hearing singing and seeing an image floating near the ceiling. Experiences are fairly rare—Vaughn Franks estimates that 1 in 50 guests report unusual activity in Mrs. West's room.

The Chaska House Bed and Breakfast 🗝🗝🗝

716 W. Main St., Waxahachie, TX 75165 • 800-931-3390

Description and History

In 1900, Edward and Marie Chaska built this gracious, two-story Greek Revival frame house, located just off what is now Highway 287. The Chaskas owned and operated a dry goods store on the square called the "Emporium of Fashion." In 1909, Edward Chaska died at age 53 in New Jersey while undergoing medical treatment for a chronic ailment. The house passed to his widow, Marie, who lived in the house until her death in 1953. The couple was childless and Marie died without a will. As a result, the property was inventoried by a court-appointed administrator and sold at auction on the courthouse steps in August of 1953. Two brothers, J.F. and O.B. Dunaway, purchased the house and its contents.

Following the Dunaway brothers, James and Ruth Saxon purchased the house and lived in it until both died within two years of each other. Mrs. A.L. Hardesty, formerly known as Miss Sadie Ralston, purchased the home from the Saxon Estate. Miss Sadie was

The Chaska House is the perfect place to spend the night in hopes of experiencing the supernatural.

a notable and colorful long-time local school teacher who lived in the house until 1968. In the next decade, two families, the Fullers and then the McBurneys, owned the property. Louis and Linda Brown bought the Chaska House in 1980 and began the restoration process. The Chaska House is a nationally registered historic landmark, described by *Texas Highways Magazine* as "Victorian Splendor." The romantic and inexpensive guest rooms feature private baths and sitting areas.

Reservations are accepted in advance by check, money order, cash, or credit card. All rates are quoted at double occupancy plus 13 percent tax; mid-week rates are available. Chaska House has a 72-hour cancellation policy. A full southern breakfast is served in the formal dining room. Call 800-931-3390 or 972-937-3390 for more information or to make reservations, or visit the website at www.hat.org.

Ghostly Visitations

Innkeepers Louis and Linda Brown moved into the Chaska House in February 1980. According to Louis, the most memorable and unexplainable event that happened in the 20 years they've lived in the house concerns one of the first changes the Browns made to their new

> **Most Haunted Areas:**
> *The upstairs, including the staircase and the Plantation Room*

home. The Browns disconnected an extensive 1950s-era phone system, which included a heavy black rotary telephone in each room. During the first week of the Brown's occupation, the Chaska House was wired for several modern telephones.

With most of their possessions still in boxes, the Browns sat down to dinner one night. During the meal, a phone began ringing. The ringing was not coming from the new telephone in the Brown's kitchen, but from somewhere upstairs. After several minutes of listening to the phone ring, checking the kitchen phone only to find a dial tone, and trying to resume dinner, the Browns headed upstairs to find the source. Louis discovered one of the old black rotary phones lying disconnected under a pile of boxes in a bedroom. This disconnected phone was ringing. As his family joined him in looking at the phone in disbelief, Louis answered it. His ear was filled with static and a croaky old woman's voice asking politely, "May I speak to Mrs. Curline?" Louis responded that she had the wrong number and hung up. He quickly picked up the receiver once more and was met with the absolute silence of a dead phone.

Months later, Louis asked a neighbor about Mrs. Curline. He found out that, indeed, a Mrs. Curline had lived across the street from the Chaska House, but had been dead for years. Louis is a no-nonsense engineer and is stymied by an experience he can't logically explain.

The Browns feel sure the spirit is female but aren't sure if it's Mrs. Chaska or Mrs. Ralston, both past owners of the elegant home. Louis claims the ghost is often helpful. One Sunday morning in the early 1980s, as the rest of the family waited in the car, Louis Jr. stood at the mirror in his bathroom combing and fussing over his hair for church as teenagers do. A distinct female voice, very close to his ear, told him, "Hurry, Louis, or you'll be late." Needless to say, young Louis rushed off to church that Sunday with his hair less than perfect.

Louis Jr. also experienced something so frightening that he didn't tell his parents about it until he left the house for college. His bedroom was at the top of the main staircase and every night he would lie awake listening for "her" footsteps to walk halfway up the staircase and then stop. Louis Jr. got to know every creak in that old staircase during the years he consistently experienced this nocturnal ghostly journey.

Activity in the house includes electrical disturbances, footsteps pacing the upstairs hallway, doors opening and closing, and water turning on and off. During many breakfasts at the Browns' table, guests have questioned late-night knocks on their doors. The Browns have also experienced the knocking phenomenon while staying in the Plantation Room, but were never able to locate the source of these tapping sounds.

Many nights, Linda will be downstairs wrapping up her day while Louis retires to the bedroom they share upstairs. He often senses a figure standing over him as he falls asleep knowing he is alone in the room...or is he?

Rose of Sharon 👶👶👶

205 Bryson, Waxahachie, TX 75165 • 972-938-8833

Description and History

Prominent attorney F.P. Powell built this home for his new bride in 1892; the Rose of Sharon is located just off Highway 77, which runs through town. The Powells had two daughters while living in the house before moving to Austin in 1912.

After the Powells' departure, the house had a long succession of owners. After World War II, a couple bought the building for use as a boarding house. The wide first- and second-story porches were enclosed for additional rooms

The very beautiful and very haunted Rose of Sharon is a favorite among visitors to Waxahachie.

during this period. The house served as a rooming house for 30 years.

In the late 1970s, a single mom moved into the house for 10 years. The building was repossessed in 1987, and it stood vacant for several years before current owner Sharon Shawn purchased it in 1991, restored it, and opened a bed-and-breakfast inn.

An overnight stay at the Rose of Sharon is moderately priced and includes a delicious home-cooked breakfast. Mine consisted of tasty muffins, sausage, grapefruit, coffee, and juice.

Ghostly Visitations

Innkeeper Sharon Shawn used to be afraid to be alone at night. That was before she moved into her beautifully restored Victorian home known as the Rose of Sharon.

These days (or, rather, nights) when Sharon has to retrieve something from another part of the house, she navigates long hallways and rooms without even turning on the lights. She feels safe, warm, and protected.

I had the same experience the night I spent at the Rose of Sharon in June 1999 while researching this book. My night's rest was peaceful and undisturbed, even though I spent the night with a family of four in my bathroom—all dead for almost 100 years.

The innkeeper described an urge to buy this house that was so strong it defied common sense. The house was in extreme disrepair and had been abandoned and neglected for years. Shawn and her husband had just purchased a new home around the corner from the derelict building. Nevertheless, Shawn felt drawn to the wisteria-vine-covered home. The house, hidden under ugly asbestos siding, had long ago been segmented into many individual apartments when it was used as a boarding house. Even in this horrible state, Shawn could see the potential and was determined to restore the Powell's dream house to its former grandeur.

Shawn and her husband purchased the home and began planning their restoration efforts. One afternoon shortly after purchasing it, Shawn made her first visit alone to the house. She entered the front door and made her way through the maze of rooms and through a tiny door into what is now the formal dining room. Her purse was heavy and cumbersome, so she left it on the floor of this room and maneuvered through another small door into an adjacent room to explore. Shawn found heaps of old newspapers and magazines that kept her occupied for longer than she had planned. Shadows stretched across the room as dusk rapidly approached. Shawn backtracked through the house, stopping to

retrieve her purse along the way. To her surprise and delight, she found two 14-carat gold hoop earrings—a favorite pair she'd lost more than a year before—lying a foot away from her bag. The earrings were totally unexplainable but much appreciated; Shawn believes they were a welcome gift from the original owners of the house, the Powell family.

Shawn has seen the four Powell family members standing in the Cathryn's Room

Does a family of four occupy this bathroom in Cathryn's Room?

bathroom on three occasions. The family is posed for a family portrait, all dressed in early twentieth-century clothing, with the man wearing a gray suit and the woman in a long dress. Two little girls wear white dresses with sashes and one carries a doll draped over her arm. The figures are a bit hazy and glow with an otherworldly light. Shawn admits the experience is a bit startling, but not frightening.

While she's making the bed, Shawn often feels a presence in Cathryn's Room. She describes it as a warm, loving sensation. Shawn thinks of the Powells as her invisible room-mates. She hears them moving through the house and just lets them do their own thing while she does hers.

Seven Gables 👦👦

501 N. College St., Waxahachie, TX 75165 • 972-938-7500

Description and History

Built in 1898 and located just off the present Highway 77, Seven Gables offers the "Old Waxahachie Charm…In a Suite Package!" in its three magnificent suites with private sit-

Keep an eye on your keys while staying at Seven Gables.

ting areas and bathrooms. The large rooms in this quaint Victorian are furnished with antiques and period-style furniture. A night at Seven Gables is an inexpensive treat with all the comforts of home including TVs and VCRs in each suite.

Reservations are accepted in advance by check, money order, or cash and must be guaranteed by a deposit equal to one night's stay or 50 percent, whichever is greater, within 10 days of making the reservation. The balance is due upon arrival, and unconfirmed reservations will be canceled. All rates are quoted at double occupancy and an additional 13 percent hotel tax applies. The cancellation policy requires seven days' notice for a full refund. Reservations canceled within seven days of arrival will be refunded only if another party assumes reservations, and the refund will be minus a $25 processing fee. Smoking is permitted only on the veranda. Pets are prohibited, but children over 12 are welcome. A gourmet breakfast is included in the room rate.

Ghostly Visitations

Helen Sturges moved into her dream house, Seven Gables, on February 28, 1992. Her granddaughter was visiting and spent the first night with her (and otherworldly others, so it

> **Most Haunted Area:**
> *The Rose Room*

seems!). Around midnight, the alarm went off, scaring grandmother and granddaughter half to death. The police made a thorough search of the house, but found nothing unusual.

Subsequently, every night between midnight and 2 a.m., the back doorbell would ring just one long peal. This activity continued for an entire year without explanation. About this time, Helen married Jim Anderson, who moved into Seven Gables in 1994. The doorbell stopped ringing as often, but other unexplained activity was just beginning. One reccurring manifestation is the smell of cigarette smoke throughout the nonsmoking guest rooms of the house.

Helen's daughter and son-in-law, Janet and Jack, came to visit and stayed in the Rose Room. This room was added during Helen's reconstruction of the front of the house. Late that night, Janet woke up to find a cloud of cigarette smoke surrounding her husband's head. Because Jack is a smoker, her first thought was "Mama will kill him!" But then Janet realized that Jack was fast asleep.

On another occasion, Helen's 19-year-old granddaughter, Carrie, felt someone bounce up and down on the bed in the Rose Room—while she was in it! One morning at breakfast, guests staying in the Rose Room casually asked, "Who does Steven love?" A confused Helen said she didn't know. Apparently, the words "Steven loves" were scrawled on the glass shower door and appeared in the steam from the couple's morning showers.

Recently, Jim and Helen returned home from an errand. Because Jim had left his keys dangling in the door, Helen removed them and put them on the kitchen counter. When Jim needed to run out again, he asked Helen where his keys were. He went to retrieve his keys but couldn't find them anywhere in the kitchen. For the next hour, the couple turned the house upside down trying to find his keys. Giving up the search, Jim made the decision to drive the 91 miles to their ranch to get his extra set of keys. Helen talked him into lying down for their afternoon nap before setting off on his journey. Helen was lying on the bed reading when she rolled over onto Jim's set of keys! They were smack in the middle of the bed—definitely not there when Helen had lain down just minutes before. Helen told Jim that the ghosts saved him a long trip!

Guests have reported broken clocks ticking in their rooms and felt invisible people getting into bed with them. This happens so frequently that Helen has stopped asking guests how they slept for fear of the responses she receives. Helen has had electrical and plumbing problems and seen strange shadows looming over her. The night before my visit in June 1999, she heard low moans coming from inside her bedroom. She and Janet have seen white blobs of light floating in Helen's bedroom and the Rose Room.

Helen believes there are two male ghosts, both in their 60s or older, "living" in her house. She calls them "Uncle Joe" and "Grandpa." Previous tenants told her the dining room was once the bedroom of Uncle Joe. During a visit to see Helen's renovations, one of Joe's descendants reported that Uncle Joe had strangled to death in his bed.

In 1993, a young woman in her 30s stopped by to tell Helen that she had lived in the house as a child with her parents, brother, and grandfather in the 1970s. Her grandpa had a massive stroke and died in the front yard in 1976.

Helen stresses that Uncle Joe and Grandpa aren't mean-spirited, just feisty old-timers who love to play tricks on Helen, Jim, and their guests. Although Helen doesn't believe in ghosts, she does believe in Uncle Joe and Grandpa!

The Catfish Plantation ☺☺☺☺☺

814 Water St., Waxahachie, TX 75165 • 972-937-9468

Description and History

Found just off of Highway 287 on Water Street, this cozy Victorian house was built in 1895 and was the birthplace of baseball great Paul Richards. Richards played for the New York Yankees and managed the Baltimore Orioles and Chicago White Sox. Two other restaurants operated in this space until the Bakers bought it in the early 1980s. The Bakers opened the Catfish Plantation in 1984.

The most haunted restaurant in Texas, the Catfish Plantation is home to at least three wandering spooks.

The Bakers completed the most extensive restoration to date. Today the Victorian is a beautiful terra cotta with gingerbread trim and dark green and cream accents. In September 1998, Jeff and Alice Hageman bought the historic building from the Bakers. The Hagemans have made few changes to the restaurant's staff and menu. The Catfish Plantation still serves the best Cajun food this side of New Orleans and is one of the most haunted vacation destinations in the state.

The Catfish Plantation's hours are Thursday 5-8 p.m., Friday 11:30 a.m.-2 p.m. and 5-9 p.m., Saturday 11:30 a.m.-9 p.m., and Sunday 11:30 a.m.-8 p.m. The Catfish Plantation offers an inexpensive, scrumptious selection of down home cookin' from the best all-you-can-eat catfish in the state to a wide variety of Cajun dishes (such as the chef's specialty Catfish New Orleans) to frog legs and stuffed crab for Creole lovers. The desserts are to die for and include homemade cobbler and chocolate chip pie topped with vanilla ice cream and hot fudge. So bring your appetites and your nerves of steel to the most haunted restaurant in the Southwest for an evening of delicious food and paranormal pranks.

Ghostly Visitations

I had the pleasure of eating a delicious southern fried chicken dinner at the Catfish Plantation, the most haunted restaurant in Texas, in June 1999. The restaurant maintains three binders full of eyewitness accounts from employees

Most Haunted Areas:
Front dining room and bathrooms

"Elizabeth" was murdered on her wedding day in front of this fireplace.

and customers of the supernatural events that take place in the house. Time and again, people report tales of feeling cold hands on legs and knees, gymnastically inclined silverware, the strong fragrance of roses, sudden strong breezes and wind, cold spots, sounds of a piano playing an unidentifiable melody, and flying coffee cups, lemon slices, and dollar bills. One group of women wrote about the maraschino cherries in their drinks at dinner. The ladies ate the cherries and left the stems on the table. Throughout their meal, the stems were constantly flipping off onto the floor, and one stem disappeared entirely. When they left the restaurant, the ladies were amazed to find the missing stem sitting on the backseat of their locked car. Another extraordinary paranormal tidbit, related in an article in the October 1994 *Dallas Morning News*, describes a positively dumbfounded customer whose old driver's license—which he believed he had lost in Vietnam—materialized during his dinner at the restaurant. More than a little intrigued, I asked owners Jeff and Alice Hageman to describe their experiences since buying the restaurant in September 1998.

The Hagemans were true skeptics at the beginning, considering the stories of ghostly blue lights and flying wineglasses as fantasies designed to ensure publicity for the restaurant. They soon changed their minds. Jeff's first experience with the restaurant's penchant for the paranormal happened the first day he toured the building with its former owner Tom Baker. The two men walked out the front door to examine the patio area. After a few minutes of discussion, they walked back to the front door to reenter the restaurant. The door was locked. Tom Baker grinned at Jeff rather sheepishly and explained that this must be the work of one of the ghosts. Jeff laughed nervously to himself as they walked around to the back door. He knew Tom had not locked the front door, so who had? This strange event was only the tip of the proverbial paranormal iceberg.

In the first nine months they owned the restaurant, the Hagemans have witnessed so many unexplainable things that they have both become believers in the unknown forces that walk the floors of their 1895 Victorian. Jeff has experienced several auditory anomalies with the female ghosts of the Catfish Plantation. He was working out back one weekday afternoon when the restaurant was closed to business. He heard a woman's voice call "Hello!" to him from the direction of the back door. Jeff thought a customer had wandered into the restaurant, not knowing they were closed. A careful inspection revealed that no one was inside and that the front door was locked. Numerous times, Jeff has heard a woman just behind his shoulder whisper his name when no one was there. He wrote this off as a fatigue symptom until a waitress, Cathleen, described the same experience to him.

The restaurant has an elaborate motion-activated alarm system that had to be disconnected during slow weekdays due to the number of times it went off unexplainably in the middle of the night. Jeff was continually roused from sleep to venture down to the dark restaurant, disarm the system, and wander around checking doors and windows. Because these nocturnal trips made him extremely uncomfortable and agitated to be alone in the building, it seemed easier just to leave the system off during the week. I can't say that I blame him one bit!

Jeff's wife, Alice, has several stories of her own encounters with the Plantation's spirits. Recently, she was sitting in a chair working on one of several wreaths decorating the tiny alcove where the restrooms are located. Her back was to the door leading to the front dining room and her chair was blocking the doors to the men's and ladies' rooms. Alice heard the dining room door open and saw someone standing just behind her left shoulder. She quickly excused herself and stood to move out of the way, but there was no one behind her.

In fact, quite a bit of activity centers on both bathrooms. Alice was using the restroom one evening during business hours when the shuttered swinging stall doors started to rattle and shake. She set a new world record for "finishing her business" that night. Customers complain of cold drafts and unseen forces flushing toilets and turning on water while they're visiting the restrooms. One customer reported approaching the men's room and hearing a man coughing behind the door. Soon the patron heard a nose being blown and a toilet flush. After several minutes of silence, the man knocked on the door. He finally opened the door to a completely empty bathroom.

Around Halloween 1998, Alice had several visiting friends come to dinner. The group was sitting in the front dining room by a window. The restaurant was busy that night and Alice was called away from the table to check out a customer. About a minute after she walked off, the group saw a figure pass outside the dark window and heard a hard knock. Startled but sure that Alice had succeeded in giving them all quite a fright, they laughed and waited for their hostess to "reappear." When Alice did return, they scolded her that they had all jumped several feet in the air after her little stunt. An innocent Alice asked them to explain, then assured her friends she'd been busy at the cash register for the last 15 minutes.

On a sunny weekend afternoon, Alice was tending to some diners on the outdoor patio. The strings to her apron were securely tied in front after being wrapped twice around her waist. While taking her customers' orders, Alice felt the apron fall to the ground. Apparently, this is a favorite ghostly trick to play on the wait staff as many employees have had their apron strings untied mysteriously.

Two formal investigations of the building occurred during the Bakers' ownership. The first one, in 1987, was a full team of parapsychologists, engineers, scientists, and psychics as well as two representatives from the University of Texas. The crew used sensitive sound equipment, laser light beams, thermometer gauges, and infrared cameras to measure the activity in the restaurant. Five separate investigations were conducted and the psychics all agreed that three entities haunt the Catfish Plantation.

A 1988 investigation sponsored by *D Magazine* turned up similar results. The magazine researched the history of the house to confirm the identities of the three ghosts. "Will" is the lone male haunting the Catfish Plantation. He was a Depression-era farmer who lived in the house. He's been sighted wearing overalls, standing by the fireplace, and watching passing cars from the front porch. Employees think "Will" is behind the apron string pranks and likes to put cold hands on the knees and legs of pretty customers and waitresses.

The Plantation's trouble-maker is "Caroline" or "Carrie," a former owner who lived and died in the house in the 1970s. She is described as a disgruntled matron who throws food and dishes in the kitchen in reaction to the presence of so many strange mortals in her home.

The third specter is the tragic "Elizabeth." The story of this lost soul explains her need for companionship with the living. She died in the front room by the fireplace on her wedding day in 1920. Although research has confirmed her death, the circumstances surrounding that unfortunate day are lost in time. One theory suggests that Elizabeth was forced to marry an older man she didn't love and was strangled to death by her young, jealous lover. Another legend says she killed herself in despair at the thought of being separated from her true love. Poor Elizabeth is still seen and has been photographed looking out a window in her wedding dress, complete with a lacy parasol.

Elizabeth is often felt in the front dining room where she died. One afternoon, Alice stood in this room thinking of her father, who had recently died. She felt a cold, but tender hand on her arm. Alice thinks this was the compassionate Elizabeth offering comfort and sympathy.

Elizabeth has also been known to follow employees home. Alice described an apparition she saw in the rearview mirror of her car while exiting the parking lot one evening. This female form was sitting in the passenger seat of a waiter's car behind hers. Kristen, a two-year veteran of the Catfish Plantation, told me about two other employees who saw a shadowy figure seated in her passenger seat as the group was leaving for the evening. Knowing how frightened Kristen could become when confronted with the odd activity in the restaurant, the employees waited two months to tell Kristen what they saw sitting next to her. A former owner, Melissa Baker, tells of Elizabeth leaving the restaurant with her and appearing in her own home. It seems this lonely spirit just wants some company. Leaving the restaurant the night of my interviews, I asked Alice and Kristen to watch my car as I drove off and be sure to call me if they saw a shadowy figure sitting next to me. I talked to my seemingly empty passenger seat just a little bit in case Elizabeth was indeed sitting next to me.

 **Less Spooky Things To Do In Waxahachie**

Every June on the "**Gingerbread Trail**," the beautiful town celebrates her rich architectural heritage by offering guided tours through manors and mansions built by the cotton barons of the nineteenth century. During this annual event, an arts and crafts fair, antique automobile show, and old-fashioned street dance round out the festivities. Other not-to-be-missed attractions include the **Scarborough Faire**, located just west of Waxahachie in the 35-acre village of Scarborough. Beginning the last weekend of April and running through mid-June, Scarborough Faire is one of the largest renaissance festivals in the country. Step back into the sixteenth century and experience all that once was, through costumed actors, period music, full-contact jousting, and bird of prey demonstrations. The **Ellis County Courthouse**, often described as one of the most photographed buildings in Texas, is famous for its curious connections to a stone mason's broken heart. The Italian stone carver, employed to sculpt the courthouse's stone columns, fell in love with a local girl. The lovesick man immortalized his love by carving her image into the building's façade. When the girl did not return the mason's affections, the rejected suitor continued to carve her likeness in the stone, making it progressively uglier.

For more information on Waxahachie, contact:
Waxahachie Chamber of Commerce
Convention and Visitors Bureau
102 YMCA Dr., P.O. Box 187,
Waxahachie, TX 75168
972-937-2390
www.waxacofc.com

Elusive Boos of the North Texas Prairie

 There are several ghost hunting clubs active in North Texas and plenty of ghosts to hunt in this area of the state. On your next visit to "Big D" or "Cowtown," why not make your trip more dimensional by staying in a haunted bed-and-breakfast or wandering a spooky cemetery? Don't forget your camera!

1896 Railroad House Hotel, Cleburne
421 E. Henderson St., Cleburne, TX 76031 • 817-517-5529
Reports of mysterious footsteps come from the owners of this historic hotel.

Baccus Cemetery, Dallas
Reportedly contains several benevolent spirits.

Mt. Pleasant Cemetery, Dallas
Local investigators report that paranormal phenomena have increased in this cemetery, possibly because a subdivision is being built nearby.

Pioneer Cemetery, Dallas
The Dallas-based organization the Ghost Preservation League has found evidence of several spirits haunting this old downtown cemetery. Members have photographed glowing orbs and unexplained streaks of light hovering among the tombstones.

Sons of Hermann Hall, Dallas
Ghostly children heard laughing and playing, paintings that fall off the walls without cause, doors slamming on their own, and disembodied voices echoing through the building when the hall is quiet and locked to visitors are reported here. Apparitions of a man and woman dressed in early twentieth-century clothing have been spotted as well.

Pangburns Chocolate Shoppe, Fort Worth
When this building housed Fort Worth Books & Video, owners and customers were plagued by the appearance of unexplained lights, footsteps, and an unseen presence.

Peter Bros. Hats, Fort Worth
909 Houston St., Fort Worth, TX 76102 • 817-335-1715
Current owners (and descendants) think the founder of this business, known as "Granddad," haunts this establishment.

Texas White House Bed & Breakfast, Fort Worth
1417 Eighth Ave., Fort Worth, TX 76104 • 817-923-3597
The owners report unexplained paranormal activity from time to time. Guests have told of a ghostly presence in their rooms.

Ghost Clubs of the North Texas Prairie

 The following groups are active in the Dallas/Fort Worth area, with some traveling to surrounding towns to hunt ghosts.

Ghost Preservation League

Founder Janis Raley has investigated many haunted locations around Dallas.

The Ghost Stalkers

P.O. Box 126033, Fort Worth, TX 76126 • 817-731-HAUNT

The two founders of this group have 12 years' experience in hunting ghosts. Both have photographic and film production backgrounds, making spirit photography and filming a specialty. Based in Fort Worth, ghost hunts have taken this team all over the world. Website: www.ghoststalkers.com, e-mail: ghosttx@ghoststalkers.com

Paranormal Research Society

I love the acronym this group uses, SPOOKS, for Supernatural Phenomenon Organization of Kindred Spirits. This group is especially interested in Texas urban legends and their origins. Website: www.geocities.com/ladellpepper.

Otherworld Investigations

This organization is affiliated with the Philadelphia Ghost Hunters Alliance, and members describe themselves as "intrepid freelance investigators in the field of parapsychology." Website: home.flash.net/~brockam/paranorm.html.

Region 3
Ghosts of the East Texas Piney Woods

The Piney Woods region of East Texas is filled with darkened forests where nature lovers can walk ankle-deep through decaying pine needles beside still lakes. Towering trees dripping with Spanish moss block out the sun and create all sorts of wonderfully hidden nooks and crannies where the spirits of long-dead Caddo Indians roam. Native East Texans speak with soft drawls, love the spicy food inspired by their Cajun neighbors' cuisine, and hold generations-old beliefs in the ghosts that inhabit their forests, towns, and homes.

These deep woods are treasure troves of Texas history, containing beautiful old towns where stately mansions remind visitors of a simpler time—and usually house a spirit or two within their ancient walls. From Nacogdoches, the oldest town in Texas, to Jefferson, the most haunted small town in Texas, this region's earthly population has grown accustomed to sharing space with specters of varying shapes and sizes.

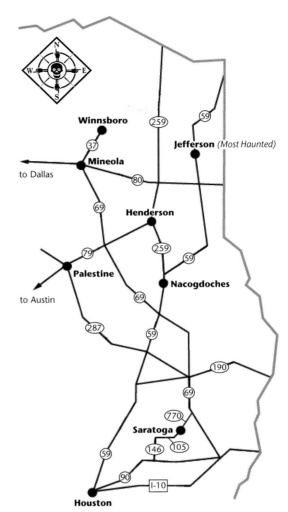

HAUNTED LOCATIONS

Henderson's Invisible Citizens

Named for J. Pickney Henderson, the first Attorney General of the Republic of Texas, the town of Henderson was created specifically to serve as the seat of Rusk County in the 1840s. It is located on Highway 259 about 30 miles north of Nacogdoches.

In the years before the Civil War, cotton was the main cash crop and several sprawling plantations flourished around the town. Having a lavish mansion with hundreds of slaves to run it was a way of life for Henderson's cotton barons and their families.

This area of East Texas lost many of its men during the War Between the States. Rusk County, the largest county in Texas, sent more men to fight in the Civil War than any other county in Texas. Following the war and reconstruction, better railroads were built through Henderson and the town prospered.

Henderson was a rural community until the Texas Oil Boom of 1930. The discovery of oil changed the lives of East Texans forever. At the turn of the century, cotton prices were low and the future looked bleak. Oil made many millions for a lucky few and brought jobs to the masses. Henderson's downtown area was designated as a National Register Historic District in 1996.

 SPIRITED BUILDINGS AND HOUSES

Howard-Dickinson House Museum 👻👻
903-657-6925

Description and History

Dave and Logan Howard built the Howard-Dickinson House in 1854. The brothers were brick masons and carpenters and the home was one of the first buildings constructed of brick in Rusk County. The Howards lived in the home from 1855 until 1905. Sam Houston, the first president of the Republic of Texas, was a cousin of and frequent visitor to Mrs. Dave Howard. In 1905, Mrs. M.A. Dickinson purchased the house. After her death, her daughter Kate Dickinson added a wing and operated the building as a boarding house until 1950.

Henderson entrepreneur Homer Bryce bought the historic home in 1964 and donated it to the Rusk County Heritage Association. The Heritage Association restored the home and furnished it with period antiques. In 1967, the Howard-Dickinson House opened to the public as a living museum and meeting place for special events. The home was presented with a Texas Historical Medallion and recorded as a Texas Historic Landmark in 1968.

The Howard-Dickinson House Museum is open by appointment only. For reservations, call the Tourist Development Department at 903-657-5528 or the Howard-Dickinson House at 903-657-6925.

Ghostly Visitations

A tragedy that took place in the mansion provides clues to the identities of the ghosts who haunt it. One day, two of the Howard brothers were in the basement cleaning their guns. A gunshot broke the stillness of the

quiet afternoon. One of the brothers staggered upstairs, mortally wounded. He died in his mother's bedroom, leaving behind a widow and two fatherless children. Bloodstains remain on the floor to this day.

Docents have reported finding a light on in the basement when they open the house for the day even though they were certain that all the lights were off the night before; an explanation for the persistent light has never been found.

Not long ago, a member of the Heritage Association witnessed a woman in white enter the house through the front door and climb the stairs to the second floor. The silent lady wore a wide gold bracelet on her wrist. Upon investigation of the upstairs, the society member found herself completely alone in the house. A discussion with Mrs. Howard's granddaughter revealed that the gold bracelet was a family heirloom that had been missing for a long time and was never found.

A frantic woman standing on the upper floor balcony once waved down a police officer who was passing by the house. The officer quickly made his way into the house to assist the stricken woman, but couldn't find her. Was this desperate woman the apparition of Mrs. Howard, trying to find help for her son who lay bleeding to death on that tragic afternoon so long ago?

Less Spooky Things To Do In Henderson

Each year, on the second Saturday in November, Henderson welcomes craftsmen and folk artists from a four-state area for the **Heritage Syrup Festival**. This is the first and largest folk art festival in East Texas. Using an antique syrup mill (powered by mules) to crush the cane, the town commemorates the traditional method of making ribbon cane syrup. The festival includes arts and crafts, folk art demonstrations, bluegrass bands, an antique-car show, and children's activities. Henderson's museums include the **Depot Museum Complex,** where visitors can tour a restored 1841 log cabin, and the **Arnold Outhouse**, a three-hole privy that is the most publicized historical marker in the state. The **New London Museum** chronicles the lives of the people of the East Texas Oil Field through the world's worst school disaster. In 1937, a natural gas explosion destroyed a junior-senior high school, killing an estimated 296 students and teachers. The tragedy inspired the Texas Legislature to pass a law to add a detectable odor to natural gas. Antique hounds will love Henderson's selection of shops and outdoor lovers can choose from several lakes and state parks.

For more information on Henderson, contact:
Rusk County Chamber of Commerce
201 North Main, Henderson, TX 75652
903-657-5528
www.hendersontx.com

Bygone Boos of Jefferson

Most Haunted Small Town in Texas

The town of Jefferson is located 15 minutes north of Marshall on County Road 390. The East Texas countryside surrounding Caddo Lake—with its moss-draped cypress trees that block out the sun and inky black waters that swallow anything unlucky enough to fall in—is as spooky as a horror-movie set.

The ghost-filled forest surrounding eerie Caddo Lake in East Texas.

Locals claim the spirits of Caddo Indians who settled this land long ago haunt the dense forests. And there may be other lost specters roaming these woods. According to Kent Biffle's "Texana" column in the *Dallas Morning News*, the lake has claimed boat-loads of victims (more than 165 to date), including 68 passengers who went down with the *Mittie Stevens*, a steamboat out of Shreveport, Louisiana. The ill-fated steamer burned and sank on the night of February 11, 1869. Blanketed by rich silt, the wreck still eludes frustrated marine archeologists. In addition, several murders took place through-out the region, with the lake serving as the perfect dumping ground to cover every ghastly (turned ghostly) misdeed.

In the middle of this ghost-infested area lies the little town of Jefferson, the final destination the *Mittie Stevens* never reached more than 130 years ago. Jefferson is a sleepy town with a gaudy past. Afternoons are spent lazily among the towering pines along the banks of the slow-moving Big Cypress Bayou. Jefferson's history is so pervasive that it covers you like a shawl, greets you at every corner, and lures you into every immaculate historical home for a peek.

Jefferson originated in the 1840s as a river port town. Second only to Galveston in port size and traffic, Jefferson's boats ventured up the Mississippi River into the Red River, through Caddo Lake, and up Big Cypress to the docks. By water, Jefferson was 100 miles from Shreveport and 720 miles from New Orleans.

In the days before railroads came to the piney woods, farmers and townspeople were dependent on port cities to import and export their goods. Jefferson became the only dependable port in North Texas, shipping more than 100,000 bales of cotton out of the region annually. Prosperous and elegant, the town's population swelled to 35,000 inhabitants in the days following the Civil War.

Enter the United States government. The government powers that be examined a huge logjam on the Red River that was damming up nearby Cypress Bayou and making it possible for riverboats to navigate through to the port of Jefferson. The government decided to blow up the obstruction. With this accomplished, the bayou's water level dropped dramatically and steamers could no longer make their way into Jefferson's port. By 1890, most folks in town (who had been in the shipping industry) left to look for work elsewhere. And so the belle of East Texas slumbered.

Formerly known as the Grove restaurant, this empty house is believed to be the most haunted building in Jefferson.

Today, Jefferson has become quite a tourist attraction due to its embrace of history and, for ghost lovers, its healthy share of haunted hotels, bed-and-breakfasts, tour homes, restaurants, and theaters. Jefferson has the distinction of being "the most haunted small town in Texas" by virtue of the high percentage of ghosts compared to the town's living population of just over 2,000 residents.

 HAUNTED HOTELS

Excelsior House 👹👹👹
211 W. Austin St., Jefferson, TX 75657 • 903-665-2513

Description and History
The second-oldest hotel in Texas (the oldest is the haunted Menger Hotel in San Antonio), the Excelsior House is located in the heart of Jefferson's Riverfront District. It has been in continuous operation since 1858, when riverboat captain William Perry, realizing the need for a hotel in the rowdy port town, purchased land and constructed the Irving House. Today, this is the oldest section of the hotel, forming the northwest portion of the Excelsior House. The southwest wing was added sometime between the end of the Civil War and 1872.

After Captain Perry died, a succession of proprietors owned the hotel, which operated as the Exchange Hotel and the Commercial Hotel. Kate Wood purchased the building in 1877 and renamed it the Excelsior House. Wood added the brick portion of the old section during her ownership. She and her daughter, Amelia Wood McNeeley, operated the hotel until 1902. From 1902 to 1920, McNeeley managed the property alone. When she died, her will granted the hotel to long-time Excelsior employee George Neidermeir.

Neidermeir and his family ran the hotel until 1954, when Mrs. Peters bought it. She contributed to the hotel's beauty through extensive restoration efforts, then sold the historical landmark to the Jessie Allen Wise Garden Club in 1961.

A ghostly experience at the Excelsior inspired Steven Spielberg to write Poltergeist.

The hotel registers boast a number of famous signatures, including the 18th and 19th presidents, Ulysses S. Grant and Rutherford B. Hayes; financiers W.H. Vanderbilt and John Jacob Astor; author Oscar Wilde; 36th president and first lady, Lyndon B. and Lady Bird Johnson; and railroad tycoon Jay Gould. City fathers denied Gould's request to bring the railroad to Jefferson, and legend has it that Gould then put a curse on the town. He assured the citizens of "the end of Jefferson," predicting that "grass would grow in the streets and bats would roost in the church belfries." During the 1840s, Gould's prophecy became reality when Jefferson's port closed to steamboat traffic and the population rapidly dwindled from 35,000 inhabitants to just over 1,000. As a reminder of what might have been, the Jessie Allen Wise Garden Club maintains and offers tours of Jay Gould's own custom railroad car, which sits across Austin Street from the Excelsior.

Most rooms in the Excelsior House are inexpensive ($75 per night), with the exception of three moderately priced ($100-$125 per night) suites: the Diamond Bessie Suite (Bridal Suite), the Hayes Presidential Room, and the Grant Presidential Room.

The Excelsior House has conference facilities available to groups. All major credit cards are accepted. For cancellations, give 10 days notice (30 days notice on holidays or special event weekends). The hotel does not allow smoking or pets. Check-in time is 2 p.m. and checkout time is 11 a.m. For more information, call 903-665-2513 or visit the website at www.jeffersontx.com/excelsior.

The hotel serves a plantation breakfast every morning featuring orange blossom muffins, sausage, eggs, biscuits, orange juice, and coffee. Hotel guests may reserve this meal upon check-in. If you're not staying at the hotel, you can request breakfast reservations one day in advance (subject to space availability).

You can catch a tour of the Excelsior House at 1 p.m. and 2 p.m. daily. For a fee of $2, visitors are treated to information about the hotel's rich history and are shown through the lobby, museum room, ballroom, dining room, courtyard, and several of the bedrooms (my tour included all the haunted rooms).

Ghostly Visitations

The Jessie Allen Wise Garden Club members are notoriously tight-lipped about the Excelsior House's bevy of ghosts. Don't expect to be regaled with ghost stories by employees during check-in. From other paranormal investigators,

I heard of a maid who repeatedly saw a headless man stalking the hallways outside the Gould Room; I also heard guest reports of covers being yanked off the bed and thrown across the Hayes Room.

The story of a guest finding a woman in black rocking her baby in the Gould Room's rocking chair is also a part of the hotel's history. Accompanying the guest back to the haunted room, the desk clerk also witnessed the apparition before the wraith disappeared. Two night clerks working alone in the hotel witnessed a woman in black gliding down a first-floor hallway. The brave souls investigated, but found no one.

Jodi Breckenridge, assistant manager at the haunted Jefferson Hotel, told of an experience she had while working at the Excelsior over a decade ago. Spending the night alone in the building, she heard footsteps pacing the hallway above. Climbing the stairs to scrutinize the situation, she heard a conversation above her emanating from the attic. Two voices spoke in what sounded like German. Jodi never solved the mystery of whom she overheard, but the owner of the hotel confirmed that she had experienced the same phenomenon on two separate occasions while alone in the hotel.

The haunted rocking chair located in the Jay Gould Room.

Two well-documented stories about Excelsior House haunts involve movie director extraordinaire, Steven Spielberg, and retired ABC newsman, Lyndon (Dave) Adams. Spielberg was in Jefferson during the 1970s, filming his movie *Sugarland Express*. He told columnist John Anders of the *Dallas Morning News*, "We dragged ourselves upstairs after a rough day. I swear my room was haunted. I made everyone wake up, pack up, and get back in the cars at about two o'clock in the morning. We had to drive 20 miles to the nearest Holiday Inn, and everybody was hot at me. I should add that I am not normally superstitious." Spielberg was staying upstairs in the east wing of the Excelsior in the Gould Room.

Retired newsman Dave Adams wrote to columnist Ken Biffle of the *Dallas Morning News* telling of a wild night that he and his wife, Carol, spent in the Gould Room on September 5, 1995.

"Any ghosts?" joked Mr. Adams, although he'd heard no stories.

"No ghosts," said the clerk.

Dave Adams wrote, "After soaking up some history, Carol and I went upstairs. As I unlocked the tall door, for some unexplainable reason a tune started running through my head, 'The Gold and Silver Waltz' by Franz Lehar."

Inside, the room had two double beds with big wooden headboards and antique chairs, one of them a rocker. The bathroom had an old footed tub.

"We sat on the pleasant veranda, which overlooks a brick courtyard, in its center a huge iron fountain. And we had a fabulous dinner a couple of doors down from the hotel at the Galley Restaurant."

After dinner, they fell asleep in bed watching TV.

Adams recalled, "I awoke because I had to go to the bathroom. I turned the TV off, then shuffled sleepily to the bathroom. I noticed that the door was starting to open slowly. I shut it, and it latched firmly. Later, when I returned to the door, I found I couldn't turn the knob. Something or someone was apparently gripping the knob on the other side, tightly. I said, 'Come on, Carol—very funny.' The pressure let up. The knob turned easily.

"I flicked off the light as I opened the door. Across the room, standing beside the bed was the figure of a woman dressed all in black, with a black veil. For one split second, I thought it was Carol, but she was in bed, wearing a white nightie. The apparition vanished.

"I became aware of the scent of perfume in the room. I stood for a moment, slightly shaken, but then got into bed and lay there wondering. I thought of waking Carol, but thought better of it. She would be frightened and want to leave....I drifted off to sleep. I awoke to the odor of cigar smoke. I heard what sounded like someone rifling through newspaper pages. I sat up, but didn't see anything. The sound stopped."

Next came "a knocking sound from the headboard near my head. Then I heard fingernails being dragged across the headboard, right above my head. My hand touched Carol, sound asleep. About 4 a.m., she woke up and asked if I was having trouble sleeping. I did go back to sleep. I had a vivid dream, a woman in black, seated at a grand piano was playing 'The Gold and Silver Waltz.' Returning from dinner, we'd peeked into the huge parlor off the main lobby and noticed a black grand piano.

"I was again awakened—to noises in the bathroom. I even heard the toilet flush. I reached over. Carol was still beside me. The knocking resumed, this time quite persistent. I really thought I was beginning to lose my marbles. I drifted off to sleep again. I awoke to bright sunshine streaming through the windows. I went into the bathroom, looked at myself in the mirror, and thought, 'Nah. It couldn't have happened.'" When Adams told his wife of his unbelievable nocturnal experiences, she did recall the knocking sounds.

In spite of these reliable reports, recent "paranormal pickings" were slim. Luckily, I met Phyllis Nance.

Nance works days at the Chamber of Commerce and is a night clerk at the Excelsior House. Nance related the story of the "jumping coffee mug." While cleaning rooms at the Excelsior one cold winter day not long ago, a maid was drinking hot chocolate. She accidentally left her green mug in one of the rooms, where the hotel manager found it later. As was the custom, the manager left the mug on top of the time clock in the office with a terse note regarding the inappropriateness of this lapse in protocol. That same evening, Nance clearly remembers seeing the mug on the time clock when she locked the office securely before going to bed. Early the next morning, she unlocked the office and was shocked to see the mug across the room, upside down, and under a desk. She had the only key and was positive that she'd locked the door. Puzzled, she mentioned the incident to several employees to gauge their reaction. The group decided the mug must have vibrated off the time clock, rolled across the floor, and up-ended itself under the desk. They put the mug back on top of the time clock and waited. The mug sat defiantly on the time clock for three weeks until it was finally taken down to be washed.

 # The Jefferson Hotel 👼👼👼👼👼

124 W. Austin St., Jefferson, TX 75657 • 800-226-9026

Description and History

Located in the heart of Jefferson's Riverfront District, the Jefferson Hotel is one of the oldest buildings in town. Originally constructed as a cotton warehouse in 1851, it was converted into a hotel when the steamboat port closed in the 1870s.

Known by several names over the years, including the Hotel Jefferson, the Grisgby Hotel, and the Austin Street Hotel, the Jefferson Hotel has a colorful past. During the 1870s, when the establishment was known as the Grisgby Hotel, the upstairs was a bordello called the Crystal Palace. At one time, there was a Chinese laundry downstairs in the back of the building. Sometime after World War I, during the Roaring Twenties, the building reopened as a respectable hotel. It became one of the finest in town, featuring big dances downstairs on Saturday nights.

During the 1960s, the hotel fell on hard times. During this period, it functioned as a boarding house for a few elderly residents. The class of the clientele slipped until Jeffersonians began to refer to the grand old hotel as a "flop house."

Since the 1970s, a series of owners has meticulously restored the hotel. From the bright front lobby to each of its comfortable rooms, period furnishings and antiques provide the ambience of turn-of-the-century Texas grandeur, when the Jefferson Hotel reigned supreme.

The Jefferson Hotel, with its small army of lost souls roaming the halls, is one of the most haunted hotels in Texas.

Currently, the hotel is owned and operated by Ron and Carol Meissner. The couple has resided at the hotel since 1996, when they started a new round of restoration efforts. Over the years, Carol, Ron, and assistant manager Jodi Breckenridge have experienced the ghosts of the Jefferson Hotel—and there seem to be quite a few occupying the historical building.

Upstairs rooms at the Jefferson are inexpensive to moderate (from $65-$100 per night) even during holidays, when prices increase slightly. Full-, queen-, and king-size beds are available. Each room has a private bath and most tubs have hand-held showers. The downstairs rooms are moderately priced (from $80-$125 per night). Two suites are available, one with a Jacuzzi and one with a fireplace. For more information on accommodations, please call 800-226-9026 or 903-665-2631, or visit the website at www.jeffersontx.com/jeffersonhotel.

Several times a year, the hotel offers special "Murder on the Bayou" mystery weekends, touted as "The Original Jefferson Murder Mystery Weekend Event." Guests are encouraged to participate in full costume and receive awards for character realism. The hotel staff mails character lists and descriptions before your visit, and the murder is solved during your weekend at the Jefferson, with prizes given to the super sleuths. The fun-filled package includes a trolley ride, a historic city tour, a historic home tour, a tour of the haunted Texas History Museum, a wine and cheese reception, and dinner at spooky Lamache's Italian Restaurant on Saturday night. Please call Jodi at 800-226-9026 for dates, prices, and reservations.

The Jefferson Hotel welcomes groups and provides information, including pricing and itineraries for local tours, restaurants, and meeting locations. All major credit cards are accepted. For cancellations, give 10 days notice (30 days notice on holidays or special event weekends). Check-in time is 2 p.m. and checkout time is 11 a.m.—or possibly during the middle of the night…BOO!

Ghostly Visitations

The award for the most spirit-infested edifice in Jefferson surely belongs to the Jefferson Hotel. Checking into this hotel is like navigating a supernatural cafeteria line. Guests can choose from 24 antique-filled rooms with 13-foot-high ceilings, offering a wide selection of

Most Haunted Areas:
Rooms 2, 5, 6, 9, 11, 14, 18, 19, 20, 21, and 23

paranormal prank possibilities, from the whispering woman in Room 14 to the knicker-clad man in Room 5, who likes things decidedly messy. For healthy ghost buffs (no heart conditions, please), try Room 19. The infamous inhabitant maintains the reputation of being the most active spirit in the 137-year-old building. One psychic identified at least seven nonpaying guests at this hotel.

When I checked into the Jefferson for my first overnight stay, I asked for the most haunted room available. Jodi Breckenridge assured me that Room 14 was a "hot bed" of ghostly activity—literally. The manifestations began when a bishop's bed, original to the old hotel, was moved from Room 12 to Room 14. It seems the ghost in Room 12 relocated with the bed. Reports of a pretty blonde apparition occupying this room were confirmed when a guest decided to snap a photo of each guest room in the hotel. She managed to capture Room 14's ghost—who appeared as a smoky figure standing by "her" bed—on film. Nodding bravely, I accepted my room key and, with my mom in tow, walked up the creaky wooden staircase to investigate our lodgings. The bishop's bed is a full-sized bed and, even though the close quarters were somewhat appealing to me, we decided to request an additional "unhaunted" room for mom so we would both be more comfortable. Assigned Room 3, she was assured there had been no recent reports of ghostly activity.

Room 14 is home to the "whispering woman" of the Jefferson Hotel.

After a full day of interviewing the friendly ghost owners of Jefferson, Mom and I returned to the hotel to change clothes for dinner. All the guest rooms are equipped with window air conditioning units. When I left before our afternoon interviews, mine was cooling on medium. When I entered my room a few hours later, I was blasted by a gust of frigid air. I hurried across the room and turned the air conditioner off, convinced that my unit was an overzealous cooler.

Following a wonderful dinner at the haunted Galley Restaurant across the street, Mom and I retired to our separate rooms for the evening. My room was decidedly warmer this time around. A storm was brewing outside, and the June evening was humid and hot. I turned the air conditioner back on and settled into bed with a book. I'll admit, I did leave the bathroom light on and forced myself to read until 11 p.m. so I'd be really tired when I turned out the light. Because of the heat, I cranked the air down to the coolest setting, but even then my room never became as cold as it was during the hottest part of the day. With thunder booming outside and the sound of driving rain on my window, I switched off the light, pulled the covers up to my chin, and dozed off.

Sometime in the middle of the night, a woman whispering in my right ear startled me awake. I don't have a sense for what was said; only that it was a woman's whisper. The sound seemed to emanate from the ceiling-high headboard of the bishop's bed. My heart was thumping so hard in my chest that I could hear it. I forced myself to open my eyes and look around the room. Only blackness met my wide eyes. I had met the "whispering woman" of Room 14.

Mom had her own adventure that rainy night. At 2:30 a.m., the window shade in her room slammed down onto the air conditioning unit and woke her up. She'd left the shade raised about a foot above the unit so the sun would wake her in the morning. She got out of bed and examined the shade. It was tight and did not easily move up or down without a good tug. We tested both her shade and my shade the next morning and couldn't come up with a reasonable explanation for hers falling the way it did. I was impressed that she'd ventured out of bed to investigate and slightly embarrassed of my own wide-eyed terror. We relayed our nighttime adventures to owner Carol Meissner, and she confirmed that another guest staying in Room 14 had reported a similar experience with the audible headboard.

My most recent visit to the hotel included a Friday night spent in nefarious Room 19 (although the only thing that kept me awake that night was the July heat) and a decidedly more eventful Saturday night in Room 21. I was in town with journalist Melissa Revere and her mother, Dee, to interview witnesses of the paranormal for a magazine article about haunted Jefferson hotels and bed-and-breakfasts. On Saturday morning, Jodi and Carol offered up a slew of stories describing the recently increased activity in Rooms 20 and 21 on the first floor, so we decided to move downstairs and try our paranormal luck.

New tales feature a central character who had not played a starring role in the hotel's paranormal play during my previous visits. Witnesses describe the "new ghost on the block" as a tall, dark, handsome man dressed in a tan coat with brown pants tucked into boots. He has been seen silently strolling down the hallway, entering Rooms 20 and 21 during the early morning hours.

An unsuspecting mother and daughter sleeping in Room 21 made the acquaintance of "the handsome man" one morning at 2:45 a.m. The mother was awakened by a hand gently stroking her hair. She distinctly heard a man's voice say, "My, don't you have pretty long hair." The startled woman jumped out of her bed and into her daughter's— in her own words—"faster than you'd expect a 60-year-old to move."

Our first indication that the move to Room 21 was indeed fateful was returning to our locked room at sundown to find every light in the room ablaze. We had intentionally left only one light on. We ventured next door to the haunted Lamache's Restaurant for a delicious Italian dinner and returned to Room 21 anticipating a good night's sleep.

Do ghostly children play on this staircase in the Jefferson Hotel?

A good night's sleep it was until 3:44 a.m., when I woke up abruptly and completely. I rolled over, looked at the clock, and glanced over at Melissa and her mom sleeping in the other bed. Suddenly, a loud rushing sound filled my ears. Seconds later, my body felt as though it had been plugged into an electrical socket—goosebumps covered my arms and legs and the hair on the back of my neck stood on end. I was unable to move or speak.

My discomfort escalated dramatically when I felt the other side of the bed depress as if someone—or something—sat down on the edge and rolled over toward me. I could feel chills racing up and down my back as I tried to calm down and regain my voice. Finally, I choked out, "Melissa!" and she responded to my terrified voice as I vaulted from my bed into hers, waking up her mom in the process. After several tense minutes, we settled down and went back to sleep (leaving a lamp on to ward off things that go bump in the night).

Oddly enough, another woman staying in Room 21 reported a similar experience of being paralyzed by a pressure on her chest just a few weeks before our visit. Other reports from this area of the hotel include the late night sounds

The Jefferson Hotel's infamous Room 19.

of a baby crying, a little girl calling "Mama" in the hallway, and a muffled conversation between a man and woman emanating from the unoccupied Rooms 20 and 21.

During the sleepy months of the hot Texas summer, the paranormal activity in the hotel tends to increase. One of my favorite episodes took place in the late 1990s when a desk clerk named Michael was wrapping up his shift. It was the middle of a slow week and there were no "paying" guests staying at the hotel. Michael made his rounds upstairs, turning off lights and locking rooms, before leaving for the night. He was closing the last door in the long, dark hallway when the guest room doors started opening and slamming shut all at once. Lights turned on and off as Michael dashed downstairs and phoned his friend Phyllis Nance, the desk clerk at the haunted Excelsior House just up the street. Nance reports that Michael was in a complete panic when he called, screaming that he was alone in the hotel but that "all hell was breaking loose upstairs!" He could hear doors slamming and the sounds of footsteps and dragging furniture upstairs. Michael locked up and waited in the street for his ride that night.

Not long ago, a traveling salesman complained of a group of children making a huge racket all night long by running up and down the creaky staircase. He was the only guest in the hotel that night. We'll encounter these ghostly children again as witnessed by several employees of the haunted Lamache's Restaurant next door.

In late 1999, a guest staying in Room 19 went downstairs to complain that her bathroom door was locked. Carol sent her visiting son, Shawn, to open the door. Shawn said the door opened easily, but he was met with a gust of freezing cold air blowing out of the bathroom. Shawn normally claims Room 19 when he's in town, but was relieved that it was occupied that night! Other stories about Room 19 include a woman who swore a petite lady woke her by laying a chilly hand on her arm, as well as guest reports of shadows moving in the corners, water faucets turning on of their own accord, and mysterious knocks coming from the headboard. One guest stepped into a cold spot with a definite 30-degree drop in room temperature; the spot smelled of cloves or allspice. More than one guest has fled in the night, leaving a note and check at the front desk.

The night before my most recent visit to the Jefferson Hotel, three women and a baby were staying in Room 18. One of the ladies decided to nap in the room during the hot afternoon and woke up to find a hovering, glowing cloud in the corner of the room. She dismissed the vision as a trick of the eye and didn't think about it again until an hour later. The woman's companions returned to prepare for dinner. The group left the room, turned off the light, and locked the door. Just a couple of steps down the hall, they realized they'd left something in the room and turned around to retrieve it. To their surprise, the door was standing wide open and the light was on. The last straw occurred when they returned to the room after dinner only to find that the phosphorescent mist was back. They packed their bags and went to the front desk to request another room. Unfortunately for them, they were shown to Room 20. The next morning, the maids found four pillows piled in one of the double beds occupying the room. All four guests had slept in one bed after experiencing coat hangers falling in the armoire, a window shade that kept flying up, and an exploding light bulb in Room 20.

In Room 5, a tidy couple lined several pairs of shoes up against the wall before going to sleep. In the night, the wife heard a ruckus at the foot of the bed. When she tried to wake her husband, he admonished her, claiming the noise was probably just a rat, and asked her to go back to sleep. (Carol and I agreed we'd rather contend with a ghost than a giant, ruckus-raising rat!) The next morning, all the neatly organized shoes were thrown into a pile in the middle of the room. Another story about Room 5 involves a young boy who woke his parents repeatedly during the night to report the presence of a man in a long, dark coat and short pants who would not go away. Jodi Breckenridge later witnessed a fog hovering about four feet from the floor in front of Room 5's bathroom. "It kind of glows and moves," she said. "I didn't stick around to see what it did. It scared me to death, and I ran downstairs three steps at a time and twisted my ankle."

Another family member of mine had a strange experience in Room 5 one recent Christmas. I brought my sister, Lara, and brother-in-law, Darrell, to town for the Jefferson Christmas Candlelight Tour. During the night, my sister woke up out of a dead sleep with the sensation that someone was sitting at the foot of the bed. She told me the next morning that she didn't open her eyes for fear of actually seeing someone perched down there watching her.

Who are these wandering specters? It's anybody's guess. Legend has it that a couple checked into the hotel in the late 1890s for their wedding. At the last minute, the groom bailed and the jilted bride hanged herself in the hotel. Is she the blonde in Room 14? Perhaps she and her cold-footed beau were supposed to share the bishop's bed on their wedding night....

Could the female specter trapped in Room 19 be a "working girl" from the days when the Crystal Palace bordello operated out of the hotel? When the hotel was used as a boarding house for the elderly in the 1960s, records show, a long-time resident died in the building. Does he roam the hallways appearing as a foggy, amorphous shape? And who are the children playing on the stairs? Spend a night or two in this lovely, spooky building and maybe you can add your own piece to this wonderful supernatural puzzle.

BED & BREAKFASTS WITH A BOO!

Claiborne House 👶👶👶

312 S. Alley, Jefferson, TX 75657 • 877-385-9236

Description and History

Captain V.H. Claiborne purchased several lots of land in 1871 and built the Claiborne House in 1872. The original bill of sale hangs in the dining room of the home. V.H. Claiborne was a captain in the Confederate army and the quartermaster in charge of supplies.

The house has had many owners over the years. By the time Karen and Bill Gleason purchased the home in 1982, it had fallen into a serious state of disrepair. The couple had just moved into the back part of the house and started restoration work when their adoptive son, Buckley, arrived. Karen and Buckley spent weeks alone in the house while Bill was away at law school, spending weekends at home with his new family. After two-and-a-half years in the house, the Gleasons decided to sell their beloved home and move to Longview, where Bill had been offered a job with the

Does "Captain Claiborne" still live in his beloved home?

district attorney's office. When Buckley was in second grade, the Gleasons had an opportunity to move back into the house and be near family in Jefferson. Two more happy years passed before the Gleasons sold the Claiborne House again.

The current owners, Steve and Elaine Holden, moved into their dream home on Halloween weekend 1998—very appropriate timing for this house! The Holdens then converted the home into a beautiful bed-and-breakfast inn a year later.

To reach the house from Highway 59, go to Highway 49 and take a right. Go to South Alley (Vinyards Grocery will be on the corner), turn right onto South Alley. Claiborne House is on the left at the corner of South Alley and Baker. Look for the white house with the red door on a hill.

The Claiborne House offers six beautifully decorated guest rooms. The Holdens named the antique-filled rooms after romantic poets: Brownings' Room, Yeats's Room, Tennyson's Room, Wilde's Room, Dickenson's Room, and Keats's Room. Prices range from moderate ($95 per night) to expensive ($140 per night). The haunted Brownings' Room is the most expensive of the six, but features a queen-size bed, wood-burning fireplace, and Jacuzzi tub for two. Room rates are based on double occupancy.

The Holdens prefer payment by cash or check, but do accept Visa, MasterCard, and American Express. Reservations are accepted in advance and may be made by Visa or MasterCard only. Whole-house bookings and holiday or special event weekends require a 50 percent advance deposit. All stays during holiday or special event weekends require a two-night minimum.

The Claiborne House will accept cancellations made at least seven days in advance (30 days notice is required to cancel holiday or special event weekend bookings). Unless the room is rebooked, a one-night lodging fee is charged for cancellations made following these restrictions. The hotel serves a full southern gourmet breakfast on crystal and china at 9 a.m. For more information, call 877-385-9236 or 903-665-8800, or visit the website at www.jeffersontx.com/claiborne. Check-in time is 3 p.m. and checkout time is 11 a.m. No children or pets are allowed.

Ghostly Visitations

At the time of this writing, Steve and Elaine Holden have yet to see the ghost of "Captain Claiborne," who is believed to haunt the Claiborne House. Elaine has noticed the oven temperature lowering by itself and lights

Most Haunted Areas:
The Brownings' Room, kitchen, and staircase

flickering on and off. The Holdens arranged a meeting with former owner Karen Gleason, president of the Jessie Allen Wise Garden Club, to join us at the Claiborne House and tell us about her supernatural experiences in the old house.

Karen's first memory of "Captain Claiborne" was of seeing someone just within her peripheral vision standing in the corner of the Gleason's bedroom, now known as the Brownings' Room. Karen saw the Captain approximately a dozen times that first year in this area of the house.

During their second year in the house, once every couple of weeks or so, Karen saw a figure standing in the kitchen while she watched TV in the sitting room (now the dining room of the Claiborne House). The figure always stood just outside the door to her son's room, which is now the Holden's private quarters.

The Captain has been seen in the lavish Brownings' Room.

Karen saw this figure several times before she was *allowed* to study him for more than a fleeting second. One night, Karen saw the figure from her peripheral vision, turned to look directly at it, and was rewarded with a long look. Long enough, in fact, to determine that the apparition was a man with a beard like Abraham Lincoln, a gaunt, thin face, and dark hair; he was wearing a long black coat and white shirt. He stood behind a floor lamp so Karen had a reference point and estimated that he was at least 6 feet tall. He appeared to watch her for several seconds before vanishing.

When Buckley was a year-and-a-half old, he began telling Karen about the "man" in his room. He asked why Daddy was in his room so long every night. Most of these nights, Bill wasn't even in town but was in Nacogdoches studying law at Stephen F. Austin University. Buckley described the position and posture of the man in great detail to Karen.

After months of experiencing the apparition, Karen was relieved when Bill also saw the "Captain" in the kitchen. Bill described the same white shirt, black coat, and beard that Karen saw. Shortly after Bill's experience, friends of the Gleasons were over for dinner one night. Ken Tomlinson, a Continental Airlines pilot, asked Karen who else was invited for dinner that evening. He thought he'd seen a man standing in the kitchen.

A commotion on this staircase turned out to be just the "Captain."

Even though Karen spent much of her time alone in the house with an infant, she says the presence was benign and never threatening. In fact, the two times Karen was frightened, she called the police because she was convinced that an intruder, rather than a ghost, was in the house.

The first incident happened in 1982. Karen had just put Buckley down for the night and was reading in bed. Suddenly a sticky door, leading from the sitting room to the bathroom connecting the master bedroom and the nursery, dragged noisily across the carpet and opened into a large houseplant. Due to the settling of the house and the height of the carpet, this door was hard to open and could not have swung open without help.

Karen always left a light on in the sitting room at night and kept this door cracked to illuminate the bathroom a bit. She could see from her bedroom that this light was spilling into the bathroom through the open door.

Karen was so frightened that she jumped out of bed and grabbed her husband's gun. After several breathless moments of complete silence, she bolted through the bathroom and noticed the open door and several leaves from the plant scattered on the floor along the way. She grabbed Buckley and ran into the kitchen, where she called the police, then ran next door to a relative's house. Police found no evidence of a break-in and Karen became convinced that "Captain Claiborne" had paid her a visit. She told us that she scolded him for scaring her so and warned him to be more careful in the future.

It seems the Captain heeded her wishes until the couple's second ownership of the house many years later. That day, Karen had come home for lunch and was walking through the dining room into the front hallway. Just as she reached the dining room door, she heard heavy footsteps on the staircase. It sounded as if a man wearing boots was clomping noisily above her. Karen backtracked through the kitchen and over to her aunt's house, where she called the police. A careful check established that all the doors were locked and the windows were nailed shut. The patrolman seemed hesitant to search the dark upstairs, which had not yet been converted into rooms. I can't say that I blame him one bit. No explanation of the footsteps was ever provided. To this day, Karen still misses Claiborne House and hopes the Holdens will take good care of the "Captain"!

McKay House 👻👻👻
306 E. Delta St., Jefferson, TX 75657 • 800-468-2627

Description and History
Daniel Nelson Alley, a founder of Jefferson, built the McKay House in 1851. Alley was an early, prominent landowner in Marion County. This antebellum Greek Revival-

Fond of setting off smoke alarms, the McKay House spirit likes to grab the attention of earthly inhabitants.

style beauty sits in a residential area known as "Quality Hill," a short walk from the historic Riverfront area, and has received both Texas and National Historic Markers.

Several families owned the house before 1884, when Hector McKay bought the property. McKay was a veteran of the Civil War and a respected attorney. His son, Arch McKay, owned the McKay House until his death. The house has recently been restored and expanded to include an 1890 Victorian Garden Cottage, known as the Sunday House, which was moved to the property from the nearby town of Nesbitt.

Guests are truly pampered in the McKay House's moderately priced rooms (from $99 per night). Considered "One of the Ten Most Romantic Inns in America" by *Vacation Magazine*, the McKay House has seven extravagantly furnished bedchambers (five in the main house and two in the Sunday House garden cottage) to choose from.

Spend the night in Lady Bird Johnson's favorite room, the McKay Room, with its collection of documents from the infamous Diamond Bessie murder trial, or compose a poem in the writer's alcove of the Garden Gables Suite. Guests can relax in the "Spinning Room" of the Jefferson Suite and "let your soul catch up with you." Seven fireplaces create a feeling of warmth year-round.

For those brave few who relish the idea of a supernatural encounter, reserve one of the rooms in the Sunday House. The Sunday Room features Victorian decor and includes some of "Aunt Pearl's" favorite outfits, complete with hats and shoes. A night spent in the Keeping Room allows guests to experience a simpler time. It's a rustic room where the family did most of its cooking and eating during the mid-1800s. This room features a large fireplace with rock mantel (and perhaps a pie-baking spirit thrown in for good measure).

Chances are—if you're lucky—a night spent in the Sunday House won't be the most peaceful.

You can cancel one week before your arrival date (groups must give a month's notice to cancel). Check in between 3 p.m. and 5 p.m. (unless other arrangements are made) and check out by 11 a.m. A complimentary gentlemen's breakfast is served in the Garden Conservatory. For more information, call 800-468-2627 or 903-665-7322, or visit the website at www.bbonline.com/tx/mckayhouse/.

Ghostly Visitations

Lisa and Roger Cantrell have named their favorite ghost "Aunt Pearl" in honor of Pearl McKay, the second owner, who lived and died in the house. Aunt Pearl walks the halls of the main McKay house. Lisa reports many strange occurrences in the house over the last 12 years, including footsteps heard in empty hallways,

> **Most Haunted Areas:**
> *Virtually all the rooms of the main house and the Sunday House's Sunday and Keeping Rooms*

electrical disturbances, and the feeling of someone watching her while she's alone in the big house. Family members and guests have reported glimpses of shadowy figures in their peripheral vision and in the many mirrors throughout the house. When witnesses turn to get a better look at the figure, they are disappointed (or thrilled, depending on their respective constitutions) to find nothing at all.

Despite years of unexplained activity, including her children's complaints of dishes and pans rattling in the deserted kitchen, Lisa was still skeptical of Aunt Pearl's presence. During my June 1999 visit to the McKay House, Lisa reported that two weeks earlier she had changed her mind.

Two couples were staying at the McKay House overnight. The Cantrells had tucked their four children in for the night and were sound asleep in their quarters downstairs in the main house. At about 11:30 p.m., the smoke detector in the upstairs hallway went off. After a quick look around to rule out a legitimate fire, the Cantrells scrambled upstairs with a stepladder to turn the noisy detector off. Roger climbed the ladder to the 12-foot ceiling and removed the cover of the detector as well as the two batteries. He climbed back down and stood holding the cover in one hand and the batteries in the other—and

"Aunt Pearl" haunts McKay House.

the smoke detector began its shrill alarm again! Lisa said she and Roger just looked at each other, at the batteries in Roger's hand, and at the alarm that was screeching above their heads in disbelief. Then Lisa noticed who was standing behind Roger.

In the dim hallway behind Roger, the smoky form of a woman stood "watching" Lisa. Lisa grabbed a protesting Roger and dragged him down the stairs after her. He was concerned that the alarm's noise was disturbing their guests, but Lisa maintained they had done everything they could and the alarm would go off when it was good and ready. She was right. A few minutes later, all was quiet in the McKay House once again. Lisa believes she saw Aunt Pearl that night standing in the darkness.

Recently, Lisa was bathing in the Quiet Room downstairs when she heard a baby crying. The child was calling plaintively for "Mama." Lisa, thinking the pitiful cries were coming from one of her children, quickly dried off and rushed to their rooms to find all sleeping soundly. She can find no explanation for this.

Betty, long-time housekeeper for the inn, reports two additional spirits who reside in the Sunday House. One is a white, middle-aged woman; the other, an older African-American woman. Betty complains of Victorian hats flying across the room while she's cleaning the Sunday and Keeping Rooms in the little cottage. Several guests staying in the cottage have complained of late-night furniture moving on the front and back porches. Interestingly, there is no furniture on the porches to move!

The Sunday Room, where Aunt Pearl's clothes are displayed.

In 1999, a preacher was staying in the Sunday House overnight. At breakfast, he told the Cantrells of an amazing nocturnal visit he'd experienced. It seems the preacher's slumber was disturbed by a round African-American woman carrying a cherry pie! She smiled to the astonished man and offered him a piece of pie. Not surprisingly, he declined.

During my visit to the McKay House, I heard an interesting story from a diminutive witness. Katie, the Cantrell's three-year-old daughter, told me about her friend, "Michael," who lives under her bed. Michael told Katie that he was struck by lightning while mowing the lawn! Maybe we should add one more ghost to the long list of resident wraiths at the McKay House.

Twin Oaks Country Inn 👤👤

P.O. Box 155, Highway 134, Jefferson, TX 75657 • 800-905-7751

Description and History

The main house and inn sit on a pre–Civil War plantation site, the oldest plantation in Northeast Texas. It is to the left of Highway 134 about 1.5 miles from Jefferson toward Caddo Lake State Park. The original Twin Oaks burned to the ground in the 1890s. Two subsequent homes built on the site also succumbed to fire.

Owners Vernon and Carol Randle moved the 104-year-old wooden Victorian home to the plantation grounds and carefully restored the home (not pictured) to its former beauty.

The Twin Oaks Country Inn brochure reads, "Moved to an idyllic site and saved from the ravages of time, this beautiful Victorian House again extends hospitality to all who would come…" Twin Oaks has five beautifully decorated guest rooms with private entrances, private baths, color TVs, original Victorian woodwork, and hardwood floors.

Rates are available upon request and based on double occupancy only. Reservations require a deposit and can be made by Visa, MasterCard, Discover, American Express, personal check, or cash. A two-night minimum stay is required on holidays and a seven-day cancellation notice is required.

Nature provides visitors with spectacular views, glorious sunrises, and romantic sunsets. Guests can relax with a walk on the plantation grounds, a cool swim in the pool, or a game of croquet, horseshoes, or badminton.

Check-in time is 4 p.m. and checkout is 11 a.m. Twin Oaks does not allow smoking, children under 12, or pets. Carol serves a wonderfully hearty breakfast on china and crystal in the main plantation house. Complimentary tours of the plantation are included. For more information, call 800-905-7751 or 903-665-3535, or visit the website at www.twinoaksinn.com.

Twin Oaks Plantation recalls a time when cotton was king and ghosts here were still alive.

Ghostly Visitations

In 1998, when the Randles were adding a sun-room to the back of Twin Oaks, they discovered a round cap of rough, rock-hard concrete in the way. When contractors removed the concrete, all were amazed to find the remains of an old cistern. Vernon

remembers smelling a strong gardenia scent while peering down into the blackness of the well. The contractor decided to drop a ladder down and visit the bottom of the pit. Afterwards, the man climbed back into the sunshine and encouraged Vernon to venture down, claiming he experienced a powerful feeling of peacefulness while inside the cistern. Vernon, who is slightly claustrophobic, says curiosity finally got the better of him and he descended into the depths of the well. He, too, experienced a strong sense of calmness that seemed otherworldly and made quite an impact on him.

The Randles removed bricks from the cistern and sent them to Civil War museums in Dallas and Atlanta for dating and analysis. The results proved that the Randles had uncovered a pre–Civil War cistern original to the Twin Oaks plantation, which stood on this site in the mid-1800s. The Randles built a wishing well on top of the cistern, which serves as a focal point for the New Orleans–style patio at the back of the house.

At this point, things started to get interesting at Twin Oaks. Vernon Randle has always been sensitive to paranormal activity. He was the first to hear the music. While watching television upstairs in his study one evening, Vernon heard the strains of an ambiguous melody floating in the distance. He turned the television's volume down and listened harder. The faint music was still there. Despite searching for the source high and low, the origin was never determined. Vernon and guests staying in the renovated Victorian inn have heard this music on several occasions. In addition, Vernon has heard the distant sound of laughter.

Uncovering this old cistern started the supernatural events at Twin Oaks.

Oddly enough, Vernon has also heard water running through the cistern while enjoying his patio late at night. Several investigations with a flashlight always end the same way—with the sight of a bone-dry cistern and no explanation for the sound of running water.

In addition to the auditory activity, Vernon also catches glimpses of strange shadowy figures out of the corner of his eye throughout the house. When he turns to look directly at the mysterious shapes, there is never anything there. During my visit to Twin Oaks, I suggested to Vernon that he has the same experience with auditory manifestations—the harder he listens, the fainter the sounds become. Vernon is planning to experiment the next time to see if the melody becomes more distinct when he's not listening as closely.

All agree that the vibes coming from the old cistern are good ones. The Randles also report that the unexplained activity has picked up, with episodes happening more often in recent months.

White Oak Manor 👶👶👶

502 Benners, Jefferson, TX 75657 • 903-665-1271

Description and History

Mr. Craver, the first Marion County extension agent, built White Oak Manor in 1911. The beautifully restored Greek Revival home is best known for the huge 200-year-old oak tree presiding over the front yard. The magnificent tree is the largest white oak in Marion County.

Over the years, 13 families have lived in the home. For a time, it functioned as a boarding house. In the early 1990s the property was owned by Gary Hurst, who operated the home as a bed-and-breakfast called Heather-in-the-Hollow. The current owners, Cindy and Larry Pinkerton, have lived in White Oak Manor for six years. After 18 months of restoration, the home reopened as White Oak Manor Bed and Breakfast.

White Oak Manor offers a choice of three antique-filled guest rooms. Miss Clara's Room has a king-size bed, fireplace, balcony, private bath with claw-foot tub and shower, and cable TV. The Rose Room offers the same amenities with a queen-size bed. For privacy-seekers, the Judge's Chamber boasts a queen-size bed, private bath with claw-foot tub, cable TV, and a large sitting area that looks out to the 200-year-old oak tree in the front yard.

A reporter with the *Fort Worth Star Telegram* stayed in the Judge's Chamber while researching an article on haunted East Texas bed-and-breakfasts. He likened the huge tree outside his window to the demonic tree in Steven Spielberg's terrifying movie *Poltergeist* (reputedly inspired by Spielberg's ghostly experiences at the haunted Excelsior House). The scared writer claimed he barely slept a wink all night, fretting about the ancient tree and imagining tapping and scratching on his windowpane.

A *little girl's spirit plays in the rooms of White Oak Manor.*

For rate information, contact Cindy Pinkerton at 903-665-1271 or 903-665-1048. A two-night minimum stay during holidays or special events is required. Cancellations will only be accepted seven days before the reservation date (30 days notice before holidays and special events). White Oak Manor accepts Visa, MasterCard, American Express, Discover, cash, or checks. For more information, visit the website at www.bbonline.com/tx/whiteoak.

Check-in time is 3 p.m. and checkout time is 11 a.m. Smoking is not permitted indoors. The Pinkertons serve a true gentleman's breakfast brimming with such home-made goodies as tiny chocolate muffins and flaky biscuits, cheesy grits, grilled ham, and fresh fruit.

Ghostly Visitations

Jodi Breckenridge, assistant manager at the haunted Jefferson Hotel, related that in 1989 a woman rented the house for six weeks. During her stay she saw an apparition of a little girl with long blond hair three or four times.

> **Most Haunted Areas:**
> *Miss Clara's Room and the Judge's Chambers*

Following these experiences, Gary Hurst owned the house in 1992, when it was known as Heather-in-the-Hollow Bed and Breakfast. Jodi's friend Elizabeth took care of the house and guests while Hurst was out of town.

One Friday afternoon, Hurst locked the deadbolts on the front and back doors before leaving town, not realizing that Elizabeth didn't have a key to these locks. Elizabeth enlisted Jodi's help to find a way into the house to turn on the air conditioning units for the expected weekend guests.

Jodi and her two-year-old daughter, Amy, were standing on the front porch trying to decide what to do. Amy peered through a window looking into the front room of the house and exclaimed, "Beth's home!" When Jodi asked who "Beth" was, Amy replied, "My friend, Beth." When questioned more, Amy described Beth as a little girl with long white hair. Jodi didn't see anyone in the house and became spooked. She remembered that, while on several visits to Heather-in-the-Hollow, she would find Amy carrying on animated conversations while playing alone—or was she really alone? Jodi never brought Amy with her to the house again.

During my relaxing stay at White Oak Manor, Cindy Pinkerton told me that a little six-year-old girl had died in the house from pneumonia. Cindy also said that her little girl's bedroom is often the scene of such unexplained activity as covers being pulled off the bed by unseen hands and a quilt that moves mysteriously from her bed to a chair.

Cindy also mentioned a guest who actually saw the little girl pull the covers from the bed in Miss Clara's Room early one morning. The laughing child ran from the foot of the bed and hid behind the door leading to the room before fading into thin air. I can report that my night's sleep was undisturbed by the small wraith, although I did tuck the covers securely around me before retiring. I like to call this particular ghost-hunting technique "the burrito procedure." It may not ward off otherworldly visitors, but it sure makes me feel braver in dark, unfamiliar rooms!

RESTAURANT REVENANTS

The Galley Restaurant ☺☺☺

121 W. Austin St., Jefferson, TX 75657 • 903-665-3641

Description and History

Located directly across from the Jefferson Hotel in downtown Jefferson, the Galley Restaurant makes its home inside a historical building constructed by the Russell family between 1862 and 1865. Over the years, the building has housed law offices, cock fights, a Chinese laundry, and a bordello, or "bawdy" house, upstairs.

Dinner is served beginning at 4 p.m. The upstairs bar opens at 5 p.m. on Friday and Saturday evenings for dinner and drinks, with live music from 7 p.m.-11 p.m. The restaurant is closed on Sunday and Monday. Dinners at the Galley are moderately priced, hearty, and delicious. The Galley, known to have the best steaks in town, also specializes in such seafood and pasta dishes as blackened snapper and garlic shrimp. A good wine selection and sinful desserts round out your dining experience.

The Galley Restaurant boasts regular ghostly activity as well as fantastic steaks.

Ghostly Visitations

My mom and I visited the Galley Restaurant on the proverbial dark and stormy night with thunder and lightning rolling through the skies outside. Just the perfect atmosphere for a good ghost hunt over dinner!

Most Haunted Area:
The second-floor bar

Nicole, a waitress at the Galley for the past few years, is no stranger to the odd happenings in this building. Nicole's most common paranormal experiences occur during the busiest times of the nights she works. Moving between tables, the bar, and the kitchen to serve diners, Nicole often hears someone saying her name directly into her ear when no one is there. She has even collided with someone who isn't visible! Nicole says she'll step back from the bar with a loaded tray and "bump" into someone behind her. When she turns to apologize, no one is there. Obviously, this ghost likes to follow Nicole very closely.

One night before dinner when Nicole opened the restaurant alone, she was in the kitchen getting ice from the ice machine. She was a bit nervous to be in the building alone and thought, "I hope nothing happens to me while I'm here by myself." No sooner had she finished her thought when the ice machine door slammed down onto her arm. Nicole said this has never happened to her or anyone else, before or since. It took all of her courage to stay in the restaurant until the other employees arrived for work.

Nicole also reports that items often turn up missing. Unfortunately, the busboys get the blame for these pranks, even though they vehemently deny the charges. Most missing items do turn up eventually.

The second floor of the building recently opened as the Galley Bar. Owner and fifth-generation Jeffersonian Bonnie Spellings claims that her employees avoid visiting this area after hours. One waitress claimed she saw a man standing in the shadows of this large room when she was alone in the building cleaning up.

Spellings confirmed that she felt this entity was male and offered a possible explanation for his presence. Approximately 35 years ago, when the Spellings family purchased the decaying building, Bonnie Spellings found two ropes hanging from the large rafter that runs the width of the second floor. The ropes had been cut through with a knife. Spellings related a story about a crooked constable who terrorized the African-American community of the small town during the 1930s. Whenever an unsolved crime came to his attention, the constable would walk through the streets and find two innocent African-American men to question. Tragically, the interrogation would take place in one of the main streets' many deserted buildings—at the end of a hangman's noose. If the faultless men did not confess to the crime, the constable would kick the chairs out from under the poor souls, causing unspeakable deaths by strangulation. Spellings believes one of these innocents may haunt the upper floor of the Galley.

Spellings has experienced the mischievous side of the Galley ghosts on more than one occasion. Checks often disappear while the owner is paying bills in the office downstairs, only to turn up in odd places hours later. One afternoon while working alone in the restaurant, Spellings paid a visit to the downstairs ladies room, only to have the door slam shut in her face.

On many occasions, Spellings has heard a muffled conversation between at least two invisible women coming from the second floor. Maybe the souls of long-dead ladies of the night are still ensconced in their former "office space."

Lamache's Italian Restaurant ☺☺☺☺☺
124 W. Austin St., Jefferson, TX 75657 • 903-665-6177

Description and History

Lamache's Italian Restaurant is located in the same building as the spectacularly spooky Jefferson Hotel. The area of the building where Lamache's now serves delicious old world recipes was once the ballroom where the Jefferson Hotel held weekly dances every Saturday night during the Roaring Twenties.

Another restaurant, Jay Gould's, was open in the same location for a few years prior to Lamache's. When Mike and Elisa Lakey opened their wonderful restaurant in September 1997, the supernatural events began immediately.

Lamache's Italian Restaurant is open for lunch and dinner Wednesday through Sunday. The restaurant is closed Monday and Tuesday.

An impressively varied menu with reasonably priced pastas, chicken, seafood, specialty pizza, and Italian subs and sandwiches offers something for everyone with an appetite. *Specialita della Casa* include lasagna, eggplant and veal parmigiana, linguine carbonara, and Pompeii pasta. A respectable wine list and delectable dessert menu, including tiramisu torte and cannoli, ensure diners a night of ghost hunting on a full stomach!

Ghostly Visitations

On a hot and lazy afternoon in July 1999, I was visiting with Carol Meissner and Jodi Breckenridge in the lobby of the Jefferson Hotel. Breckenridge mentioned some of the ghostly goings-on next door at Lamache's Italian Restaurant and offered to introduce me to the manager, Ida Lakey.

Most Haunted Area:
The kitchen

Breckenridge, Lakey, and I settled around one of the dining room tables and began to discuss the odd happenings in the restaurant. The first report comes from Breckenridge, no stranger to the strange due to her experiences as assistant manager at the Jefferson Hotel.

On a quiet afternoon during the summer months just begore Lamache's opening, Breckenridge was dusting some items in a display case in the Jefferson Hotel's lobby when she heard distinct strains of big band music coming through the wall from next door. Jay Gould's Restaurant had recently moved out and the building was deserted and dark. Breckenridge was puzzled, knowing that Jay Gould's did not even have the wiring for a sound system to account for the music.

Her curiosity piqued, she walked to the door connecting the hotel and the restaurant's dining room located under the lobby staircase. As soon as she opened the door, the music stopped. Breckenridge went back to her dusting, then heard the music start up again. Determined to find an explanation, she walked out into the street to see if the music could be coming from somewhere else. It wasn't—it was coming from inside the empty restaurant! Breckenridge listened to the music for several more minutes before it finally faded away. Several other Lamache's employees have heard this mysterious music since the restaurant moved into the building.

On many different occasions, Ida Lakey has heard someone or something knocking on the door that connects the dining room and hotel. No one is ever on the other side when she opens it. This door opens and closes on its own even though Lakey describes it as a "sticky" door. Lakey and the cook, Cedric, have heard repeated knocking on another door connecting the kitchen to the hotel. During one memorable morning when the ghost was particularly active, Lakey experienced a jumping spoon, slamming kitchen door, and disembodied knocks on the back door.

Guests staying in Rooms 16, 17, and 18 of the Jefferson Hotel have complained about pots and pans banging in the restaurant late at night. These rooms are directly above Lamache's kitchen.

Room 23 guests complained to hotel owner Carol Meissner that the kitchen staff was cleaning dishes late into the night. The travelers were sleeping soundly when their ears were assaulted at 1 a.m. by the noise of crashing pots, pans, and dishes. Carol assured them that she let the last restaurant employees out the back door at 11 p.m.

Flickering candles, clinking wineglasses, and electrical disturbances are part of the restaurant's dining experience. During a performance of an original play by Marsha Thomas (owner of the haunted Living Room Theater) held in the dining room one evening, the lights in one section dimmed dramatically as the lights in another went out completely. Lakey had to go into the kitchen to adjust the controls.

Lakey and others have heard the sounds of children laughing and running through the guest rooms overhead. And I mean *through*. The disembodied footsteps run a path through the walls of the rooms rather than down the hallway. Lakey said that many children staying at the Jefferson Hotel claim to see a little girl and boy holding a bell. No adult has ever seen the children, but many have heard the bell ringing. And let's not forget the lonely salesman whose rest was disturbed by a group of children running up and down the hotel's staircase all night.

Lakey, who considers herself psychically sensitive, believes Lamache's ghost is a female from the 1920s or 1930s who is displeased that the building is now a restaurant. Maybe she's impatiently waiting for one of the big Saturday night dances that popularized the hotel during the rowdy Roaring Twenties.

SPIRITED BUILDINGS AND HOUSES

Living Room Theatre 👶👶
112 Vale St., Jefferson, TX 75657 • 903-665-2310

Description and History

In 1869, David C. Russell designed this French-Quarter style early-Victorian building, constructed of handmade clay brick. It is located less than a block from the Jefferson Hotel on Vale Street. In 1983, the current owners, the Thomases, remodeled the old building into a private townhouse with the Living Room Theatre housed in—well, the living room.

The building has been used by many businesses over the years, including a bank, newspaper offices, an antique shop, a bawdy house, and a gambling parlor. The building received a Texas Historical Medallion in 1965 and was entered into the National Register of Historical Buildings in 1971.

Born and raised in Jefferson, Marsha Thomas followed her dream of becoming an actress all the way to London, where she

Catch a show, and possibly a ghost acting out, at the Living Room Theatre.

studied drama, dance, and voice. Nowadays, Marsha performs one-woman shows in her Living Room Theatre for audiences of 30. She presents dramatic dialogues about interesting "Texian Women," most of which she wrote herself. Performances are Friday and Saturday at 8 p.m. Call Marsha Thomas at 903-665-2310 for more information.

Ghostly Visitations

The Thomases have a cat and a small poodle that frequently stare at the staircase—with hair standing on end—obviously observing something the Thomases are unable to see. After several months of this behavior,

> **Most Haunted Areas:**
> *The private apartment and the staircase*

Marsha began noticing things rearranging themselves while she and her husband were out. Throw pillows on their bed would be moved and even neatly stacked on top of each other.

Finally, the couple began to hear rapid footsteps pacing the attic above them at night. The steps were light and seemed childlike to the incredulous couple. Marsha did some research and found out that a small house had been torn down on this property to make room for the larger building in the 1860s. The property was traded off and included in the trade was a little 12-year-old slave girl named Mary. Are the footfalls the Thomases hear at bedtime the small child rushing through her evening chores? Why not take in a little culture the next time you're in Jefferson on a Saturday night...and see if you can catch a glimpse of little "Mary" on the stairs?

GHOSTS OF THE GREAT OUTDOORS

Oakwood Cemetery

Description and History

Oakwood Cemetery occupies a tract of land that was donated to Jefferson in 1846 by Allen Urquhart, owner of the local ferry. The earliest marked grave is that of settler Benjamin Foscue, who died of cholera in 1850. The historical marker for Oakwood Cemetery reads, "The nearly 15,000 interments include ...antagonists Robertson and Rose (first names unknown), who killed each other and lie here chained together, an iron post marking the grave; sensational murder victim "Diamond Bessie," her alleged killer's captor, Sheriff Vines, and lawyers active in ensuing trials; Confederate veterans such as spy-hero John Burke and 1860s Federal occupation soldiers; and veterans of other wars.

A wraith has been seen wandering around Diamond Bessie's gravesite.

Ghostly Visitations

The spirit who walks the grassy nooks between graves in Oakwood Cemetery is one of the most famous—and infamous —inhabitants in a town long known for its colorful characters. In 1854, the beautiful Annie Stone was born into the family

of a shoemaker in Syracuse, New York. Well cared for and educated, fate called and she left home as an aspiring actress at the age of 15. Young and without the stability her parents

Annie Stone, also known as "Diamond Bessie"

provided, Stone soon became the mistress of a man named Moore. Within a few short years, she was supporting herself as a prostitute and earned the nickname "Diamond Bessie" for her custom of wearing the lavish diamond jewelry she received from her many male admirers. At the age of 20, Diamond Bessie met her future husband, Abraham Rothschild, at a bordello in Hot Springs, Arkansas. Rothschild was the son of a wealthy jeweler and loved prostitutes as much as he loved whiskey.

After traveling the country and visiting many cities, Diamond Bessie and Abraham Rothschild landed in Jefferson in December 1876. The attractive young couple spent a few days enjoying the bustling activity surrounding them before setting off for a picnic in the woods around Cypress Bayou, just off Marshall Road. Witnesses watched the couple cross the foot bridge and disappear into the trees.

Later that same afternoon, Rothschild returned to town alone. When questioned about his wife's whereabouts, Abraham replied that Bessie had stayed across the Bayou, visiting friends. The following day, Rothschild checked out of the hotel, carrying Bessie's luggage, and traveled to Cincinnati. After a period of heavy drinking and hallucinating, Rothschild

Abraham Rothschild awaits his murder trial in the jailhouse.

tried to commit suicide in a saloon, but he only succeeded in disfiguring his face by shooting out his right eye with a pistol.

On February 5, 1877, Sarah King found Bessie's body while looking for firewood along Marshall Road, just southwest of Jefferson. She had been shot in the temple. Sympathetic citizens collected money for a coffin and burial plot in Oakwood Cemetery and laid poor Bessie to rest—or so they thought!

After the body was discovered, Rothschild was arrested for Bessie's murder, hauled back to Texas, and tried in the most controversial trial ever to take place in Jefferson. Rothschild was found guilty and received a mandatory death sentence. A judge who felt that Rothschild did not receive a fair trial overturned the guilty verdict. The news infuriated the citizens of the town, who believed Rothschild was responsible for the murder of his attractive young wife. Rothschild left town a free man, but many say he returned in the 1890s, leaving red roses and praying at Bessie's grave in the Oakwood Cemetery.

Even today, townsfolk claim fresh flowers can often be found at Bessie's gravesite. No one knows who leaves the flowers. Her restless form has been seen wandering around the lonely cemetery.

Less Spooky Things To Do In Jefferson

Visit the shrouded **Caddo Lake**, in **Caddo Lake State Park,** and enjoy fishing, boating, and camping. Guests have various options for seeing the town of Jefferson. **Turning Basin Tours** offers trolley car tours of Jefferson's brick-lined streets and daily riverboat tours. History-hungry travelers flock to Jefferson for one of Texas's oldest festivals, the **Jefferson Historical Pilgrimage** held the first weekend in May each year. Several historical homes open their doors to the public, and theatrical events are held throughout the weekend. December is a special time with the **Jefferson Christmas Candlelight Tour** held during the first two weekends of the month. Four antebellum mansions are open for tours, decorated in natural greenery, with glowing candles and docents in costume.

> *For more inforamtion on Jefferson, contact:*
> Marion County Chamber of Commerce
> 118 N. Vale St., Jefferson, TX 75657
> 903-665-2672
> http://jefferson-texas.com

Mysterious Mineola

Mineola was established in the 1840s near an artesian well used by traders located at the intersection of Highways 69 and 80. In 1989, it was designated as a Texas Main Street City, with more than $3 million spent on business district building renovations to date.

HAUNTED HOTELS

The Beckham Hotel 👹👹👹
115 Commerce St., Mineola, TX 75773 • 903-569-0835

Description and History

Built by the Beckham family, the three-story Beckham Hotel housed railroad employees and passengers for many years. It is located one block south of Highway 80, facing the railroad tracks in downtown Mineola. The year of construction has been lost to time, but a State of Texas county survey map shows the original structure existed in 1885.

The lovely and ghostly "Elizabeth" haunts the Beckham Hotel's main staircase.

The building burned to the ground in 1925, but the determined Beckhams rebuilt on an even grander scale and opened for business in 1927. The historical structure has been a working hotel ever since. Stories abound of bootlegging and late-night poker games during the 1920s and 1930s, when big bands played upstairs and whiskey and mean tempers were plentiful.

When Mr. Beckham died at age 90 in 1972, he willed the building to his stepson, Lester Jay, who continued to sublease the hotel until 1985. The hotel changed hands several times over the next few years, starting with Jerry and Becky Penrod's ownership in 1987. Restoration work began and continued after the hotel was sold again, in 1991, to Warren and Lawanna Bean. Current owner John DeFoore is completing the restoration work.

Rates at the Beckham Hotel are inexpensive (less than $75 per night), with a total of 10 rooms available on the second floor, including the Western Suite, the Courtyard Room, the Music Room, and the Rose Suite. All have private baths—the Western Suite's bathroom is cleverly decorated to resemble an old outhouse and the Beckham's brochure cautions, "You might even find an eye peeking in through an old knothole!" The renovations will encompass the third floor of the old hotel, where as many as 24 "railroad" rooms furnished with just a bed and chair will be available. DeFoore is successfully transforming this historic landmark back to its original form. Much of the furniture in the hotel is original—and so is the Beckham's resident ghost, "Elizabeth"!

Ghostly Visitations

Dolly Smith wears many hats in her busy life. In addition to being an antique dealer through Rose Petals and the Bargain Barn in Mineola, she is hard at work furnishing the old Beckham Hotel with period antiques. Smith will eventu-

Most Haunted Areas:
The staircase and Western Suite

ally man the front desk of the hotel that she has been associated with for the past 10 years. She is also a psychic, having experienced the supernatural through visions and premonition dreams her entire life.

Back in 1987, when Jerry and Becky Penrod owned the Beckham, Smith worked as a cook and waitress for the hotel's restaurant. Early one morning, Smith was alone in the building preparing rolls for the day's lunch and dinner hours. She heard a loud noise upstairs, which frightened her because there were no paying guests that cold December morning. Smith was concerned that someone had broken into the hotel during the night and slept in one of the vacant guest rooms. She walked out into the lobby and stood at the foot of the staircase, where she heard a loud noise once again coming from upstairs.

Suddenly, a very solid woman appeared at the top of the staircase and "floated" down towards Smith. The pretty woman was in her early 30s and wearing a Victorian dress. Her light brown hair was pulled on top of her head and she smelled of fresh flowers. She passed directly *through* a transfixed Smith, who became extremely cold but not frightened by this strange encounter. Smith said she felt a peaceful warmth emanate from the young woman, who seemed to tell her, telepathically, that her name was "Elizabeth."

Shortly thereafter, Smith dreamed the same experience and again saw Elizabeth on the stairs that early morning. The original sighting lasted only a matter of seconds and then the apparition was gone, disappearing into thin air. The dream allowed Smith to relive the unforgettable experience in vivid detail a second time.

The experience left its mark on Smith; several years later, she had a conversation with another employee, who provided clues to Elizabeth's identity. Andy, an older man who was a caretaker at the Beckham, told Smith that his grandfather spoke of a woman named Elizabeth who haunted the hotel. Apparently, this woman died in the final days of the last century when she fell down the main staircase leading to the lobby.

Former owner Becky Penrod witnessed Elizabeth on several occasions and even claimed the ghost would periodically ride home with her in her car! Many guests and other employees have reported feeling a warm presence, smelling fresh flowers, and hearing strange noises throughout the old building. As recently as May 1999, Smith and another employee, a former skeptic named Glenda, smelled the scent of fresh flowers (signaling Elizabeth's presence) in the lobby. Glenda became a believer after this unexplainable encounter with the unknown forces trapped in the hotel. Employees often report problems with the phones and lights turning on and off inexplicably. With ongoing renovation work planned, the ghostly activity shows no signs of slowing. Elizabeth still stalks the hallways and stairways of the old Beckham Hotel.

Less Spooky Things To Do In Mineola

"Shopaholics" will not be disappointed in Mineola. In addition to the 20 antique stores in town are specialty shops featuring dolls, clocks, vintage clothing, furniture, glassware, primitives, and collectibles. Craft malls have items created by local craftsmen and artists that make unique gifts for everyone on your shopping list. The **Lake Country Playhouse**, an award-winning live-drama group headquartered at the 78-year-old **Select Theater**, offers live productions at least 12 weekends a year. The **Piney Woods Pick'n Parlor**, housed in the grand ballroom of the historic haunted **Beckham Hotel**, features monthly acoustic music concerts and cultural events. Several well-known musicians, such as the Dixie Chicks, have taken the stage at the Pick'n Parlor. Mineola offers visitors a long list of seasonal events suited for the entire family, including the beautiful **Dogwood and Azalea Trails** in the spring, July Fourth's **Freedom Fest**, the **Main Street Halloween House Of Horrors**, the **Christmas Tree Lighting** (fourth weekend in November), and the **Christmas Parade** (second Saturday in December).

The Spirits of Nacogdoches

Nacogdoches is located south of Longview on Highway 259. The oldest town in Texas, Nacogdoches is named for a famous Caddo Indian who settled the area between Lanana and Banita Creeks. He established an Indian trading post near the Sabine River. The large burial mounds of the Caddos are still visible throughout the city. Calle Del Norte, a north/south route through town, is believed to have originated as an Indian trading trail and is thought to be the oldest existing thoroughfare in North America. In 1687, the La Salle expedition visited this beautiful area of Texas and a Spanish mission was founded here in 1716. Nacogdoches has been a major gateway into Texas for more than 100 years.

BED & BREAKFASTS WITH A BOO!

The Tol Barret House 👹👹
Route 4, Box 9400, Nacogdoches, TX 75964 • 936-569-1249

Description and History

Dr. Thomas Jefferson Johnson built the Tol Barret House in 1840. Johnson founded the town of Melrose, where the house was originally located, and drilled the first oil well in Texas, in 1866. The house has been awarded National Register and Texas Historic Landmarks status. Captain and Mrs. Charles Phillips now own the house and operate a bed-and-breakfast.

Tours of the Tol Barret House are by appointment only. Contact the Phillipses at 936-569-1249 to make a reservation.

Who haunts the porch of the Tol Barret House?

Photo courtesy of Campbell Cox

Ghostly Visitations

According to Captain and Mrs. Phillips, the ghost heard pacing the front porch of the Tol Barret House may be that of Angelina Martha Thomas Barret. Angelina, the niece of Johnson, came to live with her uncle and eventually was referred to as his foster daughter.

> **Most Haunted Area:**
> *The front porch*

Ann Phillips became aware of their paranormal pacer while purchasing the house several years ago. "As I was giving the check to the previous owner, she said she hoped the ghost wouldn't bother us," Ann said. The Phillipses soon learned that many people have reported unexplained experiences while visiting the Barret House. Light footsteps are heard walking across the front porch and stopping at the front door. A persistent knocking follows, but when the door is answered, no one is there. Many witnesses have seen a woman in a gold dress walk past the front windows. These strange occurrences have continued at the house in its present location as well.

During a Christmas open house at the Barret House, visitors told Phillips they heard a recurrent knocking at the front door. Each time they opened the door, no one was there.

An article in the *Daily Sentinel,* October 24, 1993, describes two ghostly encounters: The first took place when the East Texas Historical Association awarded the Lucille Terry Preservation Award to the Phillipses for restoring the Barret House. Dr. Robert Glover, a professor at the University of Texas at Tyler and affiliated with the historical association, had visited the Tol Barret House to examine the restoration efforts. "He came, unknown to us, to look the house over for consideration," Phillips said. "He later told us he thought he saw a wisp of smoke coming from the chimney as he drove up to the house. He knocked on the front door and waited for someone to answer," Phillips said. "He heard footsteps coming toward the door and expected someone to open the door, but no one did. He went around the house and looked in all the windows and could tell there was no one in the house," Phillips said.

On another occasion, the Phillipses were hosting a dinner for antique dealers at the Barret House. "Several of us were on the front porch sitting in the swings at either end of the porch," Mrs. Phillips said. "One of the dealers drove up and came in the back door. A few minutes later, he opened the front door and asked us who had knocked on the door. But none of us had."

When in Nacogdoches, stay the night with the Phillipses and maybe you'll get to see "Angelina Martha" gliding by the front windows in a beautiful gold dress. Perhaps you can answer the persistent knock on the door. She just may be standing there waiting for you to invite her inside.

 ## Less Spooky Things To Do In Nacogdoches

Relive Texas history at the **Stone Fort Museum**, an example of Spanish Colonial architecture, which interprets East Texas and Nacogdoches history. **Millard's Crossing**, a reconstructed historic village, showcases East Texas architecture from a log cabin to a Victorian mansion furnished with antiques. Adolphus Sterne, a Texas Revolution leader, built the **Sterne-Hoya House** in 1830. Sam Houston was baptized here and Davy Crockett was a guest. Sit a spell at the **Old Time String Shop** for a Saturday afternoon jam session. Nature-lovers can hike along the **Lanana Creek Trail**, an ancient Indian footpath by **El Camino Real Park**. Visit the **Stephen F. Austin Arboretum** and enjoy rare trees, shrubs, vines, and a children's garden. **Ghosts of Nacogdoches Historical Trail**, a self-guided walking tour along historic streets, includes a 7.5-mile or a 3.5-mile hike and focuses on the history of Nacogdoches' oldest properties. Plan a visit to the **Oak Grove Cemetery**, where four signers of the Texas Declaration of Independence are buried. Don't forget your tape recorders to record that rare ghostly whisper!

For more information on Nacogdoches, contact:
Nacogdoches Convention and Visitors Bureau
P.O. Drawer 631918, Nacogdoches, TX 75963-1918
888-564-7351
http://www.visitnacogdoches.org/

Palestine's Paranormal Pranksters

Palestine, the seat of Anderson County, one of the oldest cities in East Texas, is located on the intersection of Highways 287 and 79. Established as a railroad town in 1846, Palestine is second only to Galveston in the number of historical homes (50 years old or older) that are still standing. Large magnolia trees and romantic Victorian homes welcome visitors who stroll along Palestine's historic streets.

BED & BREAKFASTS WITH A BOO!

Wiffletree Inn

1001 N. Sycamore St., Palestine, TX 75801 • 800-354-2018

Description and History

Constructed in 1911, the Wiffletree Inn exemplifies the Craftsman era of skilled home building at its finest. Philip Roquemore built the house to share with his parents and two sisters; it's believed that Roquemore's father passed away here. The house remained in the family for two generations until 1979, when the last sister passed away. From 1979 to 1989, the house served as a parsonage for a Lutheran pastor. The house stood empty for two years until the Frischs moved to town and bought it in 1991.

The Wiffletree Inn has four guest rooms with double-, queen-, and king-size beds. Two rooms have private baths and two share a hall bath. Room rates are inexpensive ($65 per night) with a $10 charge for each additional adult. Children 14 and older are welcome, but no pets are allowed.

The Frischs offer special Murder Mystery packages, designed for groups or couples, for $129 per night. This price includes overnight accommodations and a delicious dinner for two. The package includes tours of several downtown antique shops and the haunted City Cemetery (with its own mysterious ghost light, which locals believe originated when the last public hanging in Anderson County took place on these grounds).

The inn accepts cash, checks, Visa, MasterCard, American Express, and Discover. Visitors must give notification of cancellations before 6 p.m. on the day of their arrival. A full breakfast of eggs benedict or quiche, orange juice, fruit, and homemade breakfast breads starts your day. For more information, call or 903-723-6793, or visit the website at www.triple1.net/W/Wiffletree-Inn-BB/.

Ghostly Visitations

Most Haunted Area: ***Upstairs***

The Wiffletree Inn's specter has a personality that would make many bed-and-breakfast owners envious of Steve and Jan Frisch. Their ghost is a "neat freak" and has been a real help around the house.

Just after moving into the house, Steve Frisch was upstairs vacuuming. Jan was still living in Dallas at the time and Steve was expecting a call from her. When he heard the phone ringing downstairs, Steve turned off the vacuum and ran to catch his wife's call.

After their phone conversation, Steve climbed the stairs to return to his chore. To his surprise, the vacuum wasn't where he'd left it sitting in the middle of the floor. After some searching, Steve found the vacuum

A vacuuming ghost lives at the Wiffletree Inn.

sitting in the storage closet with the cord wrapped neatly around the machine.

On another occasion in 1993, Steve heard doors violently slamming upstairs. Thinking it must be the guest staying at the inn that week, Steve approached the stairs to investigate. He found the upper floor shrouded in darkness and emanating a palpable feeling of anger. Steve believed the sounds of slamming doors were part of a raging argument, even though no shouting voices accompanied the banging. Realizing that he was alone in the house, Steve became frightened and called a friend over as a witness to the 20-minute-long tirade. Later that same night, his friend claimed to see a filmy apparition descend the staircase halfway, then turn around only to disappear into thin air at the top of the stairs.

Steve informed me that most of the ghostly goings-on took place several years ago during a period of intense house renovations. More recent occurrences include a guest who swore someone sat down on his bed and Jan's feelings of being watched as she works at the kitchen sink.

 Less Spooky Things To Do In Palestine

Palestine hosts many festivals and events, including the **Dogwood Trails Festival** in late March/early April, the **Hot Pepper Festival** during the last weekend of October, and the **Cattle Baron's Ball**. The **Texas State Railroad** takes travelers back to 1896, offering rides through the piney woods surrounding Palestine to Rusk, 30 miles away. **Downtown Palestine** offers shoppers many antique shops, charming stores, and quaint restaurants featuring downhome cookin'. **The Gus Engeling Wildlife Management Area** is open seven days a week from sunrise to sunset and gives outdoor fanatics a chance to camp, fish, hike, and hunt in the hilly forests of East Texas. **Lake Palestine**, a fisherman's (or fisherwoman's) dream, is only a short drive away.

> *For more information on Palestine, contact:*
> Palestine Chamber of Commerce
> 502 N. Queen St., Palestine, TX 75801
> 800-659-3484
> www.netvoyager.com/palestinetexascc/default.htm

Saratoga's Ghost Light

Saratoga, part of Hardin County, was settled during the 1850s and is located 39 miles west of Beaumont on Highway 105. The town grew up around a cluster of subterranean springs in the area, which claimed medicinal properties. Like its namesake town in New York State, Saratoga was best known as a health resort. With the discovery of oil in 1901, the resort fell into disuse when "black gold" replaced the medicinal waters as the region's primary economy.

GHOSTS OF THE GREAT OUTDOORS

Bragg Road Light 😊😊

Description and History

Bragg Road is an 8-mile-long dirt pathway leading through a thicket that lies between the Neches and Trinity Rivers. Once a gravel bed for the Santa Fe railroad tracks that ran through the town of Bragg, the tracks and town were dismantled in 1934 after the railroad discontinued the route, leaving only the pathway to mark its existence.

To reach Bragg Road Light from Saratoga, follow Highway 770 west for 2 miles to Highway 787. Turn north on Highway 787 and travel 3.5 miles to Bragg Road. For more information, call the Big Thicket Museum at 409-274-5000.

Ghostly Visitations

Also known as the Big Thicket Light, the Bragg Road Light has baffled observers for more than 50 years. Reports of a swaying light flickering in the distance that starts out yellow, turns brilliant white as it approaches, and finally takes on a red glow before disappearing are as numerous as the explanations of the phenomenon. Some say the light is the ghost of Jake Murphy, a brakeman beheaded when he fell under a train. Others swear the lights are specters of four Mexican laborers murdered by their foreman for their money. Another theory has the light coming from a lantern carried by a phantom hunter lost long ago in these isolated lowlands. Brave souls can find out for themselves by spending a dark night out in the thicket with just the crickets…and perhaps a flickering light or two to keep them company.

Less Spooky Things To Do In Saratoga

Spend an afternoon browsing through the **Big Thicket Museum**, housing backwoods memorabilia from butter molds to logging tools, pioneer artifacts, and documents. Visitors can tour a nineteenth-century log cabin and view interpretive material on Big Thicket flora and fauna.

Winnsboro's Wraith

In 1854, John E. Winn founded this pretty, quaint town, which he called Crossroads. The town was renamed Winnsboro on April 17, 1901, in honor of its founder. Winnsboro is about 90 miles from Dallas in the northeastern corner of the state.

BED & BREAKFASTS WITH A BOO!

Oaklea Mansion and Manor House 😊😊

407 S. Main St., Winnsboro, TX 75494 • 903-342-6051

Description and History

M.D. Carlock built this stately colonial mansion in 1903. A prominent Texas attorney, Carlock was also a Confederate courier, political leader, and member of the Electoral College that named Woodrow Wilson president. The Carlock family owned the home for two generations before the last Mrs. Carlock sold the beautiful mansion to the Wilkinsons in September 1996. Mrs. Carlock died in the house just three months later.

The home's 22 rooms are lavishly furnished with the original Civil War–era antiques brought to Texas by the Carlocks at the turn of the century. Oaklea Mansion features a rare curly-pine staircase and several stunning chandeliers.

Oaklea Mansion (the main house) offers three suites—the haunted Angel Suite, the Miss Ima Hogg Suite, and the Mariposa Suite—as well as four guest rooms, including the O'Hare Room, the Oak Room, and La Paloma Room. Many rooms feature beautiful stained glass windows, queen- and king-size beds, and claw-foot tubs. The Manor House has six bedrooms, all equipped with phone/fax jacks and TVs. Guests will enjoy the tranquil koi ponds, water gardens, and cozy sitting areas and balconies, as well as the Victorian gazebo, and a bandstand featuring a stone dance floor.

Oaklea Mansion is available for weddings, receptions, parties, retreats, and seminars. Catering is available upon request. The Wilkinsons accept all major credit cards. Oaklea Mansion is not equipped for children. Norma Wilkinson serves a delicious full breakfast at 9 a.m; this includes casseroles, fruit, biscuits, and muffins. For more information, call 903-342-6051, or visit the website at www.bluebonnet.net/oaklea.

Ghostly Visitations

The friendly ghost who resides at Oaklea Mansion is known as "Mr. Shelton." An elderly neighbor of the Carlock's, lonely Mr. Shelton spent many nights at the mansion after his wife died. He always stayed in the second floor bedroom, now known as the Angel Suite. Mr. Shelton is heard pacing the floor of this room as well as opening and closing the bedroom door.

> **Most Haunted Area:**
> *Angel Suite*

Less Spooky Things To Do In Winnsboro

With the end of winter comes the annual **Winnsboro Spring Festival**. This celebration includes downtown craft shows, trail rides, scenic drives and walks, cookouts, and garden planting. October's **Trail Ride** attracts up to 10,000 horsemen to this quiet corner of the state. Often referred to as Lake Country, this region has several major lakes within a 30-mile radius of Winnsboro. **Lake Fork** makes up about 27,690 acres of the best bass fishing in Texas. **Lake Cypress Springs** is considered one of the cleanest lakes in Texas and covers 3,425 acres. The lake is spring-fed and stocked with bass, catfish, perch, and bream. **Lake Bob Sandlin** is a 9,460-acre reservoir with a 640-acre state park that provides camping and commercial marinas. **Lake Monticello** is kept warmer than usual by year-round power plant cooling and produces some of the biggest bass in Texas. Other area lakes include **Lake Winnsboro**, **Lake Hawkins**, **Lake Quitman**, and **Lake O' the Pines**.

> *For more information on Winnsboro, contact:*
> Winnsboro Area Chamber of Commerce
> 201 W. Broadway, Winnsboro, TX 75494
> 903-342-3666
> www.texasd.com/wchamber

Elusive Boos of the East Texas Piney Woods

East Texas was one of my favorite regions to visit while conducting research for this book. In the future, I plan to take many additional trips to the piney woods of East Texas to uncover more evidence of the elusive gaggle of ghosts listed below.

The Grove, Jefferson

In the most haunted house in Jefferson, this former restaurant called the Grove stands empty and for sale. (I toyed with the idea of buying it while I was in town, but decided I was too much of a chicken to own *this* house.) Several spirits roam the empty rooms, including a woman dressed in clothing from the 1800s and a little dog. The current owner and numerous former employees have experienced incredible activity. Everyone in town knows this house's reputation, so the next time you're visiting Jefferson, just ask around....

Hale House, Jefferson

702 S. Line St., Jefferson, TX 75657 • 903-665-8877

The spirit of a young girl was seen standing near the staircase in this beautiful bed-and-breakfast inn.

Noble Manor Bed and Breakfast, Mineola

411 E. Kilpatrick St., Mineola, TX 75773 • 903-569-5720

Rumors persist of a haunting in this lovely bed-and-breakfast inn.

Griffith Fine Arts Center, Nacogdoches

P.O. Box 6078, Nacogdoches, TX 75962 • 409-468-2011

A playful ghost named "Chester" haunts this theater, located on the campus of Stephen F. Austin University.

La Hacienda Restaurant, Nacogdoches

1411 North St., Nacogdoches, TX 75961 • 409-564-6450

According to manager Amy Calvery, Sam Hayter's young daughter, who died of smallpox in an upstairs room, haunts the building. This attic room was used as a quarantine area for local children who caught the deadly virus.

Charnwood Hill Bed and Breakfast, Tyler

223 E. Charnwood St., Tyler, TX 75701 • 903-597-3980

The owners of this beautiful mansion in Tyler don't like to discuss their cigarette-smoking ghost.

Ghost Clubs of the East Texas Piney Woods

 Ghost clubs are more rare than ghosts in East Texas. Most of the Dallas/Fort Worth area organizations seem open to traveling to this part of the state.

ARK-LA-TEX Ghost Hunters

This club is based in Texarkana; its website lists hauntings in East Texas, Arkansas, and Louisiana. Website: http://mypage.goplay.com/arklatexghosts.

Paranormal Phenomena Researchers of Texas

RR3, Box 335, Kempner, TX 76539 • 254-547-8522

Founder Ann Riley has conducted numerous investigations at the haunted Jefferson Hotel.

Region 4

Ghosts of the Windswept Gulf Coast

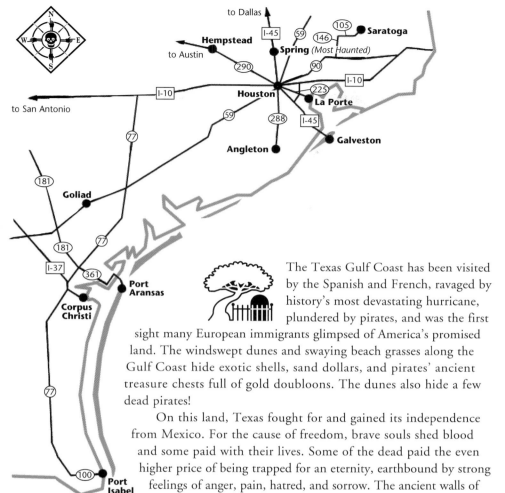

The Texas Gulf Coast has been visited by the Spanish and French, ravaged by history's most devastating hurricane, plundered by pirates, and was the first sight many European immigrants glimpsed of America's promised land. The windswept dunes and swaying beach grasses along the Gulf Coast hide exotic shells, sand dollars, and pirates' ancient treasure chests full of gold doubloons. The dunes also hide a few dead pirates!

On this land, Texas fought for and gained its independence from Mexico. For the cause of freedom, brave souls shed blood and some paid with their lives. Some of the dead paid the even higher price of being trapped for an eternity, earthbound by strong feelings of anger, pain, hatred, and sorrow. The ancient walls of the haunted fort Presidio La Bahia in Goliad held General Fannin and his Texians captive before their massacre by Santa Anna in 1836. From paranormal picaroons to the region's most haunted town of Spring, the ghosts along the Texas coast are every bit the characters in death that they once were in life!

HAUNTED LOCATIONS

Angleton's Haunts

Angleton is located 33 miles south of Houston on County Road 521. Angleton, known as the "Gateway to Historic Brazoria County," is the county seat. In the heart of Stephen F. Austin's colony, this is where Texas emerged as an independent nation.

 ## SPIRITED BUILDINGS AND HOUSES

Brazoria County Historical Museum 👁👁👁
100 E. Cedar St., Angleton, TX 77515 • 409-864-1208

Description and History

The Brazoria County Historical Museum is housed in the 1897 Brazoria County Courthouse. To reach the museum, travel north on Highway 288 and take a right on Cedar Street. The building, designed in the Italian Renaissance architectural style popular during the period, was modernized and expanded between 1913 and 1927 to its current style and size. In 1940, a new courthouse was constructed nearby and the old facility then housed the County Library and a number of public agencies.

After years of neglect, the building deteriorated to the point that it was recommended for demolition in 1978. Community leaders rallied to save it, and in 1979, the County Historical Commission signed a 100-year lease, agreeing to bring the building up to standards and open it as a County Historical Museum. Today, the old courthouse building is home to the Brazoria County Historical Museum—and to its very own ghost!

The Brazoria County Historical Museum chronicles the frontier experience and America's movement west. The 1897 County Courthouse building is a Texas Historic and Archaeological Landmark, and is listed in the National Register of Historic Places. The museum is open to the public Monday through Friday 9 a.m.-5 p.m. and Saturday 9 a.m.-3 p.m. For more information visit the website at www.bchm.org.

Ghostly Visitations

In the wonderful book *An Attic Full of Texas Ghosts*, authors Allan Turner and Richard Stewart—both experienced newspaper reporters—tell the story of the haunted Brazoria County Historical Museum. The specter thought to haunt the museum is Lavinia Perry, who was married to William Joel Bryan, nephew of Stephen F. Austin, in 1840. The couple and their seven children lived at the Durazno Plantation near the present community of Freeport. Today, many of Lavinia's belongings are displayed in the Brazoria County Historical Museum, and perhaps her ghost has returned to be among her beloved possessions.

> **Most Haunted Area:**
> *The Durazno bedroom on the second floor*

The museum includes a reconstruction of the Durazno Plantation's master bedroom, which has a haunted portrait of Lavinia Perry hanging in it. Unsettled museum employees claim that Lavinia changes her expression on occasion. "Sometimes she's smiling," said

Linda Woods, who works in the museum's library, "and sometimes she's scowling. People who know nothing about what's going on will come and tell us that the expression of the woman in the portrait has changed."

In addition to the animated photograph, museum employees and visitors have heard strange noises, including footsteps and bangs, coming from Lavinia's room. The bedroom includes a bed, armoire, dresser, sofa, and chairs—all belonging to Lavinia when she lived at Durazno more than 100 years ago. Items in the room are moved or disappear and turn up later.

Turner and Stewart tell a story about museum curator Leslie Ranking-Conger, who lost part of a favorite earring. After an exhaustive search of the museum, Leslie gave up. Almost a year later, on the day Turner and Stewart contacted Ms. Ranking-Conger about the museum's ghost, Leslie found her earring right out in the open, in plain sight. Leslie and other employees had searched the room many times when they turned the museum upside down trying to locate the missing piece of jewelry. "I was quite pleased," Leslie said, "I went and thanked Lavinia for bringing it back."

GHOSTS OF THE GREAT OUTDOORS

Bailey's Prairie

Bailey's Prairie is located 5 miles west of the town of Angleton.

Ghostly Visitations

Bailey's Prairie is named for the ghost who walks this land. A Scots-Irish colonial settler, Brit Bailey made his home on this prairie. As he lay dying, Brit asked to be buried standing up, facing the west, with his gun and a jug of whiskey by his side. His wife denied him his jug and many believe this is exactly what Brit has come back to claim.

Since Bailey's death in 1833, his specter reportedly stalks this land and peers in windows at unsuspecting settlers. After 1850, a ball of light has been seen repeatedly, floating over the prairie grasses in the early evening. Locals still spot the light in this area today. The ghost light of Bailey's Prairie is one of several famous Texas ghost lights, including the Saratoga ghost light and the Marfa Lights.

Less Spooky Things To Do In Angleton

The Father of Texas, Stephen F. Austin, considered **Peach Point Plantation** as his home in Texas. The plantation was the home of his sister, Emily Margaret Austin Bryan Perry, and her husband, James Perry, and is still owned and operated by a Perry descendent. Austin's bedroom/office is all that is left of the original plantation home. Organized groups can arrange visits through the haunted **Brazoria County Historical Museum**. The **Gulf Prairie Presbyterian Church and Cemetery** nearby is the final resting place of Stephen F. Austin, who died an untimely death at the age of 43. Although Austin's remains were removed to the state capital in 1916, his crypt remains alongside that of his beloved sister. The cemetery is open to the public. For shopping enthusiasts, **West Columbia** (first capital city of Texas) offers several antique and unique gift shops. Local restaurants feature home-cooked meals, including delicious Tex-Mex and some of the best barbeque in the state. The **Varner-Hogg Plantation State Historical Park** is located approximately 1 mile north of West Columbia. Originally built as the family home of the Pattons, an antebellum, cotton and sugar plantation family, the house changed ownership several times following the Civil War. In 1901, James Stephen Hogg, one of Texas's most famous governors, acquired the property. The Hogg family remodeled the house, significantly altering its appearance. The mansion now houses an extensive collection of historic furnishings assembled by Miss Ima Hogg. The town of **Brazoria**—the only town in Texas still operating under its original name—was established in 1828 as a port and trading center for Stephen F. Austin's colony. The peaceful town offers several antique and craft shops housed in quaint wooden buildings, as well as dinner cruises on the **San Bernard River**.

For more information on Angleton, contact:
Angleton Chamber of Commerce
445 E. Mulberry, Angleton, TX 77516
409-849-6443

Shades of Corpus Christi

Corpus Christi is located on the Gulf of Mexico, 144 miles southeast of San Antonio on I-37.

RESTAURANT REVENANTS

Blackbeard's on the Beach 👤👤

3117 Surfside Blvd., Corpus Christi, TX 78402 • 361-884-1030

Description and History

Blackbeard's on the Beach is located within sight and walking distance of the haunted *U.S.S. Lexington* and across Harbor Bridge from downtown Corpus Christi. According to the "Legend of Blackbeard's," a tale printed on the cover of the Blackbeard's menu:

In the summer of 1955 this building was not green. Nor was it a restaurant. It was a bar. The North Beach area of Corpus Christi was a fun, active, and sometimes wild place to hang out. On a warm night people would crowd to the old bar, laughing and talking. The bar itself is still in its original position, but now it is a counter to the kitchen. Legend has it that there was an argument one evening over a red-headed woman. Shots were fired, and the redhead and a fast talking New Orleans roughneck headed north on the old causeway. Neither they nor their gold Hudson were ever seen again. But they left behind a man on the floor…and possibly a ghost! Over the years many strange occurrences have been reported by customers as well as employees. Chairs move. Doors slam. Lights blink on and off. Voices in conversation have been heard long after the last customer departed. One old-timer used to order two beers every time he came in. He said that the second one on the bar was for the ghost!

In 1962 the flamboyant entrepreneur and amateur magician Colonel Larry Platt bought the little bar and added a dining room. He called it the Spanish Kitchen, and from the start, it was the "in" place to go on the North Beach. Popular for good food, fun, and a gathering place for friends and visitors, the Spanish Kitchen tradition continues today as Blackbeard's on the Beach. Next to the clean beaches of Corpus Christi Bay, the Lexington, and the Texas State Aquarium, Blackbeard's is proud to be part of the new North Beach…fun, lively, and the place to be! And while some do, and some don't, believe in ghosts, we at Blackbeard's still leave a beer on the old bar in memory of that summer of '55.

Blackbeard's menu tempts hungry ghost hunters with a yummy variety of Tex-Mex dishes, loaded burgers, healthy salads, and fresh seafood. Blackbeard's is inexpensive and open for lunch and dinner every day of the week.

Ghostly Visitations

Certainly a heck of a story, but Docia Williams reports in *Ghosts Along the Texas Coast* that a conversation she had with Colonel Platt refuted much of the

Most Haunted Area:
Throughout the restaurant

information printed on the menu. Colonel Platt asserted that the building he purchased in 1962 was so rundown that he had the building demolished and built an entirely new one in its place.

That the structure housing Blackbeard's is different from the original one doesn't negate the legend of the "redheaded woman" and the origin of Blackbeard's ghostly inhabitant. Spirits can remain attached to the location rather than the building.

Platt offered his own theory regarding the spirit who inhabits the popular restaurant. He and his wife owned the motel adjacent to the Spanish Kitchen. A sad man who actually resided at the motel was recently separated from his wife. The loner always carried his hunting rifle with him and would come into the bar every night to listen to his favorite song on the jukebox, "As Time Goes By," and drink himself into a stupor. One night, after spending the evening at the Spanish Kitchen, the man went back to his motel room, put his gun in his mouth, and pulled the trigger. Colonel Platt believes if anyone is haunting Blackbeard's, it's most likely this despondent soul.

Current employees report roving cold spots, chairs moving around the restaurant after closing, and the heavy front door blowing open when there is no wind present. A cook witnessed a set of salt and pepper shakers jump up and fly across a table.

So which man is haunting Blackbeard's—the man who lost his life because he was overly flirtatious with another man's woman or the lonely man who lost his wife and violently took his own life? Maybe a visit to Blackbeard's will shed some light and you can help solve this paranormal mystery.

FRIGHTENING FORTS AND BATTLEGROUNDS

U.S.S. Lexington 👤👤👤👤

2914 N. Shoreline Blvd., Corpus Christi, TX 78402 • 361-888-4873

Description and History

After haunting the world's seas while serving the U.S. Navy for almost 50 years, the *U.S.S. Lexington* came to rest at the port of Corpus Christi and became a museum. The museum is located just across Harbor Bridge from downtown. Tokyo Rose, who gained fame during World War II for her propaganda broadcasts to the Allied troops, nicknamed the ship the "Great Blue Ghost" with good reason. At least four times, the Japanese reported that kamikaze and torpedo attacks had sunk the ship, but each time it was repaired, restored, and returned to sea.

The *U.S.S. Lexington* received several citations and awards for her years of service, including battle stars for operations in the Gilbert Islands, Asia-Pacific raids, Lyte, Luzon, and Iwo Jima. Her hangar bays accommodated 40 aircraft ready to launch into action from her huge 910-foot flight deck.

Over the years, thousands of seamen and aircraft crewmembers bunked on the "Lady Lex," calling her home for months and years at a time. There were many casualties during the wartime years, including 9 men killed and 35 wounded by a torpedo attack, and 47 men killed and 127 injured by the 1944 Japanese kamikaze attack. Other deaths onboard due to illness and accidents are recorded. As a result of the high number of deaths, the "Great Blue Ghost" has a few ghosts of her own!

The *U.S.S. Lexington* Museum is open seven days a week, and closed on Christmas Day. Between Memorial Day and Labor Day, the museum is open 9 a.m.-6 p.m.; the rest of the year it's open 9 a.m.-5 p.m. Admission is $9 for adults, $7 for senior citizens 60 and above, $7 for active or retired military with ID; $4 for children 4 to 12, and free for children under 4. All children under 13 must be accompanied by an adult.

Ever wonder what it would be like to spend the night aboard a haunted aircraft carrier? All youth groups, including boy and girl scout troops, are invited to participate in the *U.S.S. Lexington's* Live Aboard Program. Admission includes a tour of the ship, three meals served Navy style, and overnight accommodations in an actual crew berthing compartment. Call 361-888-4873 or visit the website at www.usslexington.com for more information about this once-in-a-lifetime opportunity.

All ship tours are self-guided and involve climbing steep stairways, so comfortable clothing and shoes with non-skid soles are recommended for your safety and enjoyment (also handy for those times when you spot a transparent sailor walking toward you and you need to make a hasty retreat!).

Ghostly Visitations

Docia Williams reports in her book, *Ghosts Along the Texas Coast*, that visiting psychic and military historian Sam Nesmith sensed several earthbound spirits aboard the *U.S.S. Lexington*. In Nesmith's opinion, the dark corridors of the "fo'c'sle" area, near the anchor, and the Ready Room Number One are the most active areas.

Most Haunted Areas:
The "fo'c'sle" area and Pilot's Ready Room Number One

In the Pilot's Ready Room, Nesmith captured a spirit using his camera and high-speed film. After feeling an overwhelming presence permeating the small room, Nesmith took several photographs and was rewarded with a remarkable shot. A pilot, seen from the shoulders up, wearing a World War II–era pilot helmet and goggles, was plainly visible in one of the photos. The face of the stricken pilot appeared as a skull, and Nesmith believes this apparition is the spirit of a pilot who didn't make it back after a mission.

On my visit to the *U.S.S. Lexington*, I made exploring the "fo'c'sle" area of the ship a priority and was rewarded with a strange experience. It was late on a summer afternoon, and the ship was about to close her gangways to visitors for the night. I was alone in the "fo'c'sle" section of the ship, and the air was very warm and oppressive. As I was checking my watch and making my way back to the entrance along a dimly lit hallway, I passed through an extremely cold spot of air that felt electrified. All the hair on my arms raised and I sensed someone standing behind me, watching me. Whipping around to look behind me, I was greeted by an empty corridor. The sensation ended. I retraced my steps, and sure enough, I passed through the same cold, electrified air as before. I did attempt a couple of photographs, but embarrassingly enough, had the lens cap on. Okay, so I was nervous!

Crewmembers have reported hearing tremendous banging and rattling noises emanating from deep inside the ship's maze of passageways. A previous assistant to the museum curator, Derek Neitzel, witnessed a heavy metal door shaking and vibrating on its own. Was there someone trying to get in or get out?

A swivel chair in the seemingly empty photocopy room has been heard swiveling and squeaking by itself behind a locked door. Heavy footsteps have followed frightened crewmembers down dark hallways throughout the huge ship. On several occasions, security guards have heard voices when no one was around.

The ghosts of the "Lady Lex" have also been known to play with the water faucets in the locked and sealed admiral's quarters. People have heard the sounds of running water throughout the empty ship without ever finding a source. Sinks, toilets, and showers have been known to run, all behind locked doors, without explanation.

One crewmember's son had a frightening experience—feelings of unaccountable terror washed over him and he heard a voice, close to his ear, saying, "You'd sure hate to be here when them planes were taking off." The poor boy has never forgotten the sound of the clear, gentle voice speaking to him out of thin air. Exploration aboard the historical *U.S.S. Lexington* provides visitors with an appreciation of what life was like on a large aircraft carrier and may even hint at what death is like on a large aircraft carrier.

Less Spooky Things To Do In Corpus Christi

The **Padre Island National Seashore** boasts more than 130 miles of beautiful beaches, including **Big Shell** and **Little Shell Beaches** for great beachcombing, and

Seagull Park, a perfect site for a picnic with your family. More than 80 miles long, haunted **Padre Island** is the largest undeveloped barrier island in the continental United States. The park's facilities are open year-round for beachcombing, camping, surfing, swimming, hiking, and fishing. See sharks, jelly fish, sea otters, and countless saltwater fish at the **Texas State Aquarium**. The aquarium is within sight of the haunted *U.S.S. Lexington* and the haunted restaurant, **Blackbeard's on the Beach**. In the heart of Corpus Christi, the **Downtown Entertainment District** offers visitors fine restaurants, clubs, and shopping.

For more information on Corpus Christi, contact:
Corpus Christi Convention and Visitors Bureau
1201 N. Shoreline, Corpus Christi, TX 78401
800-766-2322
www.corpuschristi-tx-cvb.org

Ghosts of Galveston

Galveston is located 45 miles south of Houston on I-45. A great part of Galveston's appeal (in addition to its many ghosts) is its rich and exciting past. Before its discovery by Spanish explorers, including a noted visit from Cabeza de Vaca, who landed here in 1528, the island of Galveston was long occupied by Karankawa Indians.

Beginning in 1817, the infamous French pirate Jean Lafitte used the island as the home base for his miscreant maritime mayhem. Lafitte called his settlement Campeche, and by 1819 he was president of the Galveston Republic. Rumors are still whispered of Lafitte's treasure buried somewhere on the island (and guarded by Lafitte himself).

The first American colonists arrived in Galveston in 1827. In 1836, the same year Texas gained its independence from Mexico and became a republic, Galveston was born. Canadian fur trader Michel B. Menard purchased seven square miles of land for $50,000; that land became the city of Galveston.

During the late 1800s, Galveston was known as one of the finest ports on the Gulf and became a booming center for trade and industry. Islanders lived lavishly on their romantic island in beautiful Victorian mansions dripping with gingerbread ornamentation. They hosted extravagant parties for all their equally affluent friends and neighbors.

On September 8, 1900, the good life crashed down around everyone's ears. The Great Storm, a hurricane that became the worst natural disaster in U.S. history, blew in unexpectedly from the Gulf and left roughly 6,000 people dead. The devastation that followed touched the lives of all the islanders and forever changed Galveston. The change in energy this tragedy produced has contributed to the island's reputation as being one of the most haunted cities in Texas.

SPIRITED BUILDINGS AND HOUSES

Ashton Villa and Museum 👤👤👤

2328 Broadway St., Galveston, TX 77550 • 409-762-3933

Description and History

The Ashton Villa is home to a piano-playing spirit named "Miss Bettie."

James Moreau Brown, a prosperous Galveston businessman, built the lovely Italianate villa, known as Ashton Villa, in 1859. It is situated on the main street into Galveston from the mainland. The house is now a beautifully restored antebellum mansion featuring Brown family antiques, heirlooms, and original artworks.

The home stood the test of time and survived the horrendous 1885 Fire of Galveston as well as one of America's worst natural disasters, the Hurricane of 1900. In 1970, the Galveston Historical Foundation took over the house and completely restored it.

Today, the foundation holds tours every hour, on the hour. Ashton Villa's ballroom is also an integral part of annual Christmas Dickens on the Strand festivities in Galveston.

The Ashton Villa and Museum is open Monday through Saturday 10 a.m.-4 p.m. and Sunday noon-4 p.m., closed Thanksgiving and Christmas. The museum accepts personal checks and all major credit cards, and admission is $4 (children under 6 are admitted free). The museum is wheelchair-accessible and offers guests shopping opportunities at the museum store on the property.

Ghostly Visitations

The talented ghost who haunts Ashton Villa is believed to be the mansion's former mistress. Rebecca Brown, daughter of the home's builder, James Brown, was known to her friends and family as "Miss Bettie." An accomplished musician and world traveler, the liberated Miss Bettie saw the world unchaperoned, all the while drinking champagne and smoking a pipe!

> **Most Haunted Areas:**
> *The main parlor, known as the Gold Room, the main staircase, Miss Bettie's former bedroom, and the hallway on the second floor landing*

An article from Galveston County's *In Between* from October 1978 tells the story of a caretaker's encounter with the spirited Miss Bettie. While sleeping in the carriage house, he was awakened one night at 3:30 a.m. by the sound of a tinkling piano drifting across the night air from the dark mansion. Fearful of a

The spirited former mistress of Ashton Villa, "Miss Bettie."

break-in, he entered the villa and traced the piano playing to the Gold Room. As the caretaker entered the shadowed salon, he was startled to see the dim figure of a woman seated at the grand piano. The woman was dressed in what appeared to be nineteenth-century garb. She and her beautiful music soon faded into thin air, leaving the frightened caretaker alone in the dark house. He quickly turned on every available light and stayed wide awake for the rest of the long night.

Docia Williams reports in *Ghosts Along the Texas Coast* that she experienced a presence while admiring the same beautiful antique piano in the Gold Room. A shiver went through her and the hair on her arms stood up, prompting her to research the possibility of a ghost's residing in Ashton Villa.

Docents have reported that furniture unexplainably moves and that normally accurate clocks stop in the Gold Room as well as near an alcove in the living room. In another Halloween feature about haunted houses in the October 29, 1993, edition of the *Houston Chronicle*, Steven Long tells the story of Lucie Testa, weekend manager of the villa since 1988, and several of her ghostly experiences in the house.

February 18, 1991, proved to be an eventful day at Ashton Villa. Testa had to deal with the home's alarm system sounding on three separate occasions, without explanation. Then, while closing up for the night, Testa spied the ceiling fan at the top of the staircase slowly turning. She climbed the stairs to turn it off before leaving. Imagine her surprise when she opened the house the next morning to find the ceiling fan lazily spinning once again. It dawned on Testa that February 18, 1855, was Miss Bettie's birthday—the crazy day before was the 136th anniversary of the big day. Testa postulated that the electrical malfunctions on February 18 were Miss Bettie's way of drawing attention to her special day.

Testa also relays the story of a chest that Miss Bettie purchased on a trip to the Middle East, now located in the day room of the mansion. The key has been missing for many years, yet some days the chest is found locked and other days unlocked. A bed in Miss Bettie's former bedroom will not stay made. Docents straighten the cover several times a day, only to find it wrinkled and rumpled the next time they check on its condition.

Another witness saw the beautiful "handful" standing at the top of the main staircase in a formal turquoise dress, holding an ornate Victorian fan in one delicate hand. The sighting occurred during Galveston's Dickens on the Strand Christmas celebration, but a look around Ashton Villa satisfied the observer that the woman in turquoise was not a festival participant.

Turquoise is known to be one of Miss Bettie's favorite colors. The presence of so many Galvestonians dressed in nineteenth-century clothing must have inspired her to join the party as the most attractive woman—alive or dead—in attendance!

Ewing Hall on the University of Texas Medical Branch Campus ☺

301 University Blvd., Galveston, TX 77550 • 409-772-1011

Description and History

The University of Texas Medical Branch Campus is located off the Strand on the east end of the island.

Ghostly Visitations

A large 7-by-10-foot image of a bearded man, staring intently out to sea, has appeared on the side of the building facing the bay. Local legend says this portrait is of Jean Laffite, the French pirate. Drop by and decide for yourself!

 # Michel B. Menard Home ☺

1605 33rd St., Galveston, TX 77550 • 409-762-3933

Description and History

In 1838, when Texas was still a republic, Augusta Allen, the founder of Houston, built the Oaks. The oldest home in Galveston, the mansion was later sold to Michel Menard, the founder of Galveston, and is now referred to as the Michel B. Menard Home. The home sits six blocks off Broadway on 33rd Street. In 1880, the divorced wife of Michel Menard's son sold the property to the Ketchum family, who owned the house for 97 years. Mrs. Virginia Eisenhour, a Galveston

The mysterious head and shoulders of a woman have been spotted in the Menard Home.

historian and an ancestor of the Ketchum's, moved into the house in 1941 when she was just a teenager. Eisenhour's encounter with the unknown in her beautiful ancestral home provides clues to the identity of the spectral inhabitant of the Menard Home.

The Michel B. Menard Home, host to Galveston's first Mardi Gras celebration, has been restored to its former beauty and furnished with an outstanding collection of Federal and American Empire antiques.

The home is open for tours Friday through Sunday from noon-4 p.m. Admission is $6 for adults and $3 for children. The Menard Home is available for rentals and prearranged group tours by calling 409-762-3933.

Ghostly Visitations

A few days after moving into her family home, Eisenhour sat at the top of the main staircase with her dog. The night was gloomy and rainy. Eisenhour's dog began growling and

became increasingly agitated, looking down into the entryway. Following his gaze, Eisenhour was astounded to see the image of a woman's head and shoulders form in a pool of light on the front door. The ghostly woman was clearly visible, her straight hair pulled back from her face and arranged into an elaborate bun at the nape of her neck. She wore a brooch at the neckline of her dress. Eisenhour ran for her mother, who also saw the supernatural visitor on that stormy night.

Although Eisenhour and her mother looked for the ghostly woman again after the initial sighting, the mysterious woman never materialized. Perhaps there is a connection between sightings like this and the weather conditions. On stormy nights, electricity is present in the air and could provide the necessary energy that spirits need to manifest themselves on the physical plane.

Eisenhour later learned that former slaves told some of her ancestors that there had been a tragic death in the house. Colonel and Mrs. Menard had two daughters, Helen and Clara, who lived in the house during the mid-1800s. A young Clara tripped and fell down the long main staircase, breaking her neck, and died in the entry hall in front of the doorway. A visit to the Menard Home—especially on a rainy afternoon—may prove fruitful in your search into the unknown.

 ## 1839 Samuel May Williams Home ☉

3601 Bernardo de Galvez (Ave. P), Galveston, TX 77550 • 409-765-1839

Description and History

The Samuel May Williams Home, built in 1839, is Galveston's second oldest home. Williams was one of the founding fathers of Galveston and constructed the home for his family just three years after Texas won its independence from Mexico. It is located just a few blocks away from the Menard Home, on 36th and Avenue P. The mansion is a rare combination of a Creole plantation house and a New England sea captain's home.

Galveston's second oldest home, the Samuel May Williams Home, is haunted.

Williams served as secretary to Stephen F. Austin and helped finance the Texas Revolution. He was the first banker in Texas and often foreclosed on people's property, making him a man with many enemies. Shirley Homer, who works for the Galveston Historical Foundation, has been quoted as saying that Williams was the "most hated man in Texas." The negative energy felt in the old home could be a result of this hatred.

A self-guided tour of the Williams home features a short film introducing Samuel May Williams, "Father of the Texas Navy," to visitors. The home has been authentically restored and includes many family heirlooms.

The Samuel May Williams Home is open for tours on Saturdays and Sundays from noon-4 p.m. Admission is $3 for adults and $2 for children. The Williams Home is available for rentals and prearranged group tours by calling 409-762-3933.

Ghostly Visitations

A former director of the Williams House Museum claims he saw a lamp turn on in the downstairs hallway. She turned it off and watched as it started rattling "90 to nothing."

> **Most Haunted Area:**
> *Second-floor landing just outside the children's bedrooms*

Visitors have refused to enter the dwelling (even after paying their admission) due to the strange, uncomfortable energy they feel coursing through the historic home. Numerous tourists have felt a strong presence along with cold spots on the landing just outside the children's bedrooms. The next-door neighbor, Mario Ceccaci, told the story of a visiting psychic who refused to tour the home. After sensing the presence of Mr. Williams so strongly, nothing could convince the psychic to enter the house.

According to Ceccaci, the house belonged to the Tucker family for many years. When Mrs. Tucker died in 1952, the antique-filled house stood empty for several years. Ceccaci used to check on the locked house periodically to make sure everything was in order. On one of his checks, he found evidence of a recent fire in a previously empty fireplace, including ashes and still-glowing embers. Not finding evidence of forced entry into the building, Ceccaci became convinced that Mr. Williams had lit a fire to warm his old bones on a cold night! Must have been a heck of a fire to warm old, *dead* bones!

Less Spooky Things To Do In Galveston

Galveston Island offers tourists beautiful accommodations, entertainment, shopping, and 32 miles of **Gulf Coast beaches**. The temperate weather allows visitors to enjoy the wonderful beaches, golf, fishing, volleyball, and horseback riding that Galveston offers year-round. It is also home to the first nourished, or replenished, beach in Texas, a primary attraction. The beach-nourishment project added as much as 150 feet of sand to the width of the beaches on a 3.75-mile section along Seawall Boulevard. Many concessionaires provide services throughout the area, designated as alcohol-free. Children and adults alike enjoy playing in the sand while viewing the **SEE-WALL Mural**, the world's largest and longest outdoor mural. The mural, depicting marine and beach life found along the Texas Coast, is 2.4 miles long and is composed of 200 separate 88-foot frames that stretch along the seawall. Get into nature and enjoy the beauty of this part of Texas at **Moody Gardens**, a lush tropical setting for a world-class educational and recreation complex. The 10-story glass **Rainforest Pyramid** houses thousands of exotic plants, birds, butterflies, and fish, and offers visitors an incredible tropical environment complete with waterfalls, cliffs, caverns, wetlands, and forests. The **IMAX Theater** shows movies on a six-story screen, and hungry tourists dine in the restaurant overlooking sparkling **Galveston Bay**. In addition to its many outdoor activities, Galveston Island has 15 museums and historic homes open to the public for tours throughout the year. The **Strand National Historic Landmark District** offers more than 100 shops, restaurants, and art galleries conveniently located within 36 square blocks. In almost any month of the year, you can find a festival on Galveston Island. The first weekend in December brings **Dickens on the Strand**. A celebration of Charles Dickens's Victorian London during the Christmas season, the festival features authentic British foods, crafts, and costumes. **Mardi Gras! Galveston**, a 12-day event preceding Lent, is celebrated with parades, masked balls, art exhibits, sporting events, and live entertainment.

For more information on Galveston, contact:
Galveston Chamber of Commerce
621 Moody Ave., Galveston, TX 77550
409-763-5326
www.galvestoncc.com • www.galveston.com

Goliad's Ghouls

Goliad, the third oldest Spanish settlement in Texas, is one of the oldest municipalities in Texas. The town celebrated its 250th birthday in 1999 and is located at the intersection of Highways 183 and 59.

In 1749, the Spanish government transferred Mission Espiritu Santo and its royal protector, Presidio La Bahia, to the site of a small Aranama Indian village, which they named Santa Dorotea. Mission Espiritu Santo served the Aranama, Tamique, and their allies for 110 years, longer than any other Spanish colonial mission in Texas.

Spaniards lived here until 1821, when Mexico won its independence from Spain. The name of the town was officially changed to Goliad in 1829. Mexican soldiers occupied Presidio La Bahia from 1821 to 1825. Today, Goliad serves as the county seat of Goliad County.

 **FRIGHTENING FORTS AND BATTLEGROUNDS**

Goliad State Historical Park: 👹👹👹👹👹
Presidio La Bahia and the Chapel of Our Lady of Loreto
108 Park Road 6, Goliad, TX 77963 • 361-645-3405

Description and History
The Presidio La Bahia, designated a National Historic Landmark, is considered the world's finest example of a Spanish frontier fort. The fort is the oldest in the western United States. To reach the fort, travel south of Goliad on Highway 183 and 77A.

The 1721 establishment of the Royal Presidio of La Bahia ("the bay" in Spanish) was in direct response to the invasion by the French into the Spanish Province of Texas. The presidio was relocated three times, finally settling in its present location outside the town of Goliad in 1749.

When Mexico won its independence from Spain in 1821, Mexican forces took over the Presidio La Bahia. In 1835, a group of Texans led by Captain George Collinsworth stormed the fort and succeeded in capturing it from the Mexicans stationed there. Later, the *Declaration of Texas Independence* from Mexico was signed at the presidio. A total of 92 Texas settlers stated a desire for full autonomy from the dictatorial government of Mexico led by General Antonio Lopez de Santa Anna, who was responsible for the massacre at the haunted Alamo in San Antonio.

In March 1836, Texas forces stationed at the presidio and led by Colonel James Walker Fannin participated in the Battle of Coleto. Tragically, Fannin and 352 of his men were captured, tortured, and finally executed by Santa Anna and his troops on Palm Sunday. The soldiers were left naked and unburied, exposed to the elements without thought or care. This calamitous event has had horrendous and enduring consequences for the men who died here so violently. Many souls have never left the Presidio La Bahia.

For Texas State Park information, call 800-792-1112 (select "3" and "3"). To make reservations, call the Central Reservation Center at 512-389-8900 from 9 a.m.-8 p.m. Monday through Friday, or 9 a.m.-12 p.m. Saturday.

The per-person daily entrance fee ranges from $.50-$5 for anyone 13 or older; children under 12 are admitted free of charge. Goliad State Historical Park accepts MasterCard, Visa, and Discover. For more information on the park, call 361-645-3405 or visit the website at www.tpwd.state.tx.us/park/goliad/goliad.htm.

Ghostly Visitations

After studying many accounts of the hauntings of the Presidio La Bahia, I theorize that the old fort acts as a portal for paranormal energy to enter into the physical plane. The crowd of souls spending their eternities at the presidio outnumbers the living employees. The ghostly gathering consists not only of the Texas soldiers who lost their lives here under the swords of Mexican troops, but also a group of crying babies, a choir of singing women, a lady in black, a lady in white, and even an old priest thrown in for good measure. The old stone walls of this landmark have trapped a good deal of energy—negative from the battlefield and positive from the many believers who have knelt in the chapel in prayer and reverence—making the Presidio La Bahia a true paranormal hot spot.

> **Most Haunted Areas:**
> *The museum, the Chapel of Our Lady of Loreto and adjoining graveyard, the staff living quarters, and the crossing at the San Antonio River*

An article in the *Victoria Advocate* by David Tewes recounts a most remarkable tale of several haunts at the presidio. The November 1992 story features an interview with a security guard assigned to guard some equipment stored at the presidio. The guard, Jim Leos, Jr., spent a wild and woolly night at the deserted presidio. Expecting a quiet night, Leos was unprepared for the events that transpired just before midnight at the old fort.

The stillness was broken by the "eerie, shrill cries of nearly a dozen terrified infants." Feeling very agitated and concerned, Leos searched frantically for the source of the cries, which seemed to emanate from one of the dozen or so unmarked graves near the Chapel of Our Lady of Loreto. Just as the pitiful crying ended, the beautifully hypnotic sounds of a women's choir filled the Texas night. The voices came from the back wall of the fort.

After several minutes, the music ended and the apparition of a 4-foot-tall friar wearing a black robe with a hood materialized in front of the double doors leading into the chapel. The small man paced in front of the chapel for several minutes, apparently praying in Latin. He wandered to each corner of the quadrangle before disappearing into the night. Leos claimed that he observed the specter for approximately an hour and a half before it vanished.

Inexplicably, the next spirit to manifest was a woman dressed all in white. She meandered among the unmarked graves from which the babies' cries had come. Leos said, "Then she turned around and looked at me. She drifted maybe a foot or two off the ground and headed towards the back wall." Floating over the wall and out of sight, the spooky figure made her ghostly way to a 1700s-era cemetery down the road. Whoever she was looking for must be in the same situation she is!

Eight years later, on New Year's Eve 2000, members of the Lone Star Spirits spent a similarly frightening night at the Presidio La Bahia. An article in the *Victoria Advocate* by Henry Wolff, "Ghost Hunters Tap Into Spirits in Goliad," reported that group founder Katie Phillips sat in the dark waiting for the ghosts of the old fort to make themselves known. She didn't have to wait long. Although Katie Phillips couldn't make out the exact form, she says it was between 4 and 5 feet tall, "had a definite human look to it," and "it was moving behind the well, waving its arms about." This little guy sounds like the hooded friar Jim Leos saw in 1992.

Attempting to capture an electronic voice phenomenon (EVP), the researchers rigged a microphone inside the keyhole of the large old lock on the Presidio chapel doors (the chapel was locked at the time). While team member Joe Perez was outside the door filming video of the quadrangle, he heard a voice from inside the chapel declare, "Doesn't fit." Sounds recorded on the tape appear to be of furniture being dragged around inside the chapel and the old lock being actuated.

Lead investigator Pete Haviland spotted a thick mist forming in the southeast corner of the quadrangle, smelled "death" in this same corner of the courtyard, and "saw the aftermath of the Goliad massacre" while gazing out into the quadrangle. At this point, the group decided to get some shut-eye.

Evidently, sleeping peacefully is no easy trick at La Bahia. The ghost hunters reported hearing a door banging, strange mumbling sounds, and horses' hooves outside the guest quarters. When Haviland felt his bed raise up underneath him, the group made a unanimous decision to sleep in their cars. "It was the first time we ever had to leave some place to get to sleep," Haviland says. You can read the Lone Star Spirits full report of welcoming in the New Year La Bahia–style by visiting the website at www.lonestarspirits.org.

Volunteers and employees have heard organ music accompanied by a woman's beautiful soprano voice coming from inside the museum. Employees staying in the living quarters at the presidio (situated just yards from the execution spot of Fannin and his men) report roving cold spots and the feeling of being watched by unseen eyes day and night.

A visitor to the presidio was touring the chapel when she and her daughter both saw the sorrowful figure of a woman dressed all in black, with a black veil over her face, crying pitifully by the candles sitting on the altar. Sympathetically, the tourist approached the kneeling mourner to offer comfort, only to have the woman in black vanish instantly. Others report hearing the sounds of a mumbling crowd, like a group of people praying, coming from inside the empty Chapel of Our Lady of Loreto at night. Burning lights have mysteriously appeared inside the chapel when nobody is around.

Several La Bahia area residents have survived a terrifying encounter with an unknown apparition appearing in their cars while crossing the San Antonio River. The stories are frighteningly similar, with the drivers reporting confusion as to whether the paranormal passenger was sitting in the back seat or the front. Some have even claimed their horrific hitchhiker was headless! So, it seems, whether you're visiting the presidio or simply driving by, the chances of bumping into ones of these lost souls is fairly good—good as far as ghost hunting goes!

 ## Less Spooky Things To Do In Goliad

Noted Texas architect Alfred Giles designed the Second Empire–style **Goliad County Courthouse**, which was completed in 1894. The National Register of Historic Places listed the courthouse in 1976. On the north courthouse lawn stands the **Hanging Tree**, or **Cart War Oak**. At various times between 1846 and 1870, this tree served as the site for carrying out court-ordered death sentences. Under the strong limbs of this huge oak, many condemned men met their maker, swinging on the end of a rope. During the 1857 Cart War, dozens of innocent Mexican cart drivers were lynched under this tree by Texas freighters. Stop by the **Market House Museum**, built by the townspeople of Goliad in the early 1870s to house a citywide farmers' market. Today, the museum houses the Goliad County Historical Commission. Goliad visitors will enjoy touring the crumbling walls of the **Mission Nuestra Señora del Rosario**, founded in 1754 by Franciscan missionaries in an attempt to settle the Karankawa Indians, who had abandoned the first Espiritu Santo mission. The Rosario ruins are located about four miles west of **Goliad State Historical Park** headquarters and six miles west of the city, off Highway 59. To the east of Goliad, nine miles east on Highway 59, history buffs can tour the **Fannin Battleground**, the site of the Battle of Coleto Creek. In March 1836, during the Texas Revolution, Texas troops under Colonel Fannin surrendered here to superior Mexican forces after a day and a half of grueling fighting. On Palm Sunday, March 27, 1836, the captured men were massacred, their bodies left stripped and unburied. General Thomas Rusk and his army later gathered the remains and gave the soldiers a complete military funeral on Friday, June 3, 1836. The grave of Fannin and his troops remains near the fort and can be visited today. This battlefield is the perfect location for a haunting—check it out and see if you can be the first to document evidence of residual spiritual energy.

For more information on Goliad, contact:
Goliad County Chamber of Commerce
205 S. Market, Goliad, TX 77963
361-645-3563
www.goliad.org/goliad.html

Mournful Ghosts of Hempstead

Established in 1856, Hempstead is located 50 miles west of Houston on Highway 290 and Highway 6. The introduction of the railroad made Hempstead an important depot during the Civil War with several Confederate camps fixed in the area for the purpose of shipping and receiving much needed war supplies.

At the turn of the century, Hempstead earned the nickname "Six Shooter Junction" because of the violence that plagued the town. In 1905, U.S. Congressman John Pickney, his brother, and two others were gunned down outside the courthouse following a heated argument with a group of prohibitionists who had recently won a major victory in their attempt to ban alcohol. The Waller County Courthouse was riddled with more the 75 bullets during the gunfight. The violent incident shocked the nation and "Six Shooter Junction" became synonymous with the Wild West in the minds of many Americans.

Hempstead is currently the seat of Waller County. The town's economy today is based on farming, ranching, oil, and gas.

SPIRITED BUILDINGS AND HOUSES

Liendo Plantation Ranch 👶👶👶
305 10th St., Hempstead, TX 77445 • 800-826-4371

Description and History
Colonel Leonard Waller Groce built Liendo Plantation in 1853. The plantation is located north of Hempstead; take FM 1488 northeast approximately 2.5 miles to Wyatt Chapel Road and turn right into the entrance. Groce was the son of Jared Groce, one of the largest landowners in Texas during the last century. Originally a Spanish land grant of 67,000 acres assigned to Justo Liendo (the plantation's namesake), Liendo became a self-sustaining, cotton-producing community in the years before the Civil War. The Groce family loved to entertain and their home became a center of social life known throughout Texas.

After the war broke out, Liendo was saved from destruction by offering hospitality to General George Custer and his troops. The General was so impressed with the Groces and their beautiful home that he gave protection orders to spare Liendo from burning after the Civil War. Unfortunately, where Liendo was lucky, Leonard Groce was not. He lost his fortune and the plantation fell into the hands of a succession of owners over the next several years.

After much searching, Elizabet Ney and Dr. Edmond Montgomery found their true home in Liendo, and purchased the property in 1873. The couple lived in the house until 1911. The world-famous German-born sculptress and her brilliant Scottish husband caused quite a stir in the small town of Hempstead during their day. A liberated woman, Elizabet refused to use her husband's name and strolled around Liendo clad in Grecian togas, Turkish bloomers, and turbans.

Taking a sabbatical from her art to raise her two young sons, Arthur and Lorne, Elizabet knew a couple years of contentment before tragedy struck. Two-year-old Arthur contracted diphtheria in an epidemic that swept through the area in the 1870s. Little was known about the disease and despite their best efforts, the couple was unable to save their son.

What the eccentric couple did next shocked the community and caused quite a scandal: Dr. Montgomery and his grief-stricken wife cremated Arthur's tiny body in the front parlor's fireplace. An urn containing his ashes sat on the mantel for many years.

Elizabet eventually moved to Austin and built a studio she named Formosa ("beautiful" in Portuguese) and started sculpting again. During the years spent at Formosa, Elizabet sculpted the famous statesmen statues of Stephen F. Austin and Sam Houston still standing guard inside the haunted Capitol Building. She died at her studio in 1907 at the age of 74. Dr. Montgomery died four years later. Both are buried, along with their other children, in the small cemetery on Liendo's grounds.

In 1960, Carl and Phyllis Detering purchased the plantation and spent 10 years restoring Liendo to the estate's former grandeur. Today their son, Will Detering, owns the property and continues the restoration work his parents began. Liendo is a Texas Historic Landmark and listed on the National Register of Historic Places.

The plantation is open for public viewing on the first Saturday of every month at 10 a.m., 11:30 a.m., and 1 p.m. For other tours, call Will Detering at 800-826-3126 or 409-826-4400 for an appointment. A small admission is charged and the plantation is not wheelchair accessible.

Ghostly Visitations

Many believe the eccentric artist Elizabet Ney and her young son, Arthur, have never really left their beloved Liendo. Employees have heard the tiny, gasping cry of a young boy by the long white guest house at sunset. A former cowhand has heard the mournful cry coming from the tiny cemetery, where the family is buried.

> **Most Haunted Areas:**
> *Outside the guest house and the family cemetery*

Several people have claimed to see the apparition of a small child in the grove of oak trees surrounding the cemetery and on the front porch of the plantation. Owner Will Detering tells of an incident that occurred while two women were visiting Liendo in 1993. One of the women said a lady came into her room one night. She initially thought the woman was her friend, but reconsidered when she felt the "woman" get into bed with her. Finding this extremely odd, she turned over to find an empty bed. She was very frightened by this experience.

Another visitor reported feeling a sudden drop in temperature in her room. Growing colder, she also felt herself becoming very peaceful. Suddenly, a strange woman appeared and said, "I know you are a guest here." The visitor thought the woman was Detering's mother, but *it* wasn't.

Less Spooky Things To Do In Hempstead

Known as the "Watermelon Capital of Texas," Hempstead celebrates this distinction with the annual **Watermelon Festival** on the third Saturday in July. Activities include an antique car show, craft booths, a watermelon-seed spitting contest, a watermelon-eating contest and watermelon auction, and a street dance. The **Waller County Fair** is held the first weekend in October each year. Events include stock judging, a rodeo, dances, and a carnival midway.

For more information on Hempstead, contact:
Hempstead Chamber of Commerce
733 12th St., Hempstead, TX 77445
409-826-8217
www.rtis.com/reg/hempstead/default.htm

Haunted Houston

Houston is the largest city in Texas, the fourth largest city in the country, covering more ground than any other major city in America. Houston is located west of Galveston Bay at the intersection of Highway 45 and I-10. An astounding four million souls call Houston home—but this number does not include the undetermined number of the spirits of the dead. Houston is as big as Israel and El Salvador combined, proving that "Everything's Bigger in Texas!"

Houston is named for Sam Houston, general of the Texas army that won independence from Mexico by defeating Santa Anna and his men. Texans revere Sam Houston as the president of the Republic of Texas and a true state hero.

Houston has experienced phenomenal growth since 1836, when the Allen brothers established a small riverboat landing on Buffalo Bayou. The Port of Houston still thrives today, thanks to the dredging of Buffalo Bayou to form the Houston Ship Channel. In fact, Houston boasts one of the nation's largest seaports. Houston enjoys its status as a financial and industrial center for much of the state and is proud to be home to the world-famous Lyndon B. Johnson Space Center.

RESTAURANT REVENANTS

Ale House Pub 👹👹👹👹

2425 W. Alabama St., Houston, TX 77098 • 713-521-2333

Description and History

This popular restaurant, built in the English Manor style, has developed quite a reputation for serving up a variety of "spirits." It is located off Highway 59 on West Alabama between Westheimer Road and Richmond Avenue. According to an article in *Houston City Magazine* by Laura Perkins, the Ale House Pub was a "speakeasy" during Prohibition.

The owner, a woman who lived on the third floor of the building, reportedly ran an illicit drinking establishment on the middle floor and offered her customers the services of prostitutes. The enterprising businesswoman is said to have died in her bedroom on the third floor.

Join a bevy of boos at the Ale House Pub.

Managed by a string of owners, the old building has been plagued by unexplained occurrences over the years. It seems the original dead owner doesn't like to make room for the living managers.

The Ale House Pub is open seven days a week. Monday through Saturday, the restaurant is open from 11 a.m.-2 a.m., and Sunday from noon-2 a.m. The Ale House serves "pub grub," including authentic fish and chips and juicy burgers.

Ghostly Visitations

Past managers have reported that they "used to put a chair out on the top porch during business hours so she would leave the customers alone." Angela Jenkins, manager of the Ale House

Most Haunted Area:
The third floor

in 1991 said, "The place is overrun with ghosts. There are times when you feel like someone is looking at you. You'll hear noises like a party is going on when there's no one in the place. Mugs will be swinging and chairs creaking." During a radio interview between Ms. Jenkins and the *Houston Chronicle* on Halloween 1991, an unexplained voice was recorded on tape. A young woman's plaintive cry echoed across the airwaves beseeching, "Let me out! Let me out!" Jenkins theorized that the restaurant was home to two spirits, a good maid who played with the lights, and a bad sea captain who threw lit candles and smashed glassware.

The most haunted area, the third floor, where the original owner lived and passed away, has an atmosphere dense with feelings of sadness and despair, especially after closing when all the happy barflies have gone home for the evening. Employees report becoming overwhelmed with grief while cleaning up this area of the restaurant, which is currently decorated like an English pub. Lights turn themselves back on after workers have gone home for the night. Musical equipment

A paranormal investigator captured on film what appears to be an orb.

Photo courtesy of Nichole Dobrowolski

rearranges itself, dart boards rotate, and the air conditioner turns on when it's not plugged in. When customers joke about the building's ghostly owner, glasses have been known to break in their hands.

Fort Bend County Paranormal, led by Nichole Dobrowolski, investigated the Ale House Pub and captured two orbs traveling down the third-floor staircase on film. Another ghostly globe was caught on film in front of the dartboards on the third floor. The team monitored several spikes in energy measured on an electromagnetic field detector (EMF) in the same areas of the restaurant. Dobrowolski said the investigative team communicated with a spirit called "Maggie," a very timid, somewhat confused spirit trapped here. You can view these unexplained photographs posted on Fort Bend County Paranormal's website at www.angelfire.com/tx2/hauntedsugarland.

Night manager Tim Case reported that locked doors open, darkened lights turn on, and glasses fly off bar racks without explanation. Employees' keys and other personal possessions "misplace themselves," only to turn up later in strange places throughout the restaurant. A pub employee assured me that ghostly activity goes on "every day;" employees have found lit candles and broken glasses, and overheard women's voices upstairs when alone in the building.

Who is responsible for these acts of mischief? Is it the despondent former "madam" of the house, the playful maid, the irate sea captain, or a combination of all three? Maybe a meal and a beer at the popular Ale House Pub will help you draw your own conclusions.

 # Spaghetti Warehouse 😀😀😀
901 Commerce St. #2, Houston, TX 77002 • 713-229-9715

Description and History

The Spaghetti Warehouse is located less than a mile from I-10, just off Main Street on Commerce. This century-old building was originally constructed as a cotton warehouse, then later used to house pharmaceuticals. The pharmaceutical incarnation of the building produced its resident spook.

This inexpensive restaurant is open for dinner and lunch seven days a week and serves a variety of Italian specialties from spaghetti and meatballs to a fantastic lasagna. For more information, call 713-229-9715, or visit the website at www.meatballs.com.

Ghostly Visitations

The Lone Star Spirits paranormal researchers have conducted several investigations into the old warehouse and uncovered the legend of the ghost who haunts the restaurant. When the warehouse was used to store and ship pharmaceuti-

> **Most Haunted Area:**
> *The second floor dining room*

cals, the former owner was working late one night, fell down an elevator shaft, and was killed. The lady in white, who has been seen wandering the hallways on the second floor, is reportedly the wife of the unlucky owner, returning to look for her deceased husband.

Most of the paranormal activity seems confined to the second floor of the building. Busboys, waiters, and dishwashers have reported table arrangements changing spontaneously, dishes and silverware flying off of the racks in the kitchen, and restaurant equipment turning on and off of its own accord, as well as several glimpses of the lady in white. Late night crews sometimes feel as though they're being watched by someone or something standing on the second-floor stairs.

The Lone Star Spirits investigative team has recently visited the restaurant a couple of times. The first investigation provided members with a photograph of an anomalous mist in the dastardly elevator. During the second examination of the Spaghetti Warehouse, the group measured an unexplained cluster of energy in a small second-floor dining room, using an electromagnetic field detector (EMF). A photograph taken of the suspicious area at that time contained a vortex, or circular cloud of an unknown substance resembling cigarette smoke. This experiment was duplicated in a different area of the same dining room, where an energy spike caused a photograph to contain a vortex. The investigators plan to return to the popular restaurant to continue their ghost hunting efforts.

Interestingly enough, the Old Spaghetti Warehouse located in downtown Austin is also rumored to be haunted. It seems these restaurateurs have cornered the market on old warehouses…and the ghosts who dwell in them!

SPIRITED BUILDINGS AND HOUSES

Julie Ideson Building 👻👻
500 McKinney, Houston, TX 77002 • 713-247-1661

Description and History
Constructed in 1926 to house Houston's public library, the building at 500 McKinney served this purpose until a larger structure replaced it. Today, the Julie Ideson Building contains Texas and local history departments, special collections, archives, and manuscripts.

A true music lover haunts the Julie Ideson Building.

Ghostly Visitations
A former violin-playing janitor, who died in the basement of the Julie Ideson Building in 1936, walks between the stacks in the library today. His name was Mr. Cramer and he loyally polished the reading tables and floors of the old building for 10 years until his death

> **Most Haunted Areas:**
> *The Texas room, the local history room, and throughout the library*

from natural causes. After closing, when the readers and librarians had gone home for the evening, Mr. Cramer would spend his free time practicing his beloved violin.

To this day, librarians and researchers claim to hear strains of eerie, muted violin music wafting throughout the building, especially on cloudy, dreary days. Many report feeling uneasy, as if being watched. Not to fear, it's just Mr. Cramer waiting for closing time. After all, practice makes perfect!

Less Spooky Things To Do In Houston

You will find plenty to occupy your time in this busy city. A Houston must-see is the **Space Center Houston**, situated 20 miles south of Houston at the **Johnson Space Center**. This spectacular new attraction is essentially NASA's visitor center, where you are greeted by engineers, scientists, and astronauts who brief audiences through NASA update videos. Visitors can tour a **Space Shuttle Mock-Up** and the **Mission Status Center**. The **IMAX Theater** is not to be missed. Two million people are expected to tour the Space Center this year, so visitors are encouraged to go early to this popular attraction. See the final—and maybe, not so final—resting place of many famous Houston characters at the **Glenwood Cemetery**. Located at 2525 Washington Avenue, the cemetery is a 65-acre burial ground where eccentric billionaire Howard Hughes, former Texas governors Ross Sterling and William P. Hobby, Sr., and Astrodome founder Judge Roy Hofheinz are interred. Browsers and bargain-hunters should visit **Trader's Village**, a 60-acre flea market located on North Eldridge off Highway 290. Relax at the **Armand Bayou Nature Center** and the **Houston Arboretum and Nature Center** and see collections of native and exotic tropical plants. Lovers of the arts should plan a trip to the 17-block **Theater District** downtown, home to eight performing arts organizations, including the **Houston Ballet** and the **Houston Grand Opera**. Attractions such as **Six Flags AstroWorld** and the **SplashTown Waterpark** are fun summer destinations for the entire family.

For more information on Houston, contact:
Greater Houston Convention and Visitors Bureau
901 Bagby, Houston, TX 77002
800-4HOUSTON • 713-227-3100
www.houston-guide.com

La Porte's Paranormal Picaroon

LaPorte is located 5 miles east of Houston on Highway 225. French settlers gave this city its name, which means "The Door," in 1889, when the city was founded on upper Galveston Bay.

FRIGHTENING FORTS AND BATTLEGROUNDS

Battleship Texas 👣👣👣

3523 Highway 134, LaPorte, TX 77571 • 281-479-2431

Description and History

The Battleship *Texas* participated in both World War I and World War II, and is now located in the San Jacinto Battleground State Historical Park. To reach the park from 610 East, take Highway 225 east for 11 miles to Highway 134 (Battleground

Road). Continue north about 3 miles to reach the battleship.

The *Texas* was the first battleship in the U.S. Navy to mount anti-aircraft guns and to receive commercial radar. *Texas* fired on Nazi defenses at Normandy on "D-Day,"

The haunted Battleship Texas participated in both World War I and World War II.
Photo courtesy of The Battleship Texas archives

June 6, 1944. Shortly afterward, she was hit twice in a duel with German coastal defense artillery near Cherbourg; the crew suffered one fatality and 13 wounded. Could this fatality be the source of the great ship's resident spectral sailor? In 1948, *Texas* became the first battleship memorial museum in the United States; she was named a National Historic Landmark in 1977.

The Battleship *Texas* is open every day of the week from 10 a.m.-5 p.m., year-round. The ship is closed on Christmas Eve and Christmas Day. Self-guided tour routes lead to compartments above and below the decks. Contact the park at 281-479-2431 or visit the website at www.tpwd.state.tx.us/park/battlesh/battlesh.htm#battx for per-person and group admission rates.

Ghostly Visitations

The October 1988 issue of the *Texas State Parks and Wildlife* magazine featured an article titled, "In the Spirit: State Park Ghosts Wish You a Happy Halloween." The story

Most Haunted Area:
The second deck

by Mary-Love Bigony tells of the ghost of an unidentified redheaded sailor that has been spotted on the second deck of the Battleship *Texas*.

One former employee of the battleship said she often saw the young man dressed in a white sailor's suit standing by a ladder on the second deck. The apparition didn't speak, but wore a smile on his face. The witness saw the friendly ghost several times in the same place. She would feel a cold breeze blow over her just before the ladder came into sight.

Another female employee experienced a terrifying vision in a room on the second deck containing displays of guns and other military equipment. Members of a cleaning crew heard the terrified screams of the woman coming from this small room and hurried to help. The hysterical woman tearfully told the cleaning crew that as soon as she stepped across the threshold of the room, the floor became a grassy cemetery studded with white crosses. The scene she described was the image of the cemetery at Normandy. Was this psychic imprint associated with the guns and military equipment displayed in this room?

GHOSTS OF THE GREAT OUTDOORS

Trinity Bay 👧👧

Trinity Bay leads to the Gulf of Mexico at Galveston Island.

Description and History

The famous character who haunts the sand dunes and homes around La Porte is none other than Jean Laffite, the notorious French pirate who made his headquarters at La Porte. Nearly 200 years ago, when Laffite was run out of New Orleans and made his way to the Texas coast, he buried a treasure said to consist of gold doubloons and precious stones at the mouth of the Neches River near La Porte. Many witnesses believe the frightening phantom they've seen is the pirate still guarding his fabulous, as-yet-undiscovered stash.

In 1816, President Madison pardoned Laffite and the pirate moved to Galveston Island. His stay was short-lived due to his return to various nefarious activities. The U.S. Army accused him of attacking and plundering ships in the Gulf of Mexico and forcefully evicted him from the island. He is believed to have died in Yucatan in 1826, but his phantom still calls Texas home.

Ghostly Visitations

The first modern reports came to authorities during the 1920s, when several treasure hunters told terrifying stories of being choked and threatened by a nasty, paranormal picaroon. Some La Porte residents have been awakened in the middle of the night by a man wearing a red coat—believed to be Laffite—standing at the foot of their beds. The promise of untold riches continues to tempt treasure seekers from far and wide to La Porte, but I would advise "abandoning ship" if approached by a man wearing a red coat!

Less Spooky Things To Do In La Porte

At the **Battleship *Texas***, part of the **San Jacinto Battleground State Historical Park**, don't miss the **San Jacinto Monument** with the **San Jacinto Museum of History** inside. The monument is dedicated to "Heroes of the Battle of San Jacinto and all others who contributed to the independence of Texas." A 570-foot limestone shaft, the monument is topped with a 34-foot, 220-ton star symbolizing the Lone Star Republic. The San Jacinto Battleground State Historical Park encompasses the Battle of San Jacinto, the final military event of the Texas Revolution (on April 21, 1836). The 18-minute battle won independence for Texas and allowed westward expansion by the United States. Granite markers designate the locations of the Texan camps, the Mexican camp, and the site of the advance by Texan forces.

> *For more information on La Porte, contact:*
> City of La Porte
> 604 W. Fairmont Pkwy., La Porte, TX 77571
> 281-471-5020
> www.ci.la-porte.tx.us/main/main.htm

Phantoms of Port Aransas

Port Aransas is located on the northern tip of Mustang Island, about 30 minutes from Corpus Christi. The Karankawa Indians, known for their fierceness and cannibalism, are the earliest known inhabitants of Mustang Island. The Karankawas were also known for their size—some accounts report they stood over 7 feet tall. A hunter-gatherer people, they depended heavily on shellfish and mussels for food. The Karankawa used an ingenious, if stinky, insect repellent to protect them from the swarms of mosquitoes that plagued the wetlands they frequented—they rubbed alligator fat all over their bodies. According to some historians, the smell of the fat was so pungent that members of rival tribes could often smell their enemies before they could actually see them. The Karankawas survived in the region until the nineteenth century.

The first historical record of Mustang Island was by Alonso Alvarez de Pineda, who charted this section of the Gulf coast in 1519. The island was first named "Wild Horse Island," then "Mustang," because of the wild horses (called *mestenos*) brought to the island by Spanish explorers in the 1800s.

In the early nineteenth century, the colorful pirate Jean Lafitte and his band of buccaneers are said to have built bonfires on Mustang Island to lure ships navigating through Aransas Pass. When the vessels ran aground, the pirates plundered the booty. Among the many legends of Laffite and his presence on Mustang Island, one tells of an undiscovered Spanish dagger with a silver spike driven through the hilt, under which Laffite buried a chest of gold and jewels.

Historical records show that an Englishman named Robert A. Mercer ran a cattle ranch on Mustang Island around 1855. Over the years, a small fishing village grew up around the Mercer homestead. Mercer's Dock was destroyed by a hurricane in 1875 and replaced by another called Mustang Island. In the passing years, the community was known as Ropesville and Tarpon, before finally settling on Port Aransas around 1910.

Today, Port Aransas is one of the most popular tourist destinations along the Texas Gulf Coast due to its expanses of beautiful beaches. The spot offers fantastic free fishing and is known as a place where "they bite every day."

RESTAURANT REVENANTS

Beulah's Tarpon Inn Restaurant 👹👹👹

200 E. Cotter Ave., Port Aransas, TX 78373 • 361-749-4888

Description and History

As part of the historic Tarpon Inn, Beulah's Restaurant is a favorite among tourists and locals alike. The name Tarpon Inn comes from the impressively large game fish that live in the waters off the island. The restaurant is located at the north end of town near Highway 361.

Three Tarpon Inns have actually existed on this spot since 1886. The first was destroyed by fire, the second by hurricane, and the third—constructed with extra-long pier pilings for the foundation in 1923—is (keep your figures crossed) still standing today. The inn's most famous guest was President Franklin Delano Roosevelt, who came to Port Aransas for a couple days of tarpon fishing.

Beulah's Restaurant occupies two buildings that sit directly behind the inn. At one time, the space served as the bar for the original Tarpon Inn. In 1992, the restaurant's name was changed in honor of the head housekeeper at the Tarpon Inn, Miss Beulah Mae Williams. The moderately priced restaurant combines good home cooking with the added flair of gourmet cuisine.

Ghostly Visitations

Many employees and diners have witnessed the antics at Beulah's over the years. Some of the best stories come from Beulah herself. One day while walking outside past the kitchen, she heard a terrible hubbub of pots and pans crashing

Most Haunted Areas:
The kitchen and the room behind the bar

and banging loudly inside the closed restaurant. When she went inside to investigate, the commotion stopped and Beulah found everything in its proper place.

The noisy kitchen ghosts were reported again in 1993 by two teenagers who returned to the restaurant after closing to retrieve a bicycle. The friends were startled to hear the wildest racket conceivable coming from the darkened kitchen. The pair described the noises as sounding as though every pot and pan in the place was being thrown across the room. They beat a hasty retreat and have steered clear of the kitchen ever since.

A couple of workers have seen the misty form of a middle-aged woman, believed to be from a different era judging by her hair style and clothing, materialize in the kitchen. Some say this is a former cook from the original Tarpon Inn who lost her valued pearl necklace in a kitchen fire and returns to look for her missing jewelry from time to time.

Others believe a second spirit named "Sammy" is in residence at Beulah's. Sammy was also a cook at the restaurant and still comes around to help prepare meals at breakfast time. Manager Julie Caraker was working alone early one morning and was astonished by Sammy's presence in the kitchen. The floor had been freshly mopped and was still damp. Julie could clearly see two sets of footprints on the kitchen floor—her own and a set of large footprints following hers around the room! Sammy has also been known to turn light switches on and off and open doors to get a little attention.

 **Less Spooky Things To Do In Port Aransas**

Visitors to Port Aransas can expect bountiful beachcombing and great seafood meals. The city by the sea has a **free trolley** that runs daily from 10 a.m.-5:30 p.m. **Mustang Island State Park** is 3,954 acres with 5 miles of beach on the Gulf just south of Port Aransas. Activities include camping, picnicking, fishing, swimming, hiking, mountain biking, sunbathing, surfing, and birding. The **Aransas National Wildlife Refuge** was established in 1937 to protect the vanishing wildlife of coastal Texas. The refuge is home to alligators and

6-foot-tall whooping cranes. Our favorite pirate, Jean Lafitte, is reputed to have disbanded his crew of hooligans in this area and buried "enough treasure in those woods to ransom an entire nation."

For more information on Port Aransas, contact:
Port Aransas Chamber of Commerce and
Tourist and Convention Bureau
421 W. Cotter, Port Aransas, TX 78373
800-45-COAST • 361-749-5919
www.portaransas.org

Port Isabel's Transparent Treasure Hounds

Port Isabel is a small, picturesque village on Laguna Madre, the body of water between the Texas mainland and Padre Island. It is located on the southern tip of Padre Island, 23 miles north of Brownsville on Highway 48. The town is named for the Spanish Queen Isabella, who financed the voyage of Christopher Columbus that led to America's discovery.

 ## GHOSTS OF THE GREAT OUTDOORS

Padre Island 👧👦

Description and History

Padre Island is a 3-mile wide, 132-mile long sandbar barrier island that naturally protects the bays and harbors along the Texas coastline. The island's southernmost end is located near the mouth of the Rio Grande River off Port Isabel, with the northern end 132 miles away near Corpus Christi. Spanish explorers discovered Corpus Christi harbor and bay on Corpus Christi Day in 1519, hence the name. The island was given the name *Isla de Corpus Christi*.

Padre Nicholas Balli purchased the island from King Charles IV of Spain in 1880 and started a cattle ranch among the dunes and beach grasses. Over time, the island acquired the nickname "Padre Island" and the name stuck.

Dennis William Hauck tells an interesting story about one of the first white men to live on the island in his marvelous guide, *The National Directory of Haunted Places*. John Singer, brother of the sewing-machine tycoon, discovered the island by a curious twist of fate. Shipwrecked here in 1847, he loved the location so much that he decided to build a house and raise cattle on the island.

While digging a foundation for his house, Singer discovered a pirate's treasure chest containing $800,000 worth of gold doubloons. Texas was on the brink of entering into the Civil War, so Singer decided to hide his glorious find on the mainland between two huge oak trees. Singer buried his treasure in a cast-iron bathtub along with his own sizeable fortune and left to join the South's cause with the peace of mind that he would be a very rich man after the war. Unfortunately, when Singer returned to Texas after the war and tried to locate the two oaks that "marked the spot," he was unable to find them. He spent the rest of his life trying to find his treasure, but died unlucky and poor. To this day, Singer's loot has never been found.

Ghostly Visitations

The wandering specters of Padre Island all seem to be searching for buried treasure. Due to the many shipwrecks that occurred in the Gulf over the centuries, treasure hunters have discovered Spanish jewels and gold coins (and ghostly pirates) on the island for more than 100 years. For example, a notable event occurred in 1553 when a Spanish treasure fleet encountered a hurricane off Padre Island. Many ships were lost and only two survivors lived to reach Mexico. The prospect of discovering Spanish doubloons that have washed ashore as well as rumors of buried chests full of treasure keep modern seekers coming back to Padre Island, dreaming of wealth beyond their wildest dreams.

The buried riches also seem to have quite a hold on the island's supernatural inhabitants. Numerous reports from residents and visitors alike speak of encounters with transparent figures met among the dunes on moonlit nights. My advice to fortune hunters is to keep one eye on your metal detector and one eye on the misty figures roaming the beach ahead of you. One just may be a greedy, gold-hungry phantom ready to protect his plunder!

 **Less Spooky Things To Do In Port Isabel**

History buffs will treasure a visit to the **Port Isabel Lighthouse** and the **Port Isabel Historical Museum**. The 145-year-old lighthouse is the only one of the 16 lighthouses along the Texas coast that allows visitors. The Port Isabel Historical Museum tells the unique story of this area of Texas, from which both the first volley of the Mexican/American War and the last shot of the Civil War could be heard. Enjoy fishing for trophy speckled trout, redfish, and snook in the **Laguna Madre**, or venture not too far into the **Gulf of Mexico** for kingfish, marlin, red snapper, and tuna. Sail the coast and enter the shallow waters of the bay from the **Brazos-Santiago Pass**, just like Jean Lafitte, the pirate who buried plundered treasure troves all along the Texas coast. The location of a horrible massacre, 300 shipwrecked Spaniards were pursued to their deaths by Karankawa Indians across the Brazos-Santiago Pass. This pass opens to **Port Isabel Bay** and **Brazos Harbor**, and has been described as the favorite hangout of "cutthroats, pirates, and smugglers."

> *For more information on Port Isabel, contact:*
> Port Isabel Chamber of Commerce
> Lighthouse Square
> 421 Queen Isabella Blvd., Port Isabel, TX 78578
> 800-527-6102 • 956-943-2262
> www.portisabel.org

Eerie Spirits of Spring

Most Haunted City Along the Texas Gulf Coast

Spring is located 20 miles north of Houston, between I-45 and the Hardy Toll Road. From I-45 north, take Exit 70S to the first traffic light at Spring-Cypress Road and turn east, one mile to Old Town Spring. Traveling north from the toll road, take the FM 1960 exit and stay on the feeder road to Old Town Spring.

The Orcoquisac Indians were the first people to settle this area, north of present-day Houston. Spanish and French explorers followed, and the town of Spring sprung up as a trading post in 1838. In the mid-1800s, German farmers migrating inland from the port of haunted Galveston settled in the Spring area. Folks with surnames such as Fischer, Mueller, Kaiser, and Wunsche bought land for 10 to 25 cents per acre. The German pioneers brought with them their commitment to family, religion, and honest, hard work. They also brought their old-world superstitions regarding ghosts and spirits, continuing to the present day as local myths (and tangible truths!).

In 1873, the Houston and Great Northern Railroad came to the German settlement and the town of Spring blossomed almost overnight. An opera house, hospital, lumber mill, several hotels, and saloons were built close to the railroad tracks to entertain, feed, fete, and house more than 200 railroad men stationed nearby. Spring's population steadily climbed. With the transfer of the railyard to Houston, the onset of Prohibition during the 1920s, and the Great Depression of the 1930s, the bustling little town was reduced to a sleepy country village.

Spring owes her renaissance to a big, juicy hamburger. The Spring Café, operating out of the haunted Wunsche Bros. Building, gained a reputation for "the best food and the slowest service anywhere." The Spring Café attracted other retailers to the area, providing visitors with something to do while they waited for their hot burgers. Restoration began in the late 1970s, creating the continued development and growth of Old Town Spring as a shopping village and recreational area—and a lasting reputation for lodging wandering spooks in many downtown public buildings.

RESTAURANT REVENANTS

Puffabelly's Old Depot Restaurant 😀😀

100 Main St., Spring, TX 77373 • 281-350-3376

Description and History

The building housing Puffabelly's Old Depot Restaurant is a railroad depot built in 1902. Located at the far edge of town near the railroad tracks, it is not the original Spring railroad depot, which burned to the ground in the late 1950s. Puffabelly's building comes from a small town in East Texas called Lovelady. The old depot was bought by Bob and John Sanders in 1985 and moved to Spring as a storage facility and leather goods shop. In 1994, it was restored and converted into Puffabelly's Old Depot Restaurant.

The restaurant's name comes from the toddlers' song, "Down by the Station." The rhyme contains the phrase, "See the little 'puffabellys' all in a row," referring to little black steam engines puffing out white smoke.

Puffabelly's Old Depot Restaurant is known for its great homemade hamburgers, chicken fried steak, and desserts, and offers patrons an atmosphere so comfortable, "you can throw the peanut shells on the floor!" Just be on the lookout for the headless switchman, who might have a tendency to spoil your appetite!

Ghostly Visitations

A headless railroad yard switchman haunts the railroad tracks running alongside this popular restaurant. The dead switchman seems to have relocated to Spring from Lovelady, along with the old railroad depot.

> **Most Haunted Area:**
> *Along the railroad tracks beside the restaurant*

For years, the headless ghost terrorized Lovelady inhabitants by appearing near the terminal, swinging a lantern above his headless body. Legend has it that the switchman was involved in a terrible accident while trying to avert a train disaster. As the hapless man was attempting to flag down an engineer whose train was headed down the wrong track, he tripped and fell underneath the oncoming train. The horrible accident decapitated the worker and his mangled, bloody corpse was taken into the railroad depot by his coworkers.

The spooky sightings were all but forgotten by Lovelady residents after the depot's move, but the supernatural fun was just beginning for Spring's unknowing population. Shortly after the station was reassembled, reports began trickling in to local authorities describing a lone figure stalking the railroad tracks late at night and strange lights flickering near the tracks and inside Puffabelly's restaurant.

One man, Ralph Hutchins, reported to police that as he was returning home late one evening, he noticed eerie lights coming from the area just to the east of Puffabelly's restaurant. At first Hutchins thought the light might be an oncoming train, so he stopped at the crossing, expecting a slow-moving freight to pass. But there was no sound, nor was there a train. At this time, Hutchins said he felt a sudden rush of ice-cold air, even though the incident occurred in the heat of a Texas August evening. Hutchins next saw what he described as "a headless man in overalls" waving a lantern and approaching him. He gunned his engine and sped across the tracks to escape the ghastly apparition.

Local ghost hunting groups have captured several interesting anomalies on film. Smoky clouds, glowing orbs, and tufts of "spiritual residue" have been captured in and around the old depot and can be viewed on the *Old Town Spring Souvenir* website at www.oldtownspringonline.com.

Rose's Patio Café 😊😊

219 Spring Cypress/Main, Spring, TX 77373 • 281-288-0512

Description and History

Visitors to Old Town Spring can't miss Rose's Patio Café. The quaint pink house is located in the center of town on Main. Rose is famous for her home-baked bread, which she bakes fresh daily. Subsequently, the sandwiches served at Rose's Café are delicious. The café also serves fresh soup; garden, chicken, and tuna salads; and cappuccino and cookies. You can dine inside—with Luther —or outside.

The Walking Horse Gallery occupies a room in the café and showcases artist Donny Hickmott's beautiful paintings of Indians and frontiersmen; he is also available for portrait commissions. For more information about the Walking Horse Gallery, call 281-528-9023.

Rose's Patio Café boasts a spirit named "Luther."

Ghostly Visitations

Rose's Patio Café is home to a flying iron and a haunted rocking chair. Both items can be found in the dining room nearest the kitchen. A word of advice—watch out for the flying iron! Actually, the iron has never beaned a diner, but

> **Most Haunted Area:**
> *The dining area next to the kitchen*

the little metal watering can sitting next to it did hit an employee over the head. Rose stores the iron on top of a refrigerator and has found the heavy object sitting in the middle of the dining room several times without explanation.

While waiting for one of Rose's mouth-watering sandwiches, have a seat in Luther's rocking chair. Luther was an old friend of the family who owned this chair and died in it. Rose has stationed the chair against the wall to deter Luther from rocking and frightening restaurant patrons. Interested visitors can take a seat in Luther's chair. Many have reported that when they placed their hands under the arms of the chair, they felt a slight drop in temperature.

Although her husband had witnessed and reported the chair rocking by itself on numerous occasions, Rose was a nonbeliever until she came into the room one day to find

"Luther's" favorite chair.

the empty chair in a deep rock. The chair is not on runners and uses an old spring assembly to rock. Rose found the chair tilted as far back as it would go without tipping over, just as if someone was leaning back in it. Suddenly, the chair pitched forward into its upright position, then was still. I'm sure Luther was simply being a gentleman and standing up as a lady entered the room!

Members of the Lone Star Spirits paranormal investigations team recently visited the haunted café and captured some anomalies with a video camera. During the investigation, researchers secured the building from the outside and left a video camera recording in the front room. The camera was focused on a table with assorted items placed on it. The investigators' video camera captured a piece of paper being flicked off the table, as if someone had just walked by and created a breeze. Even more amazing, the audio recorder on the camera caught the sound of the front door's deadbolt lock actuating—repeatedly locking and unlocking. Rose—who has been locked out of the building several times—claims this deadbolt will lock itself when no one is in the building. An old lock in need of regular greasing, the deadbolt could not accidentally slip into the locked position. In fact, it takes some effort to actuate it.

Other unexplained activity includes the sound of footsteps throughout the old house and the locked front door opening and closing. Donny Hickmott, an artist whose Walking Horse Gallery occupies a room in Rose's Patio Café, often senses a presence in the old house, especially at night. Hickmott often hears approaching footsteps, but has never seen an apparition. Both Rose and Hickmott are in the habit of calling out to one another upon entering the building in the mornings. This routine became necessary the day Rose heard the locked front door open and close three or four times before Hickmott arrived for work.

 ## Wunsche Bros. Café and Saloon 👶👶👶👶
103 Midway, Spring, TX 77373 • 281-350-1902

Description and History

At the far edge of town next to the railroad tracks at Midway and Hardy Road is where you'll find the Wunsche Bros. Café and Saloon, Spring's most famous historical landmark. The first two-story building erected in Spring, the café remains the oldest survivor of the town's rowdy past.

The Wunsche brothers, Dell, Charlie, and Willie, were the grandchildren of immigrant German farmers who settled in Spring in 1846. The brothers acquired the property beside the railroad tracks and began construction of the Wunsche Bros. Hotel and Saloon in 1902.

The saloon was the last to close in Harris County by law of Prohibition. Old timers claim that patrons from Houston to Palestine rallied in the dirt street in front of Wunsche Bros. and drank the bottles dry the night before the authorities arrived to close the establishment.

In 1949, the Spring Café, operating out of the Wunsche Bros. building, gained a reputation for "the best food and the

Come to Wunsche Bros. Café for a possible glimpse of the brother who never left.

slowest service anywhere." Folks from Houston began frequenting the café, forming lines out the door, for a taste of the thick, hand-patted hamburgers served by owner and cook Viola Burke. When Burke passed away in 1976, her daughter, Irma Ansley, followed in her mother's footsteps, running the Spring Café and making the famous burgers for visitors from far and wide. Since 1982, current owners Brenda and Scott Mitchell have continued the traditions of the Wunsche Bros. Café and Saloon by serving the "best hamburgers in Texas."

Along with its famous Best Burger in Texas Wunsche Burger, the café serves a Gotta Have a Shiner Bock With It Char-grilled Chicken Sandwich, Cajun-grilled catfish, and chicken-fried steak. Dessert options include the Wunsche Bros. Famous Chocolate Whiskey Cake, a dark chocolate creation with pecans and a little kick (recommended to boost your nerve for ghost hunting!).

Wunsche Bros. Café and Saloon is open Monday from 11 a.m.-3 p.m.; Tuesday through Thursday from 11 a.m.-10 p.m.; Friday and Saturday from 11 a.m.-11 p.m.; and Sunday from 11 a.m.-8 p.m.

Ghostly Visitations

The owners, current management, and employees all agree that someone is haunting the Wunsche Bros. building. Most think the wandering wraith is

> **Most Haunted Area:**
> *Throughout the restaurant*

Charlie Wunsche. As the story goes, Charlie Wunsche fell in love with a pretty young lady who, unfortunately, didn't return his affections. "Uncle Charlie," as he was known, mourned the loss of his true love and never married. He lived in an upstairs room of the Wunsche Bros. Hotel for the rest of his life and became a permanent fixture at the saloon's bar, downing his treasured bourbons with branch water.

A retired cook once heard a man's mumbling voice emanate from a linen closet. The woman couldn't make out what was being said and didn't stick around long enough to listen any harder. While opening the restaurant in the mornings, employees have found a single candle burning on one of the dining tables. The location of the candle changes every time. Burning candles are carefully extinguished every night before leaving the wooden building unattended and workers cannot explain this recurring phenomenon. Chairs rattle and move around, salt and pepper shakers and packets of sugar are found scattered all over the tables and the floor, and pictures of the Wunsche family members hanging on the walls turn up crooked and rearranged in the night.

One former employee actually saw a ghost early one morning in October 1984. Ilona Langlinais was carrying a pot of freshly brewed coffee down the upstairs hallway when she glanced into a room and saw an elderly man seated at a table, staring out the window. He had white hair down past his collar and was wearing a black suit and tall-crowned, old-fashioned black hat. Ms. Langlinais felt sad watching him and decided to offer him a cup of hot coffee to raise his spirits. As she asked, "Would you like a hot cup of coffee?" a gust of wind hit her and the man sitting in front of her vanished without a trace! Her offer certainly does seem to have "raised his spirits!"

While in Spring conducting research for this book, I was browsing through a beautiful store called Thad's, located next to the haunted Puffabelly's Old Depot Restaurant and within view of the Wunsche Bros. Café. Thad's offers shoppers a wonderful collection of jewelry, garden décor, topiaries, lamps, fountains, and candles.

As I was chatting with Thad about the ghosts of Old Town Spring, he told me of a recent experience he had late one night involving the Wunsche Bros. Café. Thad and a couple of his employees were organizing a new shipment of collectibles, working late at night into the early morning hours. From midnight until 2 a.m., the late-night workers heard the alarm at the Wunsche Bros. Café sound repeatedly. On his way home, Thad drove past the darkened restaurant and was startled to see a white figure glide past the first-floor windows. Taking a closer look into the building, Thad couldn't see anyone inside and decided he would rather be at home in a warm bed than waiting outside a haunted restaurant for a ghost to return!

SPIRITED BUILDINGS AND HOUSES

Shirley's Cat House and Old Town Spring Souvenir Office 😊😊😊

211 Gentry St., Spring, TX 77373 • 281-288-4777 (Shirley's); 281-528-0200 (Newspaper)

Description and History

In 1881, Mary Kelly bought the land that is now Doering Court from Charles Wunsche (original builder and owner of the haunted Wunsche Bros. Café) and later sold it to M.E. Hamilton, who built a large house on the property in 1917. This gray dwelling still stands in Doering Court. In addition to the house, Hamilton built a large barn of hard oak at the rear of the property. The property is located at the back of Doering Court off Gentry/Midway Streets. The newspaper office is located directly behind Shirley's Cat House.

The Doering family—consisting of Henry C. Doering; his wife, Ella Klein; and the couple's four children, Vernon, Henry John, LaVerne, and Marilyn—later bought the large home and barn. Mr. Doering died of pneumonia in 1940 and left his wife to support the family by renting the upstairs of their home to several railroad men and a teacher. Ella lived in the house on Doering Court until her death in 1973.

The playful ghost who inhabits the old Doering barn is thought to be a 12-year-old playmate of Marilyn Doering, known only as "Sarah." Marilyn, Sarah, and several friends

enjoyed playing hide-and-seek in the large Doering barn. During her last fateful game, Sarah fell from the loft of the barn and badly fractured her leg. Complications set in and the girl developed blood poisoning and died within a few short months of her spill. Sarah may have left

A young wraith walks the building housing Shirley's Cat House and the Old Town Spring Souvenir *offices.*

her physical body, but seems caught on the earthly plane within the confines of the old Doering barn. Today, part of the original barn, including its spacious loft, houses Shirley's Cat House and the newspaper offices for the *Old Town Spring Souvenir.*

Along with the mischievous Sarah, Shirley's Cat House harbors a huge selection of noteworthy collectibles and gifts chosen especially for cat aficionados. Shirley's Cat House is open Thursday through Saturday from 10 a.m.-5 p.m. and Sunday from noon-5 p.m. The store is open on all holiday Mondays, with extended hours during Spring's festival events and the Christmas season. For more information on these locations, visit the websites at www.shirleyscathouse.com or www.oldtownspringonline.com for the newspaper office.

Ghostly Visitations

Current tenants Shirley Lawler and Randy Woods and his newspaper staff have witnessed "Sarah's" ongoing antics for some time. Both have heard the sounds of running footsteps and a bouncing ball coming from the

> **Most Haunted Area:**
> *The loft at Shirley's and the newspaper office*

loft above. The loft is carpeted, but the footsteps and bouncing ball sound as though they're taking place on a hard surface. Lawler's cat and Woods' dog both refuse to go upstairs into this area.

The week Lawler moved into the building, a Southwestern Bell technician was on the property for a phone installation when he heard what he thought was a customer in the upstairs loft area. Out of courtesy, he stopped working and told Lawler he would wait until the shopper had vacated the upstairs before finishing his work. Lawler assured him it was "just their ghost" and to go about his business installing the telephone. Not surprisingly, the spooked technician fled and Lawler's phones had to be installed another day!

One recurring anomaly has turned into a bit of a game. Lawler regularly opens the store in the morning to find a small yellow Beanie Baby dog sitting just inside the front door. The display for these toys is at the back of the store and Lawler cannot logically explain the dog's movement during the night. After several nocturnal "trips" across the room, the yellow toy was getting dirty, so Lawler asked Sarah if she would please play with a similar orange dog instead. Sure enough, the next morning, the orange Beanie Baby was waiting inside the threshold to greet Lawler.

Woods was working late one night when the plant on his desk began rocking. He calmly told the invisible Sarah to "Please stop shaking the plant—you're scaring me." The plant stopped rocking and Woods heard a voice calling, "Sarah, Sarah," very faintly, but he could not tell whether the voice was male or female.

Woods said he senses Sarah watching him work late at night. "It's an eerie feeling," he said. "Sometimes I feel a rush of cold air around me for no apparent reason. Sometimes when I open the office in the morning, I know that things on my desk have been rearranged; but I have this sensation that the spirit, or whatever it might be, is friendly and means no harm."

Woods's wife, Linda, claims she walked *through* Sarah one day. Linda was walking up the stairs into the loft when she felt herself pass through an extreme cold spot located at the top of the stairs. Reports of mysterious chilly breezes blowing through the building are common.

Several investigators with Lone Star Spirits Paranormal brought a psychic, Lorraine Ross, to the building that houses the *Spring Souvenir* and Shirley's Cat House for a reading. Ross detected the spirit of a young woman (much older than Sarah is reported to have been) who was murdered on the property. Ross had the impression that the woman had witnessed something she wasn't supposed to see and was subsequently murdered as a result. Are there two spirits roaming the old Doering barn? The romantic in me hopes there is another woman around to look after Sarah during the darkness of night.

The Spring Historical Museum
403 Main St., Spring, TX 77373 • 281-651-0055

Description and History

This old building housed the town's courthouse for many years before becoming the Spring Historical Museum. It is located at the entrance to Old Town Spring.

The Spring Historical Museum is open Thursday through Saturday from 10 a.m.-5 p.m. and Sunday from 1 p.m.-5 p.m. Admission is free and donations are appreciated.

The museum is home to a couple so in love that they continue to dance after their deaths.

Ghostly Visitations

Randy Woods, editor of the *Spring Souvenir* newspaper (housed in a haunted building), told the story of "The Dancing Couple and the Victrola." The story concerns a 1900s Victrola owned by Marie Bailey, who brought it

Most Haunted Area:
The front display room near the Victrola

with her from St. Louis when she moved to Spring to marry her beloved, Albert Paetzold. Although Marie's father had forbidden her to see Albert, love won out; the couple married in Spring and spent a lifetime together until their deaths in the 1970s.

One of the couple's pastimes was listening and dancing to their favorite music playing on the Victrola. They would spend hours in each other's arms gliding around their small farmhouse, lost in the lilting music. After their deaths, the hand-crank machine became the property of the Lemm family and was later sold to the Malcotts, who donated it to the Spring Historical Museum.

Witnesses from the Old Town Spring Historical Society have reported the haunting sounds of music playing on the old Victrola wafting out of the locked, darkened museum after it was closed. On moonlit nights, passersby have seen a young couple dancing inside the Spring Historical Museum. The woman is wearing a white satin and lace wedding dress and the man is in typical formal attire of the early twentieth century. It seems that Marie and Albert just might spend an eternity dancing in each other's arms—just where they belong!

Whitehall Home 👥

303 Spring Cypress/Main, Spring, TX 77373 • 281-350-2859

Description and History

The Mintz family built Whitehall, one of the original homes in Old Town Spring, in 1895. Located in the middle of Old Town Spring on the corner of Spring Cypress/Main and Keith Streets, this beautiful, 25-room Victorian mansion cost a reputed $300 to construct.

Over the years, the grand home served as McGowen's boarding house, giving shelter to local railroad workers, until it was purchased by the Kleins in the 1920s as the family residence. The Klein family owned and operated the town's funeral parlor. When their business on Spring Cypress burned down, the Kleins moved the funeral parlor and embalming area into the downstairs rooms of Whitehall. Later owners converted the house into wartime apartments, a church, and a schoolhouse.

The lovely mansion was almost demolished in the 1960s after a colony of hippies moved into the historical home and turned it into Spring's only commune. These "free spirits" nearly destroyed the house in the process. The Hudson family purchased the property in the 1970s and completed extensive renovations inside and out. Leasing part of the house to area merchants and using the rest of the building for their residence, the Hudsons spent many happy years in the home.

Several years ago, owner Raymond Hudson decided to make the entire home his private residence. He restored the rooms and refurnished them with original Hudson family heirlooms. Today, Mr. Hudson gives tours of his home to interested parties for a modest fee. Call the owner, Raymond Hudson, at 281-350-2859 for information regarding tour times and fees.

Ghostly Visitations

Two lovers haunt the upper rooms of the Whitehall mansion. Known as the "Courting Ghosts of Whitehall," the young couple met their fate in a fatal car crash back in 1933, during the height of the Great Depression. Out on a moonlit joyride, the young man lost control of the car and

> **Most Haunted Areas:**
> *The upstairs rooms including the screened-in porch*

it careened off the bridge crossing Spring Creek, plunged into a ravine, and instantly killed the tragic sweethearts. Locals discovered the dead couple the next morning and the bodies were brought to the Klein funeral parlor, located inside Whitehall, to prepare them for burial.

Since the joint wake and subsequent funerals, several Whitehall residents have reported hearing strange, unexplained noises coming from the upstairs rooms of Whitehall. Other witnesses have reported seeing a cozy pair of apparitions swinging in the large swing on the upstairs screened-in porch.

Over the years, the Whitehall ghosts have been known to enjoy frightening children living in the house. Three boys built a tree house in the large pecan at the back of the property. The boys claimed that their retreat became a house of horrors when the spooky sweethearts shook the tree and made ghostly noises until the boys fled in terror. The remains of this tree house are still visible to passersby.

GHOSTS OF THE GREAT OUTDOORS

Civil War Museum 👥👥

206-6 Noble, Spring, TX 77373 • 281-288-7252

Description and History

Located back of Thyme Square, the Civil War Museum displays an extensive collection of Civil War–era artifacts and is home to the 11th Texas Calvary. The museum sponsors several Civil War reenactments throughout the year.

The Civil War Museum is open Tuesday through Saturday from 10 a.m.-5 p.m., and Sunday from 1 p.m.-5 p.m.

The Civil War Museum is home to dozens of historical artifacts—and some of their original owners!

Ghostly Visitations

Ghostly phenomena are said to occur during the Civil War reenactments. During an investigation conducted by Lone Star Spirits, psychic Lorraine Ross detected the spirit of a disfigured Civil War soldier standing in Thyme Square watching the researchers work. An investigator snapped a photograph of the area of the square pinpointed by Lorraine and captured a glowing orb on film.

> **Most Haunted Area:**
> *Outside the museum in Thyme Square*

SPOOKY SIDELINES

Walking Ghost Tours of Old Town Spring

Stroll through the Texas Gulf Coast's most haunted town and hear the stories behind this 1900s railroad community as narrated by storyteller Boxcar Bill. Tours leave nightly from the *Old Town Spring Souvenir* offices at 6:30 p.m. and last approximately an hour and a half. The cost is $10 per person (no children under 12). For information and reservations, call 281-528-0200.

Less Spooky Things To Do In Spring

In 1980, a handful of merchants set up shop in Spring. Today, the lovely town boasts more than 150 shops, restaurants, and museums. Many of the merchants in the 10-square block area known as Old Town Spring occupy the original homes, bank, and post office of the town. Other century-old buildings were brought to Old Town Spring from surrounding towns for the purpose of housing retail establishments. Local artisans display their crafts alongside specialty shops and two wineries, the **Red River Winery** and the **Wimberly Valley Winery**, both with tasting rooms. Spring loves good food and a good party. Annual festivals draw crowds to Old Town Spring every year. The **Texas Crawfish Festival** occupies two weekends in May and advertises an event where "the crawfish is spicy and the music is hot." Visitors can munch on crawfish, étouffé, gumbo, chicken-on-a-stick, and funnel cakes while listening to swing, rock, and Zydeco music. **Old Town Spring Heritage Days** take place in September and feature more than 300 vintage cars on display. Historic reenactments take place in several areas of town, including the haunted Civil War Museum, where an authentic Civil War encampment is constructed complete with antique cannon, covered wagon, and participants in period dress. Christmas is a favorite time of year in Old Town Spring. The **Home for the Holidays** celebration runs from mid-November through Christmas and features more than 180 decorated shops, thousands of Christmas lights, and seasonal entertainment.

For more information on Spring, contact:
The Old Town Spring Preservation League
123-F Midway, Spring, TX 77373
800-OLD-TOWN • 281-353-9310
www.oldtownspringtx.com

Elusive Boos of the Texas Gulf Coast

The roster of possible paranormal pranksters inhabiting the cities and towns along the Texas Gulf Coast is a long one. Not all the leads I uncovered during my research provided enough information to warrant inclusion in this guide. Some are very promising and deserve further investigation. Try your ghost hunting techniques out by visiting the following locations—and please let me know if you discover a brand new Texas haunt.

Alley Theater, Houston

615 Texas St., Houston, TX 77002 • 713-228-9341

The ghost who inhabits this modern theater in downtown Houston is thought to be longtime managing director Iris Siff. A security guard robbed and strangled her with a telephone cord outside her office on a cold January night in 1982.

Bookstop, Houston

Located on Alabama Street in the old Tower Theater, this spot has experienced unidentified paranormal activity.

Cactus Moon Restaurant, Humble

7 W. Main St., Humble, TX 77338 • 281-446-2202

A very friendly female spirit reportedly sits on the laps on unsuspecting diners.

Craven-Ellis Cemetery, Stafford

Wispy ectoplasm and orbs have been captured on film by Fort Bend County Paranormal researchers.

Hodges Bend Cemetery, Sugar Land

Another Fort Bend County Paranormal find, team members have investigated this haunted cemetery and photographed floating orbs among the tombstones.

KLOL Radio Station, Houston

510 Lovett Blvd., Houston, TX 77006 • 713-390-5565

Reports of phenomena include apparition sightings, jumping telephone handsets, stuffed animals moving of their own accord, anomalous shadows, and elevator malfunctions.

La Carafe, Houston

813 Congress St., Houston, TX 77002 • 713-229-9399

This bar in downtown Houston is home away from grave for a former bartender who has been spotted on the premises on several occasions.

Theater Suburbia, Houston

1410 W. 43rd St., Houston TX 77018 • 713-682-3525

Ghosts, as we all know, have a flair for the dramatic and really do love old theaters. A ghost named Gurden McKay reportedly puts in an appearance here from time to time.

Ghost Clubs of the Texas Gulf Coast

The two active ghost hunting clubs along the Gulf coast both welcome new members with open arms. Whether to inquire about joining these researchers for a local haunting investigation or simply to read ghost stories that promise to set your hair on end, check out the following ghostly websites.

Fort Bend County (FBC) Paranormal

P.O. Box 1462, Sugar Land, TX 77487

Nichole Dobrowolski's group, Fort Bend County Paranormal, is based in Sugar Land and conducts paranormal investigations in the Fort Bend County, Brazoria County, Harris County, and Houston area. The club's website includes some interesting photographs of ghostly mists, orbs, and vortexes captured at various haunted locations in this part of Texas. Nicole encourages paranormal buffs to correspond with FBC Paranormal regarding supernatural encounters and is happy to answer questions about the paranormal. Website: www.angelfire.com/tx2/hauntedsugarland.

Lone Star Spirits Paranormal Investigations

The Lone Star Spirits researchers have conducted several investigations in and around Houston. They've captured some remarkable anomalies on film in several of the haunted buildings located in Spring, the most haunted town along the Texas coast. The group's website is very informative, offering lists of haunted locations, ghostly tales, and a networking area where you can find other ghost hunters in your corner of Texas. The Lone Star Spirits website is definitely one of the more comprehensive of the Texas ghost club sites today. Website: www.lonestarspirits.org; e-mail: webmaster@lonestarspirits.org.

Ghosts of the Central Texas Hill Country

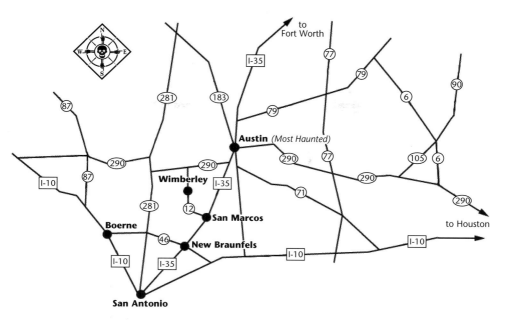

Just as North Texas is known for endless oceans of waving prairie grasses and West Texas is defined by a chalky limestone landscape speckled by cacti, Central Texas boasts the green and fertile Hill Country crisscrossed with rivers, dotted by lakes, and full of true Texas treasures. Austin in particular, the state's capital city and home to the progressive University of Texas, helps give the region an intellectual and political feel uncharacteristic of the rest of the state. As you will see, Austin is also the most spirit-infested city in Central Texas.

Agriculture has been the mainstay of the economy in Austin ever since the resistant Comanche Indian population was packed off to reservations in the 1840s. The small communities set up by German, Polish, Czech, Norwegian, and Swedish immigrants in the Hill Country have maintained the traditions, architecture, and languages of their homelands. These early European settlers brought with them traditional beliefs in the spirit world. Quietly, yet consistently maintained, legends of ghosts roaming the beautiful old towns of Central Texas and the Hill Country are handed down from generation to generation.

Apparitions of Austin
Most Haunted City in Central Texas

Austin is located in southeastern Texas, 60 miles northeast of San Antonio on I-35. Long ago, Tonkawa Indians settled in this beautiful area of Texas where rich, fertile blacklands meet the rolling green hills of the Texas Hill Country. White men called the settlement Waterloo because of the abundance of springs and creeks surrounding the area.

In early 1839, five mounted scouts seeking a new capital city for the Republic of Texas rediscovered Austin and renamed the village after "The Father of Texas," Stephen F. Austin. In September 1839, archives and furniture of the state government were transported from Houston to the fledgling capital by 50 ox-drawn wagons, and Austin was born.

Today, Austin is best known not only as the state capital of Texas but also as the "Live Music Capital of the World." The city's historic streets and buildings are filled with more than simply scheming politicians and talented musicians. Austin is home to many otherworldly inhabitants as well. From the myriad apparitions carrying on in the newly renovated Driskill Hotel on historic Sixth Street to the strange mists and shadows wandering through the trendy downtown bistro and brewery, the Bitter End, these ghosts have one thing in common—they're all happy to spend eternity roaming the Capital City.

HAUNTED HOTELS

Driskill Hotel 👤👤👤👤👤
604 Brazos St., Austin, TX 78701 • 800-252-9367

Description and History

Jesse L. Driskill, a flamboyant character made an honorary colonel by the Confederate army during the Civil War, built the Driskill Hotel. The hotel is on historic Sixth Street in downtown Austin. Driskill built his showpiece for the unheard cost of $400,000; he opened the Driskill Hotel on December 20, 1886, as Austin's premier "frontier queen" hostelry.

The building was said to "loom like a palace over surrounding structures" and was the second tallest building in Austin for many years (the haunted State Capitol Building being the tallest). Designed by the architectural firm Jasper N. Preston and Sons in the popular Richardsonian Romanesque style, the building is massive and romantic at the same time; it has the largest floor-to-floor arched doorways ever built in Texas. Colonel Driskill insisted upon installing busts of himself and his two sons, Tobe and Bud, as well as stylized heads of Texas longhorn steers and leering gargoyles high atop each entrance to greet the endless stream of legislators, lobbyists, rising socialites, and traveling salesmen who passed out of the blistering Texas heat and into the hotel's immense marble lobby.

Folks told Driskill he was foolish to spend so much money on a hotel and he soon proved his detractors correct. Within four months of the hostelry's grand opening, Driskill was bankrupt and lost the hotel in a high-stakes poker game to J.M. "Doc" Day. The Driskill Hotel closed its doors in May 1887. Three years later, Driskill died, flat broke.

Spend the night with the "ghost of a Texas ladies' man" at the haunted Driskill Hotel.

The beautiful hotel reopened under new management and embarked on a long, sometimes rocky career as the reigning queen of Sixth Street. It stood through several range wars, Prohibition, and the Suffrage Movement, events all hotly debated by the numerous politicians frequenting her secret speakeasy, not to mention a succession of owners and years of neglect. The Driskill stands today as a reminder of Austin's rowdy past and promises a future full of nights slumbering amid the memories (and ghosts) of years gone by.

A massive renovation of the hotel in recent years has resulted in heightened ghostly activity and produced a historic building that combines the luxuriousness of the past with the most modern amenities. Rooms and suites contain not only high ceilings, ornate furnishings, and tasteful artwork, but also state-of-the-art features such as large work desks, remote control TVs with cable, and telephones with computer modem capabilities, as a reminder that you need not forego convenience for tradition. Rooms are moderately priced from $100-$130 per night. For more information about the hotel, call 800-252-9367 or 512-474-5911 or visit the website at www.driskillhotel.com.

The hotel staff offers the famous Driskill Walking Tour, where you'll learn more about the fascinating past of this Texas treasure and the era in which it was constructed. One of Austin's finest restaurants, the Driskill Grill, is located inside the hotel and is well known for good conversation and even better food. The lobby piano bar offers live entertainment nightly. So come in, stay a while, and be sure to keep your eyes and ears open for supernatural shenanigans by one of the many ghosts who walk the historic halls of the Driskill Hotel!

Ghostly Visitations

The Driskill Hotel has the distinction of being one of the most haunted hotels in Texas. An ongoing $12 million face-lift to the aging landmark has stirred up the "locals," creating a frenzy of ghostly activity within her century-old walls. Boasting as many as seven named shades and a whole passel of unidentified paranormal pranksters, a night at the Driskill promises travelers a bit more than the usual soft bed and HBO.

> **Most Haunted Areas:**
> *Rooms 26 and 29, the fourth-and fifth-floor hallways on the traditional side of the hotel, the lobby, the elevators, the balcony-level ladies room, the grand staircase...pretty much the whole darn hotel!*

Appropriately enough, Driskill's first ghost is the hotel's builder and namesake, Colonel Driskill. Rumor has it that since he was unable to enjoy his creation in life, he spends time here in death. He makes his presence known by smoking cigars and turning bathroom lights on and off in several guest rooms on the top floors of the hotel.

The daughter of a U.S. Senator haunts the grand staircase leading from the mezzanine down to the lobby. According to hotel lore, the senator was visiting Austin to participate in a political event at the hotel. His unattended four-year-old daughter was playing with a ball near the staircase when she slipped, fell, and died on the marble floor at the bottom of the stairs. Late at night, the front desk staff has heard the child bouncing her ball down the steps as her giggling echoes through the empty lobby.

Mrs. Bridge's shade is another nocturnal visitor to the hotel. The stately woman worked at the hotel for many years during the early 1900s. Although she died elsewhere, Mrs. Bridges often returns to her workplace late at night to fuss over invisible flower arrangements in the lobby. Clothed in a long Victorian dress, she is usually seen walking from the vault into the middle of the lobby, where the old front desk once stood.

Yet another character in the Driskill's paranormal parade is the spirit of Peter J. Lawless. He lived in the hotel from 1886 to 1916. Over the course of the 30 years Lawless lived under her roof, the Driskill was closed to the public many times. Lawless stayed on, often without staff, possessing his own key to the front door of the hotel. He is sometimes spotted on the haunted fifth floor's traditional side by the elevators. When the doors open, Lawless has been seen checking his pocket watch.

Two "suicide brides" linger at the Driskill. During the 1940s, a young woman who planned to marry and spend her honeymoon at the hotel met a tragic end by her own hand. After her fiancé canceled the wedding at the last minute, she hanged herself in her rose-filled room. Known as one of the Driskill's more active apparitions, many employees and guests have witnessed the sad figure of Suicide Bride #1 pacing the hallways of the haunted fourth floor traditional side in her wedding dress. The apparition is often seen by guests who are at the hotel to attend a wedding or bachelorette party.

A few years ago, Suicide Bride #1 was seen in the ladies restroom on the balcony level. A guest visited this bathroom while her husband waited outside. An unknown female leered up at the unprepared woman from under the stall door, causing the poor witness to cry out in surprise. Her worried husband rushed into the tiny restroom, feeling someone (or something) invisible brush past him. When his wife described the intruder to the front desk staff, the employees recognized her as Suicide Bride #1.

More recently, a South-by-Southwest Music Festival attendee reportedly saw Suicide Bride #1 in the same balcony-level ladies room early one evening. The woman ducked into the restroom while her friends waited

"Check out" the ghosts in the lobby of the Driskill Hotel.

Photo courtesy of Mike Wilson

outside. She was shocked to see a woman with dark hair looking up at her from under the stall door. The indignant witness asked the odd woman what she was doing and the encounter ended with the stranger's sudden disappearance. The witness didn't hear the door to the bathroom open or close, but she did smell roses very distinctly.

Upon rejoining her friends waiting outside, the flustered witness described her experience and questioned what they had seen of the mysterious brunette. Her friends assured her that no one had entered or exited the bathroom while they'd been standing outside. This ladies room, obviously a paranormal hot spot, also features the macabre appearance of a severed head! Reportedly, it's the head of a prostitute who was murdered more than 100 years ago. She was chased into the bathroom by an angry "customer" and decapitated with a razor blade. Her head still appears on occasion as a reminder of her grisly death.

Suicide Bride #2 was a Houston socialite engaged to be married in the early 1990s. When her fiancé had second thoughts and called off their wedding, the young woman took a trip to Austin to recuperate from her shock and depression. She booked Room 29 on the haunted traditional side and went on a week-long shopping spree, using her ex-fiancé's credit cards.

The young woman was last seen coming out of the fourth-floor elevator, her arms filled with numerous bags and packages. Her body was discovered three days later when housekeepers became concerned that she hadn't left the room to eat. She was found lying in the bathtub, having shot herself in the stomach through a pillow. This sorrowful specter is seen most often during October wandering the hallways in a modern wedding gown and with a gun in hand.

Suicide Bride #2 appeared late one night to two amateur ghost hunters. Two friends from Dallas had heard the stories surrounding the traditional side's fourth-floor hauntings and decided to spend the night trying to catch a ghost in the act. At the time, the fourth floor was undergoing extensive restoration and no rooms were available for overnight stays. The disappointed ladies were assigned a room on the other side of the hotel.

After a night down on Sixth Street, the women returned to the hotel around 2 a.m. and decided to journey into the darkness of the closed fourth floor to attempt a ghost sighting. After several minutes of walking the plastic-draped hallways, the tired friends gave up and summoned the elevator to take them back to their room.

The elevator doors slid open and a woman, arms laden with packages, stepped out. She walked past the women without looking at them and proceeded down the dark hallway. One of the witnesses claims her first thought was, "Now, where has she been shopping at 3 o'clock in the morning?" Curious, the girls decided to follow the woman and ask her. They called out to the woman who, ignoring them, turned a corner and entered Room 26 without opening the door. Upon seeing this, the startled visitors grew a bit wary of the scene they had just witnessed and decided to call it a night.

While the women were checking out the next morning, the front desk staff assured them that the entire fourth floor was being renovated and that no one (living, at least) had spent the night in Room 26 the night before. The women insisted that the front desk clerk accompany them up to Room 26 for a look. The group found the room draped in plastic, without a bed, but with a bathroom sink sitting in the middle of the floor. The amateur ghost hunters had unwittingly succeeded in catching one of the Driskill's more famous resident ghosts in the act.

Additional apparitions are believed to roam the guest rooms and hallways of the Driskill. Housekeepers report elevator doors opening without buttons being pushed, and finding the button to their intended destination floor already lit. The elevators run consistently without passengers, and several thorough maintenance checks have offered no explanations. Employees hear the sounds associated with a noisy crowd of people, talking and laughing, descending in one of the elevators, only to find an eerie emptiness when the doors open.

Several construction workers tell stories of misplaced tools, disembodied footsteps, and faces appearing in elevator mirrors. One worker quit after seeing two people—who were transparent—walking toward him!

Guests have called the front desk in the middle of the night to say they awoke to the sensation of being pushed out of bed by unseen hands. Other guests claim they find that their bedroom furniture has moved during the night. In several guest rooms on the traditional side, maids have etched crosses in the windows to denote a haunted room.

Two of the more famous witnesses to the paranormal phenomena at the hotel belong to rock groups. The lead singer for the group Concrete Blonde, Johnette Napolitano, stayed at the Driskill in the early 1990s and wrote a song called "Ghost of a Texas Ladies' Man," commemorating the Driskill's ghosts.

Annie Lennox of the Eurythmics stayed at the Driskill while in Austin for a concert. Having trouble deciding what to wear, she laid two dresses on her bed and stepped into the shower. A few minutes later, she found her decision had been made for her—one of the dresses was neatly hanging in the closet. So she wore the dress that remained on the bed that night!

BED & BREAKFASTS WITH A BOO!

The Inn at Pearl Street 👥

809 W. Martin Luther King Blvd., Austin, TX 78701 • 800-494-2203

Description and History

The 1896 Greek Revival home known today as the Inn at Pearl Street sits just five blocks from the University of Texas atop Judge's Hill, an area named for the number of jurists who built homes in this area of Austin. The first official record of the property in the Austin City Directory of 1914 lists it as the residence of prominent Texas Judge Wilcox. He and his wife, Stella Snider, lived in the home for many years, raising 5 children, three of whom lived to adulthood. Two sons both died at the tender of age of two. Coincidentally, both boys died on Easter Sunday, a couple of years apart. The couple's three daughters never married and they lived in the big house throughout their lives.

A stay at the Inn at Pearl Street just may include an apparition sighting.

The second daughter, Darthula (bless her heart), obtained a degree from the University of Texas at Austin and a master's degree in Library Science from Columbia University. She was appointed the first director of the new Austin Public Library in 1933.

Jill Bickford, owner of Austin Executive Lodging, purchased the beautiful home in 1993. She and her parents spent two years restoring the three-story structure before opening it for business. During the extensive renovations to the house, live-in workmen reported strange happenings in the old home.

The Austin Symphony League featured the Inn at Pearl Street as the Designer Showhouse in 1995. Jill has furnished the home with art and collectibles from her world travels.

All guest rooms are moderately priced and feature private baths and balconies, phones with private answering machines, and cable TV. Amenities include a newspaper with breakfast, evening turndown service, cozy bathrobes, and complimentary wine and snacks. A full breakfast is served on weekends, and a champagne brunch on Sunday.

For the romantics, the Gothic Suite features a cathedral bed and a gold-and-marble shower/jacuzzi. In addition, the Inn at Pearl Street's Celebration Package includes a five-course candlelight dinner served in your room.

The innkeeper requires a credit card to make reservations, and accepts personal checks, MasterCard, Visa, Discover, and American Express. For a complete refund, cancellations must be made seven days prior to arrival. For more information, call 800-494-2203 or 512-477-2233 or visit the website at www.innpearl.com.

Ghostly Visitations

Two carpenters who lived upstairs in the building during part of the restoration project sensed a female presence. One of the men saw the silent apparition of a woman carrying a child from the Gothic Room down the hallway into the French Room. He later saw this same spirit sitting in a rocking chair inside the French

> **Most Haunted Areas:**
> *Outside the Gothic and European rooms, and inside the French Room and the Carriage House*

Room, rocking a little one. Bickford's mother, Vicki, believes this woman could be former owner Stella Snider, perhaps comforting one of her terminally ill boys. In addition to the strange sightings, construction workers reported hearing unaccountable noises in the night—noises that could not be attributed to the settling of an old house.

One evening, as Bickford drove up to the house during renovations, she noticed a light burning in the upstairs European Room. Strange indeed, considering that the house had not been wired for electricity! The puzzled owner drove around to the back of the house and went upstairs to have a look. She found the house dark and can't explain the presence of the otherworldly light.

Bickford always loved the energy in this beautiful place, even when it was a dilapidated wreck. She says she never feels alone and is never afraid in the big house. Visiting parapsychologists have confirmed Bickford's suspicions that several spirits are inhabiting the Inn at Pearl Street. One psychic sensed the additional presence of a very tall elderly man in the Carriage House behind the inn.

As a side note, Bickford has been hard at work restoring the house next door, with plans to open it as the Burton House Bed and Breakfast during the summer of 2000. As luck would have it, Bickford says this house seems to have its own "bevy of boos." One painter refused to stay after nightfall because he believed the house to be haunted, complaining of spirits watching him at work. A plumber and his dog both had heard unexplained noises and sensed a presence while the plumber was working at the Burton House. We'll just have to wait and see what happens after renovations are complete. Meanwhile, all the spirits who reside at the Inn at Pearl Street seem very positive about the marvelous changes Bickford and her parents have made to the home and have no plans to leave anytime soon!

RESTAURANT REVENANTS

B Side Bar, Bitter End Bistro and Brewery 😀😀😀😀

311 Colorado, Austin, TX 78701 • 512-478-2337

Description and History

The B Side Bar and the Bitter End Bistro and Brewery are located in the heart of Austin's Warehouse District, downtown at Fourth and Colorado Streets. This part of downtown Austin was known as "Guytown," the largest redlight district in the Southwest at the turn of the nineteenth century. Numerous gambling establishments, opium dens, and brothels operated in this part of town. Legislators and University of Texas students alike frequented this seedier part of Austin during the late 1800s.

Other well-known ghost-infested buildings are within walking distance of the haunted Bitter End Brewery in the area known today as Austin's Warehouse District, which includes the Old Spaghetti Warehouse and Speakeasy's.

The Bitter End Bistro and Brewery serves excellent nouvelle American cuisine and brews several varieties of beer—including a Bat City Lager—all worth sampling. Full bar and patio area outside. For more information, call 512-478-2337 or visit the website at www.sgrg.com/code/bitt.htm.

Enjoy spirits with your spirits at the B Side Bar and Bitter End.

Ghostly Visitations

In 1996, the owners of the Bitter End discovered a basement running beneath their restaurant and a building housing the reportedly haunted Old Spaghetti Warehouse.

> **Most Haunted Area:**
> *The B Side Bar area*

The owners decided to create an atmospheric addition to the restaurant called the B Side Bar, where patrons could sit on comfortable couches amid red velvet-draped walls, sipping martinis in the low light. Because the B Side has only one door leading outside, Austin historian Jeanine Plumer believes this basement was used as a speakeasy featuring bootleg alcohol, prostitutes, and gambling during the 1920s.

Shortly after this new bar opened, the paranormal activity started and hasn't slowed since. Many Bitter End employees refuse to go into the B Side alone, even during the day. After closing late one night, manager Rob Davis witnessed a dark figure moving from the left side of the bar toward the bathroom alcove. Thinking the shadow was a customer who had overstayed his or her welcome, Rob followed the moving shape into this dead-end area. The stray "patron" was nowhere to be found. A storage closet in this area is often discovered in disarray, with supplies from top shelves found knocked to the floor.

In August of 1997, Austin experienced a terrible drought. Without rain for more than two months, temperatures soared into the triple digits almost every day. During this dry period, customers and employees witnessed a strange mist that poured out of a corner of the B Side ceiling for several hours one night. One brave soul scaled the wall to the exit sign to determine the origin of the fog. Expecting to find condensation on the ceiling, the intrepid individual was unable to locate a source for the mist, finding the ceiling and surrounding walls to be as dry as a bone.

More recently, a bartender found a damp stack of magazines in this area. Initially thinking someone had spilled a drink, she was mystified to find that it was "raining" in this dark corner. The unexplained mist that hovered in the air did not originate from the ceiling or walls.

Waiter and musician Ian Kasnoff experienced a frightening presence in the B Side's upstairs area where he takes naps on occasion. Ian's first encounter began as a dream that mirrored reality. He dreamt he was standing in the upstairs area and gradually found himself being drained of energy. The more he struggled to gain his strength, the weaker he became, until he was dragging himself along the floor trying desperately to escape the upstairs room.

He awoke from his nightmare to find that he was completely paralyzed—unable to open his eyes or move his arms and legs. Frightened but determined, he willed himself to roll off the couch and flopped onto the floor, where he regained movement in his limbs. Sensing a heavy presence retreating toward a back corner (leading into the haunted Old Spaghetti Warehouse next door), Ian didn't waste another second getting as far away from the B Side's upstairs room as he could! Ian hasn't given up his favorite place to nap and has sensed the presence of a male spirit in this area of the bar a few times since his first dramatic experience.

Another restaurant manager had a hair-raising experience one night while closing down the Bitter End's main bar. A long, copper-topped bar with 25 barstools runs along one side of the restaurant. To complete his nightly closing duties, the manager pushed each stool under the bar on his way to the kitchen. After checking the kitchen for a few minutes, the employee made his way back out into the restaurant. An unexplainable sight greeted him—every single barstool had been pushed a few feet from the bar. The manager was alone in the restaurant and cannot explain this occurrence.

Clay Pit 👁👁

1601 Guadalupe, Austin, TX 78701 • 512-322-5131

Description and History

Located just a few blocks from downtown, this historic Austin landmark was built by a group of early settlers in 1853 as a trading post—a business where white men (residing in and around the village of Austin) and Indians (camping on the hills where the University of Texas now stands) could carry on their trading. Cowboys and Comanches alike were known to spend many hours loafing in the saloon at the back of the store.

In 1872, O.R. Bertram purchased the building to house his family as well as his dry goods business. Bertram's General Store occupied the premises for the next eight years. The first

Once a dry goods store, this historic building now houses the Clay Pit restaurant—and a ghost or two.

floor continued to be used as a store with the saloon in back. The second floor became the Bertram family residence, with a parlor in front and bedrooms in back.

The building continued to serve as a general store in the 34 years following Bertram's departure. During the 1880s, the State Treasury was stored in the building's wine cellar along with barrels of gunpowder, molasses, wine, and whiskey. The wine cellar itself is famous for its double-arched construction. For years, University of Texas architectural professors have brought their students here to marvel at the design inspired by the medieval castles and monasteries of Europe.

Starting in the 1940s, a series of restaurants occupied the property. The first was the Old Madrid Café, followed by the Old Seville, then Old Toro—all popular hangouts for University of Texas students throughout the 1940s and 1950s.

In 1977, the building opened as the Red Tomato Italian restaurant and remained so for several years. More recently known as Bertram's (so named for the building's most illustrious owner) and currently the Clay Pit, the structure continues to enjoy a reputation for serving delicious food and housing a spirit or two within its stone walls.

The Clay Pit features scrumptious Indian cuisine. Lunch is served daily from 11 a.m.- 2 p.m. Happy hour begins at 4 p.m. and ends at 6 p.m. The kitchen reopens for dinner at 5 p.m. For more information on the restaurant, call 512-322-5131 or visit the website at www.claypit.com.

Ghostly Visitations

The most frequently reported manifestations in this beautiful old restaurant are the sounds of a party going on in one of the upstairs banquet rooms when

Most Haunted Area:
The upstairs dining room

no one is in the restaurant. An employee responsible for opening the restaurant was shocked one morning to hear the sounds of singing, laughing, and clinking glasses coming from upstairs. Miffed that the owner didn't tell her about a morning function they were hosting, she headed up the stairs to see who was working. As soon as she began to ascend the staircase, the party sounds diminished. The closer she got, the less distinct the sounds became. When she opened the door, she was surprised to find chairs on the tables and a decidedly empty room. She ran downstairs and outside, where she called the manager. Needless to say, she waited until her employer arrived before entering the building again that morning.

A few years ago, a visiting psychic felt the presence of a small boy's spirit in an upstairs room. In the late 1800s, Bertram's five-year-old son died from typhoid fever while quarantined in his upstairs bedroom. It is believed that the tiny child remains in his old home, perhaps not understanding that he has passed on.

HighLife Café 👻👻👻👻

407 E. 7th St., Austin, TX 78701 • 512-474-5338

Description and History

The HighLife Café is located just a few blocks from I-35 on 7th Street. According to the Austin City Directory, this old building dates back to at least 1885.

Considered a hip place for an array of reasonably priced wines and a good selection of beer, the HighLife Café also serves delicious food, including something for everyone, from homemade couscous and wonderfully fresh salads to peanut-butter-and-jelly sandwiches on crusty bread. Cozy couches and overstuffed armchairs are scattered invitingly among shelves of old books while soft jazz music pipes through the sound system. Sunday afternoons spent lounging at the HighLife Café are a relaxing experience not to be missed.

Ghostly Visitations

Most witnesses agree that the ghost who haunts the HighLife Café is a woman. Employees closing the restaurant after hours have seen her on numerous occasions. At times, she wears a white period dress and at

Share a bowl of delicious soup with the HighLife Café's "lady in blue."

other times, she's garbed in blue. Late one night, a waitress spotted her sitting just to the left of the front door, watching as she prepared the bar for the next day's business. The waitress looked away for a second and the mysterious woman vanished.

Another late night after closing the bar, the owner was listening to classical music. The same piece of music, called *Oboe Concerto #9,* played again and again, even though the CD player had not been programmed to do this. The befuddled owner turned everything off (including the CD player) and walked next door to get a cup of coffee before heading home. About 30 minutes later, as he passed the darkened café on his way to his car, he heard the sound of classical music playing inside. You guessed it—*Oboe Concerto #9.* The shocked owner kept right on walking!

A journalist held his bachelor party in the basement of the café one night. His buddies had hired a group of exotic dancers for entertainment. During the show, all the men observed colored lights swirling through the air around the dancers. The men were impressed with the light show and complimented the dancers, but the women assured them they hadn't produced it. Instantly, all the lights in the basement went out. The journalist walked upstairs to remedy the problem and, after double-checking, the owner and a bartender told him the light switch was left on at all times because the beer coolers ran off the same breaker. Just as the journalist protested that the lights were definitely off downstairs, the basement lights came back on.

Another night, a group of employees stayed after closing to have a glass of wine and discuss the ghost. They tried summoning the apparition by playing Alfred Hitchcock's theme song on the piano, to no avail. After deciding to go home, the group stood outside the front door while locking up and heard a single, plaintive note played on the piano inside the darkened café. Playing Hitchcock's song had worked after all!

 # Speakeasy's 😊😊😊

412 Congress Ave., Austin, TX 78701 • 512-476-8017

Description and History

Speakeasy's is located downtown in the heart of the Warehouse District in an alley that runs between Congress Avenue and Colorado Street (behind Gilligan's Seafood Restaurant). The building at 412 Congress Avenue dates back to 1889, when owners Mr. and Mrs. William Kreisle operated a wholesale and retail furniture store from this location. The Kreisles sold home furnishings such as carpets and pianos for several years until they sold the building to Southwestern Telephone and Telegraph Company in 1899.

An article in the *Waco Semi-Weekly Tribune* on July 26, 1916, reported a tragic fire in the Southwestern Telephone and Telegraph building in which five Austin firefighters were injured—one critically. James Glass was caught beneath a falling stairway and his spine was crushed. Is this the lonely soul who haunts the popular bar known today as Speakeasy's?

Speakeasy's is a large, upscale bar in Austin's Warehouse District. Speakeasy's features live swing, lounge, and other retro-type bands. The bar has a large upstairs area, a back room with pool tables, and a pleasant rooftop area with a second bar open on weekends.

Ghostly Visitations

This trendy Austin nightspot is popular with both the living and the dead. One report from an employee is indicative of a paranormal scenario that replays from time to time. Setting up the bar one afternoon before

Most Haunted Areas:
The upstairs mezzanine and back pool room

opening, a young bartender was startled by the front doors banging open quite violently and the sounds of heavy footsteps rushing inside and up the staircase. If this wasn't enough, a frantic knocking on the walls upstairs commenced until the frightening event ended with the piercing scream of a woman. The thoroughly terrified witness ran into the freezer and stayed put until the chaos upstairs had ended.

Another strange occurrence happened during a power outage one weeknight when the bar was evacuated and the patrons sent home. Several employees sat around drinking wine and discussing the ghost while waiting for the power to return. Their musings were interrupted by a blood-curdling woman's scream coming from the back poolroom. Thinking someone from the group was playing tricks, they investigated the poolroom, only to find it quite empty and all employees accounted for. Sitting in the dark bar telling ghost stories suddenly lost its appeal and the group decided to call it a night!

The Tavern 🐾🐾🐾
922 W. 12th St., Austin, TX 78703 • 512-474-7496

Description and History

The Tavern is located on the corner of Lamar and 12th Streets. Inspired by the pubs found in England, Niles Graham brought his dreams and plans for The Tavern to Austin at the end of World War I.

When the building was completed in 1921, Prohibition kept Graham from opening the building as a pub. Leased for the next 12 years as a grocery store/meat market known as Enfield Grocery, the building was finally converted into Graham's dream pub when Prohibition was repealed. The Tavern has been a favorite watering hole in Austin ever since.

Many Austinites can be found at The Tavern on Sunday afternoons, drinking cold beer and watching football on the numerous TVs situated about the restaurant. To satisfy hungry appetites, The Tavern features tasty burgers and chicken-fried steak—rumored to be Emily's favorite!

Ghostly "Emily" likes to play pool and change the TV stations at The Tavern.

Ghostly Visitations

Employees have given the specter that inhabits The Tavern the name "Emily." Footsteps are often heard crossing the third-floor offices when no one is up there. Employees closing the bar downstairs have

> **Most Haunted Areas:**
> *The third-floor offices and the second-floor bar*

heard the pool balls break in the upstairs poolroom and have witnessed glasses flying off shelves located behind the downstairs bar. Emily also likes to change the stations on the many televisions throughout the restaurant.

One rainy Saturday morning, an employee working at the convenience store across Lamar Boulevard from The Tavern sat looking out at the gray day and saw more than she bargained for. Across the street in an upstairs window of the restaurant, a woman stood looking out at the rain as well. The store clerk watched the pensive lady for a few minutes until a customer needed assistance. Strangely moved by the woman's sad demeanor, the clerk later inquired at The Tavern, trying to determine the woman's identity, and was told the restaurant was not open for business at that hour. In fact, no employee was in the building that stormy morning. Was this melancholy figure Emily waiting for the sun to shine?

 # SPIRITED BUILDINGS AND HOUSES

Governor's Mansion 😀😀😀

1010 Colorado St., Austin, TX 78701 • 512-463-5518

Description and History

The Texas Legislature authorized $17,000 in 1854 to build the Governor's Mansion, located in the heart of downtown Austin. Of that amount, $14,000 was designated for the home and $2,500 for furnishings. Richard Payne designed the lovely, dignified neoclassic home, which was constructed in 1856 by master builder Abner Hugh Cook. The fourth governor of Texas, Elisha Peace, moved his family into the mansion in 1856.

Actually a museum, the mansion is filled with exquisite treasures (and, some say, spirits) from past administrations. By custom, each departing governor leaves a personal possession behind for posterity. The Governor's Mansion became a Texas Historical Landmark in 1962. The home is also a National Historical Landmark and part of the National Register of Historical Places.

The mansion is the fourth oldest governor's mansion continuously occupied in the United States. Thirty-seven governors and their families have lived in the mansion. For many decades, the home was the center of social activity in Austin, and theatricals, formal receptions, huge parties, and dances filled every room.

The mansion has seen its share of tragedy as well. A governor died in the house, a huge fire almost destroyed the building in the 1870s, and one suicide occurred within its walls. According to numerous reliable accounts, the pitiful spirit of the young man who committed suicide remains tied to the property because of a life cut short over unrequited love.

The public is welcome to view the elegant rooms and furnishings during tours offered Monday through Friday from 10 a.m.-11:40 a.m. For information, group tours, and

Steeped in tradition, the Governor's Mansion also is reportedly filled with an assortment of apparitions.

handicap access, call 512-463-5518 weekdays 9 a.m.-4 p.m., or the 24-hour hotline at 512-463-5516. Groups must have advance reservations. The mansion is closed weekends, some holidays, and at the discretion of the governor. For more information, visit the mansion's website at www.governor.state.tx.us/Mansion

While enjoying your tour and learning more about the history of the great state of Texas, remember to keep your eyes peeled for empty chairs that rock, doors that open and close on their own, and that fleeting shadow that may signal the presence of one of the Mansion's melancholy spirits.

Ghostly Visitations

The most famous ghost in Austin, mostly due to his famous address, is the sorrowful spirit of Governor Pendleton Murrah's 19-year-old nephew. The heart-broken lad committed suicide in the small north

> **Most Haunted Areas:**
> *Small north bedroom and Sam Houston Bedroom*

bedroom of the mansion in 1864 after a flirtatious niece of Mrs. Murrah refused his marriage proposal. Following a shot heard just after midnight, the horrified family found the young man sprawled across his bed, having shot himself in the head.

After the death, servants refused to enter the room, asserting it was haunted by the boy's anguished spirit. No one could sleep in the ice-cold room because of unexplained banging sounds and troubled moans. Soon after the tragedy, Governor Murrah and his family fled the home, fearing repercussions of the end of the Confederacy, leaving the sealed north bedroom without even washing the bloodstains off the walls and ceiling.

In 1870, Governor A.J. Hamilton became the governor of Texas and moved into the mansion. He had his servants clean the gore from the room. The mournful ghost remained, as evidenced by the opened doors, disembodied footsteps, and mysterious cold spot plaguing the mansion's occupants. It is said that the muffled sobbing of the heartbroken boy can still be heard today, especially on quiet Sunday afternoons.

In addition, the Houston Bedroom in the mansion is said to be haunted by none other than Sam Houston, the third governor of Texas. Houston was forced out of office for his refusal to support the Confederacy. The statesman's shadow lurks in the corner of the room. The wife and daughter of Governor Mark White both encountered his restless spirit in the 1980s.

David Grimes Photography Studio 👹👹👹

500 E. 5th St., Austin, TX 78701 • 512-478-0089

Description and History

The David Grimes Photography Studio, listed on the National Register of Historical Sites, is located on the corner of Fifth and Neches Streets in downtown Austin. Grimes uncovered the fascinating history of the building shortly after purchasing the property and beginning renovations.

According to Grimes, in 1870 an Italian man named Michael Paggi came to Austin seeking his fortune. In 1874, after a successful venture in the ice business, Paggi built a blacksmith shop on the spot where David Grimes houses his photography studio today. The various artifacts Grimes found during renovations show that Paggi built and repaired carriages; the artifacts include old blacksmith tools, hammers, twisted pieces of metal, and even the receipt for a carriage repair totaling a whopping $1.50.

In 1911, the building was bought by an African-American man named Rhambo, who converted the property into the only black funeral parlor in Austin. His was a lucrative business and Rhambo became a bit of a celebrity around town, always wearing white suits and traveling through the streets of Austin in a white carriage pulled by a team of white horses. Rhambo was popular and moved easily through the upper-class circles of Austin society.

Tragically, the success and flashy behavior of an African-American man was not to be tolerated in this part of the country at the turn of nineteenth century: Rhambo was lynched in Round Rock. After Rhambo's murder, the building at the corner of Fifth and Neches changed hands numerous times until Grimes's purchase in 1993.

David Grimes Studio is open Monday through Friday from 9 a.m.-5 p.m.

Ghostly Visitations

David Grimes has experienced the unexplainable in his photography studio, from witnessing a remote control car running at high speed with no one (visible) controlling it to seeing an apparition while working late at night. Grimes describes

Most Haunted Area:
Throughout the old building

the vision as the silhouette of an elderly woman who stands in a doorway watching him.

In fact, the sightings became so numerous that Grimes and his wife invited a psychic to tour the building and provide answers as to who might be haunting the old building. Without being told the history of the building, the psychic told the couple, "A black man is laughing here. He's laughing because he never thought he'd be his own client."

In the kitchen of his studio, Grimes keeps a beer glass, cut almost perfectly in half, as a reminder of a personal encounter with the paranormal forces that reside inside his building. "The cutting of this glass is one of the most remarkable things I have ever seen," Grimes says. "I took this out of the cabinet, not the dishwasher, but the cabinet, filled it about halfway with water, and set it on the corner of the counter. Phone rings. I pick it up and am talking to a client, just looking around at nothing in particular, and finally look at the glass. I'm staring at it, and suddenly the thing just splits in half, perfectly, without shattering—just the way it is now. I almost dropped the phone."

The Neill-Cochran House 👁️👁️
2310 San Gabriel, Austin, TX 78705 • 512-478-2335

Description and History

In 1853, Georgia emigrant Washington L. Hill built this beautiful historic home, located at the corner of 23rd and San Gabriel Streets near the University of Texas campus. In 1856, the Texas Asylum for the Blind rented the house, which was later purchased by Governor Fletcher Stockdale.

In the spring of 1865, during the last days of the Civil War, Shoal Creek flooded and Union soldiers camped along its banks were hit by a yellow fever epidemic. The house was confiscated and set up as a hospital. Many troops died in the house during the outbreak and were buried on the grounds. Several years later, Shoal Creek again overflowed her banks and many uniform-clad corpses washed downstream, confirming the haste with which the poor souls had been buried. In late 1865, General George Custer used the house for his staff offices and Governor Hamilton spent his term on the premises while the haunted Governor's Mansion underwent repairs after a fire.

In 1875, Colonel Andrew Neill, a native Scotsman and veteran of San Jacinto and the Confederate army, took up residence in the house. As Neill was a well-respected Austin lawyer, the house became the meeting place of some of the most brilliant and famous men in Texas. Governors Roberts, Ireland, and Lubbock, Judge E.B. Turner, Temple Houston, and Henry McCullough often sat around the library table and discussed affairs of state. Neill lived in the house until his death in 1883. He died at home after an accident had aggravated an old wound. Many believe he never really left his beloved home.

At one point, Judge Thomas Cochran bought the house for his family; they continued to live there until it was sold to the Colonial Dames of America in 1958. The house is now a museum and the state headquarters for the Colonial Dames.

The Neill-Cochran House is open to the public Wednesday through Sunday from 2-5 p.m. A small, cash-only admission fee is charged. For more information, visit the web site at http://austin.citysearch.com/E/V/AUSTX/0003/00/16.

Ghostly Visitations

Colonel Andrew Neill became the property's first identifiable ghostly inhabitant. Neighbors reported seeing Neill riding his white horse around the grounds, rocking on his balcony in the evening twilight, and even sitting on the front porch having tea with none other than General Robert E. Lee.

> **Most Haunted Areas:**
> *The main staircase, balcony, and porch, as well as the surrounding grounds*

But there are other specters associated with the mansion as well. Visitors have reported hearing disembodied footsteps wandering through the house at night, walking up and down the stairs and hallways. The wife of caretaker Rachid Moussid has felt the presence of unseen people on the stairs. Likewise, neighbors claim that on chilly autumn nights the ghostly footfalls of long-dead Union soldiers echo in the deserted streets outside the house.

Paramount Theatre for the Performing Arts 👻👻

713 Congress, Austin, TX 78701 • 512-472-5411

Description and History

Located in the heart of downtown Austin, this landmark was built for $200,000 in 1915 as the Majestic Theater. Its stage hosted the leading vaudeville entertainers of the day. Over the years, Big Bands, magicians such as Harry Houdini, and performers including Cab Calloway and Mae West thrilled audiences with their talent. Housing the largest stage in Texas, the theater's atmosphere of dazzling chandeliers, vaulted ceilings, and rococo decor made patrons feel as if they'd wandered into a Moorish palace. Austinites today flock to the theater, now called the Paramount Theatre, for concerts, classic movie showings, and major movie premieres. Visit the Paramount Theatre website at www.theparamount.org/ or call 512-472-5411 for prices and a calendar of events.

Ghostly Visitations

Many employees and actors have reported seeing strange lights in the projection room and sensing a presence behind them on the stairs. Props are reportedly moved mysteriously during performances.

> **Most Haunted Area:**
> *Main stage area*

One stagehand tried to spend the night on a small couch just off stage left. He was awakened by the sensation of something holding him down even though he was frantically trying to sit up. The incapacity lasted for several seconds until he felt a cold breeze and an electrical charge passing by; at that point, the man sat bolt upright, staring into the darkness of the empty theater.

Catch a performance and a ghost in the act at the Paramount Theatre.

Zachary Scott Theatre ☺
1510 Toomey Rd., Austin, TX 78704 • 512-476-6378

Description and History
The Zachary Scott Theatre is located near Town Lake at the First Street Bridge. The beginnings of the Zachary Scott Theatre go back to 1933, when the company originally was incorporated as the Austin Civic Theatre. The Zachary Scott is the oldest resident theater in Central Texas.

Almost 40 years later, an 8,000-square-foot theater facility with a 200-seat thrust stage was constructed; the name was changed from the Austin Civic Theatre to the Zachary Scott Theatre Center in honor of Zachary Scott. Zachary Scott was an Austin-reared actor who enjoyed a successful Hollywood film career, which included his role as Joan Crawford's love interest in the 1945 Academy Award-winning movie *Mildred Pierce*. In his memory, Mr. Scott's family provided the final funding necessary to build the 200-seat theater.

Visit the Zachary Scott Theatre Center website at www.zachscott.com/, or call the box office at 512-476-0541 for prices and a calendar of events, or call the administrative office at 512-476-0594.

Ghostly Visitations
Unidentified spirits haunt the stage area at this theater. The poltergeists are blamed for moving props, changing lighting, and stealing the actors' personal possessions and then returning them.

> **Most Haunted Area:**
> *The Kleberg Stage*

State Capitol Building ☺☺
112 E. 11th St., Austin, TX 78701 • 512-305-8400

Description and History
The Capitol is located in Midtown Austin at the beginning of Congress Avenue. Respected architect Elijah E. Myers won a nationwide design contest for the Texas State Capitol building in 1881. Myers was initially paid $1,700 for his plan. The original Capitol building, constructed in 1853, burned to the ground in a fire in 1881 while Myers's plans for a redesign were under way.

Construction on the new Texas Capitol began in February 1882. Myers specified limestone or sandstone for the exterior of the building, as the State wanted as much of the material as possible to come from Texas. Myers recommended using "Sunset Red" granite from a quarry in what is now Marble Falls, Texas, due to its strength as a building material, weather resistance, and beautiful pink color.

The Texas Capitol is an impressive building by any measure and for many years was the tallest building to grace the Austin skyline. It took 1,000 men working every day for four years to complete the 360,000-square-foot building in 1888. The Capitol stands over 300 feet tall, and in 1888 covered 2¼ acres; contained reportedly 392 rooms, 18 vaults, 924 windows, 404 doors, 4,000 railroad cars of granite, 11,000 railroad cars of limestone and other materials; and cost $3,744,600 to build.

The State Capitol building is open weekdays from 7 a.m.-10 p.m. and on Saturday and Sunday from 9 a.m.-8 p.m. All facilities and services are accessible to persons with disabilities. Parking, available in the Capitol Visitors Parking Garage located between Trinity and San Jacinto Streets, is free for the first two hours and $.75 for each half-hour thereafter (maximum charge $6). Metered spaces are available throughout the complex. Free guided tours, provided by the Capitol Information and Guide Service, begin every 15 minutes in the South Foyer of the Capitol from 8:30 a.m.-4:15 p.m. weekdays and 9:30 a.m.-4:15 p.m. weekends. Tours take approximately 30 to 45 minutes. To schedule a tour, please call 512-463-0063. Self-guided tour information is available in large print and in English, Spanish, French, and German. For Capitol Guided Tours, call 512-463-0063. For more information about the Capitol, visit the website at www.tspb.state.tx.us/tspb.htm.

Ghostly Visitations

The oldest ghostly event in Austin took place on the grounds surrounding the Texas State Capitol. When the Capitol building was nothing more than a log cabin, a well-respected Texas scout and his forbidden love, an Indian maiden, had their fates sealed in the dead of a long-ago night. The girl's father, an ill-tempered Comanche chief, caught the two young lovers in a secret tryst inside the cabin and murdered the scout in a fit of rage. Grief-stricken, the maiden plunged a knife into her heart and ended her life as well.

> **Most Haunted Area:**
> *The rotunda*

An 1898 article in the *Austin Daily Statesman* reported that several witnesses "still insist that the ghost of the scout and his lover can still be seen near the place of the tragedy and they won't go near (the area) at night." Talk of the wandering wraiths continued into the twentieth century and many still wonder whether or not the couple lingers among the stately oaks and bronze statues of famous Texans lining the Capitol's drive.

Specters and politicians alike walk the halls of the State Capitol.

Another less-known ghostly tale associated with the Capitol building begins with a cigarette fire in then-Lieutenant Governor Bill Hobby's apartment in 1983. Mathew Hansen, a horse trainer for Hobby's daughter, was asleep in one of the rooms that night. Hansen tried to escape the fire by climbing out of a window, but it had been sealed shut and the trainer died from smoke inhalation. The apartment rooms were repaired and restored after the tragic fire, but for years the cleaning staff continued to find fingerprints —with no explanation—on the fated window after cleaning it.

Two suicides have taken place in the Capitol's rotunda over the years. The first occurred in 1937 and the most recent in the mid-1980s, when a lunatic escaped from a nearby asylum and jumped from the dome of the building before shocked onlookers could stop him. Since then, witnesses claim to have seen a mournful, confused specter wandering the rotunda.

SPOOKY SIDELINES

Austin Promenade Tours

5100 Trading Bend, Austin, TX 78735 • 512-498-4686

Austin Promenade Tours offer two paranormal trips to the most haunted buildings and cemeteries in and around Austin. For more information, visit the website at www.promenadetours.com.

The Ghost, Murder, and Mayhem Walking Tour of haunted downtown Austin is offered every Friday and Saturday night beginning at 7 p.m. and lasts two hours. The cost is $10 per person or $8 per person for groups of 15 or more. Daytime and Monday through Thursday night tours are available for groups of 8 or more. Call for reservations and meeting locations.

The Graveyard Chronicles tour van, which takes ghost hunters to four cemeteries in the Austin area, goes out once a month. For history and ghost lovers alike, this tour is chock full of tales of the men and women who settled the state's capital almost 200 years ago. The minimum group size is 6 and the maximum is 10; the cost is $25 per person. Reservations are required. Call for upcoming tour dates.

Less Spooky Things To Do In Austin

History buffs will find plenty to hold their interest in the state's capital. From the **Lyndon B. Johnson Presidential Library and Museum** to the **Texas State Cemetery**, visitors can learn about the unforgettable characters who made the state of Texas great. Art lovers shouldn't miss a visit to the **Austin Museum of Art–Laguna Gloria**, nationally known for its art exhibits and listed in the National Register of Historic Places as the home of Clara Driscoll, savior of the Alamo. **Laguna Gloria** is a 1916 Mediterranean-style villa with 12-acre grounds on the banks of Lake Austin. The **Elisabet Ney Museum** is a stone castle set in a wild garden and filled with the carved statues of its namesake, German sculptress Elisabet Ney. Austin is famous for its lively performing arts scene as well as the number of outdoor activities that celebrate the great weather Austin experiences most of the year. With live music every night of the week, Austin has something for everyone's musical taste—from blues to rock to reggae. Take a stroll along **Sixth Street** to experience the festive atmosphere and spirited nightlife with live music pouring out of the bars and restaurants that line the historic street. Each year on October 31, tens of thousands of revelers flock to Sixth Street for the **nation's biggest Halloween party**. The annual **South by Southwest (SXSW) Music Festival**, held every March, has won international acclaim for merging bands from around the world with music promoters, record label executives, and music lovers who fill local clubs for the four-day festival. The **SXSW Interactive and Film Festivals** are held in Austin during the same week in March. No haunted city would be complete without bats, and Austin has more bats in her belfry than most—a million and a half, to be exact. As the **largest urban bat colony in North America**, the Mexican free-tails provide nightly entertainment from mid-March to late October as they make their dramatic nightly exodus from their roost under the Congress Avenue Bridge. For a few minutes just before dusk, the darkening sky is thick with their sheer numbers and filled with the sounds of their high-pitched cries. **Mt. Bonnell** offers one of the best views in Texas. Climb the 99 steps and savor a beautiful Texas sunset high above **Lake Austin**. **Zilker Park's Barton Springs** have lured locals for at least 15,000 years, when the predecessors of the Tonkawa tribe bathed here. Swimmers share the 68-degree artesian water of this old-fashioned swimmin' hole with schools of catfish and crawdads. The **Lady Bird Johnson Wildflower Research Center** is a native plant botanical garden. The 600-year-old **Treaty Oak**, once called North America's most perfect tree, was poisoned in 1989. Experts were able to save only one massive branch of greenery. The stately tree is the last of the Council Oaks where, according to legend, treaties with Indians were signed.

For more information on Austin, contact:
Austin Convention and Visitors Bureau
201 E. 2nd St., Austin, TX 78701
Phone: 800-926-ACVB
Web: www.austin360.com/acvb/

Boerne's Boos and Ghouls

German immigrants established a small village originally known as Tusculum in 1848. In 1851, the small village changed its name to Boerne after a German political writer. To reach Boerne, take I-10 West 22 miles northwest of San Antonio to Highway 87.

BED & BREAKFASTS WITH A BOO!

Ye Kendall Inn Bed & Breakfast 👀👻

128 W. Blanco, Boerne, TX 78006 • 830-249-2138

Description and History

In 1859, Erastus and Sarah Reed built this lovely Southern Colonial style home, located next to the Dienger Building on Main Square. The couple started the hotel tradition by renting out their spare rooms. Today, the center section of the inn is the original homestead. The building has given shelter to many famous people including Jefferson Davis, Dwight D. Eisenhower, and Robert E. Lee. Over the years, there has been a succession of owners, many of whom built additions while still using the home as an inn. The owners included Edmund King and his wife, Selina, who came to Boerne from England in 1882. King was killed in a hunting accident in back of the hotel on September 26, 1882. In 1982, Ed and Vicki Schleyer purchased the building and began extensive restorations.

Ye Kendall Inn is both a Texas and a national landmark. This inexpensive to moderately priced inn features 12 guest rooms furnished with English and American antiques including four-poster beds, claw-foot tubs, and perhaps a ghost or two.

Ghostly Visitations

Heavy, measured footsteps are heard treading overhead, but no originator can be found. Perhaps they belong to previous owner Edmund King, who was killed here.

> **Most Haunted Area:**
> *The Marcella Booth Room*

One night, Ed Schleyer was working late and heard doors opening and slamming shut. When he checked the doors, he found all entrances locked and secured. So he packed up and vowed never to work late alone in the inn again.

Restaurant employees have reported crystal prisms falling off a chandelier, a rattling doorknob between the restaurant and Victoria's Boutique, and electricity that sometimes won't turn on.

In 1991, a guest strolling the grounds after lunch reported a ghostly encounter with an elderly woman wearing old-fashioned Victorian clothes and her hair in a bun. The apparition introduced herself to the gentleman as "Sarah." Could this have been original owner, Sarah Reed?

The Marcella Booth Room is the most active room. Booth was born at the inn and still lives in Boerne, so who haunts the room today is a mystery. Many employees tell of entering the empty room to find the bed covers disturbed as if someone had been sitting on the bed.

RESTAURANT REVENANTS

Country Spirit Restaurant and Bar ☻☻☻☻
707 S. Main St., Boerne, TX 78006 • 830-249-3607

Description and History

The Country Spirit Restaurant and Bar, one of Boerne's first two-story homes, was built in the early 1870s by French architect Lamott. In 1872, Rudolph Carstanjen bought the home, which was known locally as the "Mansion House." In the early 1900s, the Mansion House became an annex to the Phillip Manor Hotel across the street. Later, Augusta Phillip used the house as a personal residence prior to her marriage to Henry Graham.

In the early 1950s, the Gilman Hall family bought the house and continued to use it as a private residence. In the late 1970s, the home was sold and converted into a restaurant. Finally, Sue Martin remodeled the building with respect for its historic architectural integrity, then opened the Country Spirit in 1984.

The Country Spirit has a wonderful selection of delicacies including chicken-fried steak (a Texas favorite) and a south-of-the-border treat, Acapulco Chicken. The menu also includes burgers, seafood, and salads. The Margarita Pie is made with tequila, lime, Triple Sec, and whipped cream. There is a full bar and

The Country Spirit is inhabited by three ghostly characters.

comprehensive wine list. The restaurant is open Sunday through Thursday from 11 a.m.-9 p.m. and Friday and Saturday from 11 a.m.-10 p.m. It is closed on Tuesdays.

Ghostly Visitations

According to local psychic Gharith Pendragon, three ghosts haunt the Country Spirit. Pendragon has been communicating with these ghosts for a few years now. The oldest ghost—and the ghost who has been in

> **Most Haunted Area:**
> *"David's" bathroom and "Augusta's" couch*

the house the longest, ever since Augusta Phillip's time—is "Fred." Fred, a late middle-aged man, hangs out in the cellar and likes to sit down at tables after people have left, and pretend to eat their food. He lived and died in Boerne in the 1860s, then moved into the Country Spirit because it was the grandest place he knew in life.

Ghost number two is "David." A young boy between the ages of 13 and 16, he was killed on the property in the 1890s. Psychics believe he was kicked in the head by a horse outside a window at the bottom of a staircase leading to the bathrooms. A lot of trauma is felt here. David likes to hang out in the men's room (he even has his own pillow in the

"David's" beloved bathroom.

bathtub and says he likes this room because of the cows on the wallpaper). He also likes to flip potato chips off plates and throw wineglasses off the bar.

Augusta Phillip, a middle-aged woman who used to be the mistress of the house, died in 1949. The last of the three ghosts to haunt the house, "Augusta" likes to hang out on the green couch upstairs near the bathrooms.

With the help of police sketch artist Betty Cooper from San Antonio, Pendragon created portraits of the three haunts. The sketches hang proudly in Martin's office upstairs, Fred complete with his floppy hat and Augusta with surprisingly few wrinkles—an omission Augusta herself insisted on!

Ghostly activity includes candles moving across tables; also, a previous owner was locked in the bathroom. Martin and Gharith believe the ghosts are friendly and actually help them out from time to time. Through the ghosts' communication with Gharith, Martin learned of an electrical problem in the house early in the spring of 1996. Electricians spent a morning alone in the house fixing the problem

"Augusta's" favorite couch.

despite hearing footsteps upstairs and what they described as the sound of someone falling down repeatedly. After going upstairs a couple of times to assure themselves they were alone in the house, they managed to complete a three-hour job in only an hour. Along with Martin, three local high school teachers witnessed the levitation of a wineglass while sitting at the bar one evening. The glass did a somersault in the air before settling back on the bar.

One of the most impressive accounts is from a San Antonio couple who had come to Boerne for a romantic Valentine's Day dinner in 1994. The couple didn't know the restaurant is closed Tuesdays—the day of Valentine's Day that year. As they drove past the restaurant on Main Street, they noticed an older man in a floppy hat gazing out of one of the floor-to-ceiling dining room windows. After parking, they found themselves confronted by a locked door (and growling bellies!). No amount of knocking could bring around the older gentleman they had seen inside the restaurant just moments before. They finally gave up and drove back to San Antonio.

A few weeks later, they tried again and were rewarded with a typically delicious Country Spirits meal. When they mentioned to a waitress their experience with the man wearing the floppy hat, she recognized Fred from their description. Sure enough, when shown his portrait, the couple identified Fred as the man they had seen gazing out onto Main Street on Valentine's Day. Maybe he was wishing for a date.

SPIRITED BUILDINGS AND HOUSES

Dienger Building—Boerne Public Library 👹👹

210 N. Main St., Boerne, TX 78006 • 830-249-3053

Description and History

Joseph Dienger and his wife, Ida, had this limestone building constructed in 1884. It sits on the square in downtown Boerne, next door to Ye Kendall Inn. The structure became the first building in Boerne to combine a business and residence under one roof, with the Diengers living in the upper levels and running the Dienger General Merchandise Store below. The Diengers loved to entertain but were notorious teetotalers, not allowing a drop of liquor on the premises. Mr. Dienger lived a full life and died at age 90 in his upstairs bedroom.

In 1969, Bob Pegram bought the building and, after extensive restoration, opened a restaurant called Antlers. Pegram found dozens of mounted trophy heads and deer antlers in the basement of the building. Apparently, Joseph Dienger had been quite an outdoorsman. Pegram turned Dienger's upstairs bedroom into a club with a bar called the Trophy Room and displayed many of the mounted heads and antlers. This is when all the trouble began. Dienger, who strongly disapproved of drinking in life, was not going to sit still while his bedroom was turned into a bar.

Today, the building houses the Boerne Public Library, which opens at 9 a.m. Monday through Saturday and closes at 6 p.m. Monday and Thursday; 8 p.m. Tuesday and Wednesday; 4 p.m. Friday; and 1 p.m. Saturday.

The Boerne Public Library is home to a spook who prefers books to booze.

Ghostly Visitations

Joseph Dienger's ghost began showing disapproval by slamming doors, rattling windows, and turning lights on and off. Apparently, he enlisted Ida Dienger for some of the demonstrations—once a woman's silhouette was seen crossing the Trophy Room and disappearing into the wall.

To appease the angry former proprietors, Pegram started a custom that other owners have followed over the years. He set a table at the entrance to the bedroom, displaying the finest china and linens along with the Diengers' favorite drink—water. Employees who left things on the table would later find them on the floor, and often the water glasses were half-empty.

Over the years, owners have reported many strange manifestations. During a party, Dienger appeared to a local salesman in the men's bathroom; he tapped the salesman on the shoulder, perhaps displeased with the freely flowing liquor that night. Dienger has also been observed walking up the stairs wearing an old-fashioned suit and carrying a briefcase. In 1979, Dienger was photographed at an office party, appearing in a shot with four people.

A staff member once witnessed the appearance of a young woman with long, flowing hair wearing an old-fashioned petticoat. The wraith stood where a window had once overlooked the park below. After a few minutes, she turned, walked toward the ladies' room, and disappeared. The identity of this ghost is unknown.

Sounds of laughing and talking often drift down from the upper rooms without an apparent source. A telephone is heard ringing where there is no phone, and a voice saying, "kitchen...kitchen" is heard over the intercom.

Now that the building houses the public library, the activity has calmed down a bit. No doubt Mr. Dienger prefers books to booze!

Less Spooky Things To Do In Boerne

The Texas Hill County surrounding Boerne is as pretty underground as it is above ground. The beautiful **Cascade Caverns** and the **Cave Without a Name** are two popular tourist attractions that have been open since the 1930s. Skilled guides provide interpretive tours of the **Cascade Caverns**. Highlights include huge rooms, crystal pools, and a 90-foot waterfall. The caverns are on Cascade Caverns Road, 3 miles southeast off I-10. In 1939, the **Cave Without a Name** was named in a contest in which a little boy said, "This cave is too pretty to name." It is located northeast of Boerne 6 miles on FM 474 and right on Kreutzberg Road 4.6 miles. The lakes, streams, and hills surrounding Boerne are full of fish and native game. Birdwatching is also popular. The 19,000-acre **Guadalupe River State Park** is a great place to fish, canoe, hike, and swim. The park's access is on Texas 46, 13 miles east of Boerne. Visitors will find several antique and specialty shops lining Main Street in Boerne.

Invisible Inhabitants of New Braunfels

Prince Carl Solms Braunfels of Germany founded the town of New Braunfels on March 21, 1845. New Braunfels is located 35 miles to the north of San Antonio on I-35. The first wagons of immigrants crossed the Guadalupe River and built an encampment on a bluff overlooking the Comal River.

In this part of Texas, cannibalism thrived in the 1840s and shortly after the colonists' arrival, Tonkawa Indians consumed the cooked flesh of a Waco Indian nearby. As the Tonkawa women returned from the feast the following morning, they met a number of the New Braunfels settlers. The women pounded their stomachs and happily proclaimed their hope that, by eating the Waco warrior's flesh, their unborn children would be as brave as the Waco warrior had been. One wonders how the German pioneers reacted to this bit of news coming from their new neighbors!

The founding of New Braunfels, often referred to as the "City of a Prince," had a major impact on the Texas Hill Country. The many artisans and craftsmen among the 6,000 original settlers generated industry and commerce for the entire Central Texas area. In addition to economic growth, this early colony brought religion, organized public education, and other socioeconomic benefits to the area.

For a small town, New Braunfels definitely has its fair share of haunted inns and bed-and-breakfasts, all extremely reasonably priced and perfect for an evening's stay or a wonderful weekend of ghost hunting in the Texas Hill Country.

HAUNTED HOTELS

The Faust Hotel 👹👹👹👹👹

240 S. Seguin St., New Braunfels, TX 78130 • 830-625-7791

Description and History

In the 1920s, the citizens of New Braunfels realized that a modern hotel was needed to attract tourists and traveling salesmen to the area. Walter Faust Jr., vice president of the local chamber of commerce and president of the First National Bank, raised funds for the construction of the Travelers Hotel.

Construction began on the original site of the Faust home-stead, which was moved across the street. The grand hostelry opened

"Walter" is up to his tricks at the Faust Hotel.

Witnesses have seen original hotel owner Walter Faust walking the hallways.

on October 12, 1929, to the cheers of 2,000 townspeople who turned out for the event. Designed in art-nouveau Spanish Renaissance style, the hotel was considered one of the finest small hotels of its kind in the southern United States. Faust and his wife became the first owners of the establishment and lived in a suite on the premises until his death in 1933. The hotel was renamed The Faust in his honor.

Bob and Judy Abbey purchased The Faust Hotel, located in downtown New Braunfels, in 1990 and added a microbrewery and a gourmet dining room. The Faust Hotel is listed on the National Registry of Historic Places. Evidently, Walter Faust is pleased with the changes, as it seems he never really left his grand old hotel.

Enjoy great service, beautiful rooms, and affordable rates at The Faust Hotel. The 70-year-old, four-story facility features 62 rooms (all with private bathrooms), a brewpub, and a gourmet restaurant. The Faust is only minutes away from such local attractions as Schlitterbahn and other types of water recreation, antique and outlet shopping, and the historic village of Gruene.

The guest rooms contain touches from the 1920s such as ornate tile, wrought-iron ceiling fans, and candlesticks, along with every modern convenience. And they may include a visit from Walter! The rate for single occupancy is $59-$69 per night and double occupancy is $79-$145 per night. The Faust Brewing Company offers guests a chance to enjoy a gourmet dinner and sample handcrafted ales while watching the brewmasters ply their trade behind the polished granite bar.

Smoking is allowed in limited areas. Children are welcome, but pets are not permitted. The Faust Hotel accepts all major credit cards. Reservations are advised; call 830-625-7791 from 7 a.m.-11 p.m., seven days a week. For more information, visit the website at www.fausthotel.com.

Ghostly Visitations

Several occupants of the suite Walter Faust once occupied have seen him standing at the foot of the bed. "Walter" also turns ceiling fans on and locks guests out of their rooms.

> **Most Haunted Areas:**
> *The second and third floor hallways*

One day, a visiting couple commented on the "quaint and old-fashioned" bellman they saw running the elevator. They described the bellman as an older man wearing a plaid jacket. The desk clerk assured them that the hotel did not employ an elevator operator or bellman, but that they had, in fact, seen the resident ghost, Walter.

One of the strangest sightings involved a painting contractor, Mr. Abram, who was working at the hotel. While working on the fourth floor, Abram saw a man in his early 70s—well-groomed, wearing metal-rimmed glasses and a well-tailored suit—going in and out of all the rooms without using a key. Abram knew all the doors were locked and couldn't imagine how this was possible. Yet the old gentleman would first look down the hallway at Abram, run into a room, stay a couple minutes, then dart back out into the hallway. When he questioned employees downstairs, they showed him a portrait of Walter Faust that was hanging in the dining room. Abram said "without a doubt" the strange man he saw that day was Faust, the former owner of the hotel.

While painting the doorframe to room 326, Abram also witnessed the apparition of a woman holding a baby. She and her child were surrounded by a faint blue glow. As he called to a woman working down the hall, the lovely lady and her baby disappeared.

A housekeeper was cleaning a third-floor bathroom when she felt a tap on her shoulder. She spun around and saw a four- or five-year-old girl standing behind her. The child ran into the hallway and straight through a wall. She is believed to be Christine, an ancestor of Walter Faust, who lived on

"Christine" and her cat roam the Faust Hotel.

the homestead where the hotel now stands. Christine's portrait (above) hangs on the third-floor hallway next to Room 306. Others have heard and seen a child playing hopscotch in the hallways and a white cat running down the corridors.

There are apparently no malevolent or negative phantoms staying at the Faust, but don't be surprised if you see Walter, Christine, or one of the other friendly spirits hovering around during your stay at the lovely old Faust Hotel.

The Prince Solms Inn 😊😊😊

295 E. San Antonio St., New Braunfels, TX 78130 • 800-625-9169

Description and History

Constructed by German craftsmen in 1898, The Prince Solms Inn has always been a hotel. It is located just down from the town's main square. The hotel's plain Texan exterior belies an exquisite interior filled with antique furnishings, 14-foot ceilings, and a garden and patio flagged with huge stones from a nineteenth-century prison.

The hotel's eight rooms with baths and two suites are decorated with Victorian furnishings and antiques. A continental breakfast is included. The inn's restaurant, Wolfgang's Keller, offers continental cuisine in a quiet, relaxed atmosphere. Murder mystery weekend packages are also available. For information, call 830-625-9169 or visit the website at www.princesolmsinn.com.

A jilted bride and Union soldier haunt The Prince Solms Inn.

Ghostly Visitations

People have seen and felt the spirit of a young woman in the bar area of the inn's restaurant, Wolfgang's Keller, which is located in the basement. She is believed to be a waitress or bartender who once worked there.

> **Most Haunted Areas:**
> *The inn's restaurant, staircase, and Huntsman's Room*

Tales of a sad wraith said to haunt the stairs waiting for her lover to return are legendary. She and her family stayed at The Prince Solms before her wedding, but as the wedding party waited, the groom never showed up. The jilted bride is still present in the inn, seen waiting at the top of the stairs.

The Huntsman Room is said to be haunted by a Union soldier who lived at the inn when it was used as a boarding house. He came to New Braunfels to live after the Civil War because the German community was more sympathetic to the Union. This man supposedly passed away in this room. He's back...

BED & BREAKFASTS WITH A BOO!

Karbach Haus Bed and Breakfast Home 👶👶👶

487 W. San Antonio St., New Braunfels, TX 78130 • 800-972-5941

Description and History

In 1906, George and Hulda Eiband built this beautiful home, considered one of the finest homes in New Braunfels. George Eiband died in 1935 and the house passed to his

three nephews, who all declined to live there. In 1938, Dr. Hylmar Emil Karbach Sr. purchased the property. He, his wife, Katherine, and their four children moved into the house, where the couple spent many happy years raising the big family and entertaining New Braunfels's society. Dr. Karbach died in

The haunting of the Karbach Haus is a family affair.

1959, and his wife died in 1985. Karbach's oldest daughter, Kathy, and her husband, Ben, restored the house and converted it into a wonderful bed-and-breakfast inn.

The Karbach Haus Bed and Breakfast Inn, with its four guest rooms and a carriage house, features a huge backyard, complete with a large swimming pool and spa surrounded by ancient pecans, cypress, and magnolia trees.

Each guest room has its own private tile bath and a comfortable sitting area. Equipped with cable TV, VCR, bathrobes, down comforters, designer linens, queen- or king-size beds, ceiling fans, and many antiques and family heirlooms, rooms at the Karbach Haus are a perfect blend of historic ambience and modern convenience. Room rates range from $105-$160, including breakfast.

Start your morning with a full German-style, multi-course breakfast. Later, spend the evening on the wraparound porch watching the sunset and waiting for the warm and friendly ghosts of the Karbach Haus to make an appearance.

To reach the house from the Main Plaza traffic circle, drive west on San Antonio Street past the second traffic light at Academy Avenue. For more information, call 800-972-5941 or 830-625-2131, or visit the website at www.texasbedandbreakfast.com/karbach.htm.

Ghostly Visitations

Kathy is convinced their home is occupied by several happy spirits. Many guests have commented on the "children" and the sound of laughing in the night. The Karbachs lost

> **Most Haunted Area:**
> *Throughout the home*

their youngest child, Roy, in a tragic playground accident several years ago. Kathy believes Roy has returned to his grandmother's home, where he spent so many happy summers and where his parents now live.

Kathy's mother, Katherine, also visits—turning out lights left on in unoccupied rooms and making sure everything is kept tidy. Katherine also rocks in her favorite chair on the wide, cool porch. The loving presence of Kathy's younger sister, Martha Jo, is also felt in the house. Finally, Hulda Eiband comes around from time to time to check on her house as well.

Less Spooky Things To Do In New Braunfels

While visiting the quaint German town of New Braunfels, water lovers can enjoy a day of "tubing" down the **Guadalupe River**. Or spend a day at **Schlitterbahn** ("slippery road" in German), one of the world's largest and most popular water parks, filled with one-of-a-kind rides. The historic community of **Gruene** nearby has monthly **Old Gruene Market Days** that attract art lovers from all over Texas. November brings the annual **New Braunfels Wurstfest** —a world-renowned festival of German heritage, beer, and sausage-making—on the banks of the **Comal River**.

For more information on New Braunfels, contact:
Greater New Braunfels
Chamber of Commerce, Inc.
390 S. Seguin, New Braunfels, TX 78131
800-572-2626 • 830-625-2385
www.nbcham.org/

San Marcos Spirits

San Marcos is 35 miles southwest of Austin on I-35. Archeologists say that the land San Marcos occupies is one of the oldest continuously inhabited sites in North America. Evidence of Indians living along the San Marcos River dates back 12,000 years. Spanish explorers discovered the springs that form the river on Saint Mark's Day, and named the river for the saint. Nearly 120 years later, the Spanish established a settlement, *Villa San Marcos de Neve,* near present-day San Marcos. In 1844, the vice president of the Republic of Texas chose San Marcos for a settlement. By 1851, the town was the County Seat.

GHOSTS OF THE GREAT OUTDOORS

San Marcos Bridge

Ghostly Visitations

The bridge runs across the San Marcos River on the road between San Marcos and Nixon. Legend says the ghost of the San Marcos Bridge is a young man who lived in the 1800s. Leaving to fight for the South in the War Between the States, he promised to return home. He seems to have kept that long-ago promise.

Since the 1920s, motorists have reported a transparent apparition of a Confederate soldier carrying a muzzle-loading rifle who walks the area on dark nights. In 1939, two businessmen fixing a flat tire were surprised by a tall, shirtless figure wearing a rebel cap, who approached them silently. Fearful because of the rifle the odd man was carrying, one of the men went for his own gun hidden in the car. The rebel ghost disappeared before them.

Less Spooky Things To Do In San Marcos

Take the **Living History Trolley Tour** or the **Heritage Tours of Old San Marcos**. Stroll along the tree-lined streets to view the historic mansions of San Marcos or watch the scenery from an old trolley car. Visitors to **Aquarena Center** can ride a glass-bottom boat for a look at the unique plant and animal species that live in the clear San Marcos River. Aquarena Center also has a historic gristmill, ruins of a Spanish mission, and many bird-watching trails. At **Wonder World**, you can explore an earthquake-formed cavern and ride to the top of the 110-foot **Tejas Observation Tower**. You can also take a unique train ride through **Mystery Mountain** into the largest wildlife-petting park in Texas.

> *For more information on San Marcos, contact:*
> San Marcos Chamber of Commerce
> 202 NCM Allen Pkwy., San Marcos, TX 78666
> 512-393-5900
> www.sanmarcostexas.com/chamber

Wimberley's Haunted Well

Established in 1848, Wimberley is a resort, retirement community, and artists' colony all rolled into one picturesque village located on the banks of the Blanco River and Cypress Creek. Wimberley is located in the beautiful Texas Hill Country on Ranch Road 12 just 45 miles southwest of Austin and 60 miles northeast of San Antonio.

 ## GHOSTS OF THE GREAT OUTDOORS

Jacob's Well 👳👳

Description and History

The source of water for Cypress Creek, Jacob's Well is a huge rock hole at least 240 feet deep. Mammoth rocks frame a spring of clear blue water that comes from deep within the earth, creating a natural amphitheater around the pool. It's a beautiful and dangerous place.

Ghostly Visitations

Several witnesses have reported seeing the "Ghost Lights of Jacob's Well" over the years. A campground bordered by a 100-year-old rock wall and cemetery and the natural pool that is Jacob's Well is a treasured spot for locals and visitors alike.

Recently, three families from Wimberley were sitting around the campfire after a summer day spent swimming in the pool. Three women—two sisters and a sister-in-law—put their children and husbands to bed and decided to take a midnight swim before retiring for the night. They had the pool to themselves and the night was very dark, with a new moon.

The women were talking and giggling softly, deciding to go skinny dipping, when they noticed that the air became very still—almost thicker—and the night sounds of the woods died away. One sister reported feeling as though she had been put on "alert." Suddenly, three identical golden glowing spheres appeared on the winding path running alongside the pool. They moved quickly and succinctly, perfectly spaced apart and following each other with great precision. The frightened women scrambled up the banks of the pool and back to their welcoming campfire for the night.

Long a favorite of divers and spelunkers, Jacob's Well has three chambers connected by tunnels running between them that pose challenging exploration possibilities for many adventurous folks. Of the three chambers, the third is the most dangerous. The opening to this cave is so small that divers have to remove their scuba tanks and push them through ahead of themselves to enter. The interior of this cavern is very unstable and cave-ins are frequent occurrences. Of the nine people who have gone into this third cavern, only one has returned alive. The bodies of most of the unlucky ones have never been recovered from the deep, dark hole. Are the "Ghost Lights of Jacob's Well" the wandering souls of the lost divers? Spend an evening in the dark waters of Jacob's Well and draw your own conclusions!

Less Spooky Things To Do In Wimberley

Step into **Billie Bob's Knob** (12 miles north of Wimberley on Ranch Road 12), an eclectic shop filled with arts and crafts and out-of-the-ordinary treasures. **Artists' galleries and studios** are clustered around Wimberley's town square. From watercolors of the surrounding green hills of the Texas Hill Country to glass creations and ceramics, there is something for every art lover. Natural beauty abounds along **Devil's Backbone**, one of the most scenic drives in Texas. Officially known as FM 32, it goes from FM 12 south of Wimberley and west 24 miles to Blanco.

> *For more information on Wimberley, contact:*
> Wimberley Chamber of Commerce
> and Visitor Center
> P.O. Box 12, Wimberley, TX 78676
> 512-847-2201
> http://wimberley.org/

Elusive Boos of Central Texas

Many of the "haunts" listed below are literally in my own backyard. My ghost club, the Capital City Ghost Research Society, continues to investigate the ghostly goings on and research the historical backgrounds of these locations in the future. We'd be delighted to have you join us!

Bellevue Place "Old North Castle," Austin

Since 1929, the Austin Women's Club has owned this beautiful historic structure near downtown Austin. For years, rumors of haunting activity in the old home have circulated around Austin.

Carrington's Bluff Bed & Breakfast, Austin

1900 David St., Austin, TX 78705 • 512-479-0638
This historic bed-and-breakfast inn is home to at least one ghost. Stay tuned for ghostly developments on this one!

Cleo's Hair Salon, Austin

503 Neches St., Austin, TX 78701 • 512-478-9323
Next door to the haunted David Grimes Photography Studio, stylists at this hair salon have also experienced paranormal activity.

Fado Irish Pub, Austin

214 W. 4th St., Austin, TX 78701 • 512-457-0172
Reports of a furniture-moving ghost were plentiful when the Capitol City Playhouse was located in this building. Now that the property has become a rowdy Irish pub, the activity seems to have ceased.

Jessen Auditorium, University of Texas, Austin

2613 Wichita St., Austin, TX 78705 • 512-471-3434

The auditorium is haunted by the ghost of Dallis Franz, a famous pianist and professor at the university.

Littlefield Home, University of Texas, Austin

2613 Wichita St., Austin, TX 78705 • 512-471-3434

The ghost of Mrs. George Washington Littlefield walks the halls of this beautiful Victorian on campus. The Littlefield dormitory nearby also experiences strange goings on.

Logan's, Austin

200 E. 6th St. #A, Austin, TX 78701 • 512-236-0300

This bar is located on the state's rowdiest party street, Sixth Street. Logan's is located in a turn-of-the century building that used to serve as a coffee refinery. Swinging glasses and doors, as well as a loud cackling emanating from the second floor, are attributed to a man who died in the building.

Old Spaghetti Warehouse, Austin

117 W. 4th St., Austin, TX 78701 • 512-476-4059

Employees have seen an entire ghostly family, dressed in old-fashioned clothing, sitting in one of the trolley cars inside after closing. This restaurant is next door to the haunted Bitter End, and many believe the buildings share the same ghosts.

Ghost Clubs of Central Texas

 Historically, researchers devoted to investigating the ghosts of Central Texas were few and far between. Today, a handful of groups are active in this area of the state.

Capital City Ghost Research Society

The mission of the Capital City Ghost Research Society (CCGRS) is to provide a forum for people interested in ghosts, supernatural activity, and hauntings to meet and discuss Austin hauntings, plan and participate in investigations, and provide information to the public about these haunted places. The CCGRS meets once every month at a haunted Austin locale to discuss upcoming activities and share a spirit or two! Website: www.ghostlyguide.com, e-mail: ghostlyguide@austinrr.com.

Ghost Hunters Inc.

420 Quail Valley Dr., Marble Falls, TX 78654

This Central Texas-based group is dedicated to the discovery of scientific proof that ghosts exist. The members of Ghost Hunters Inc. strive for proof and accuracy while at the same time enjoying the hunt! Website: www.angelfire.com/tx3/ghost.html e-mail: medinaghosts@hotmail.com.

Region 6

Ghosts of the Lonely South Texas Plains

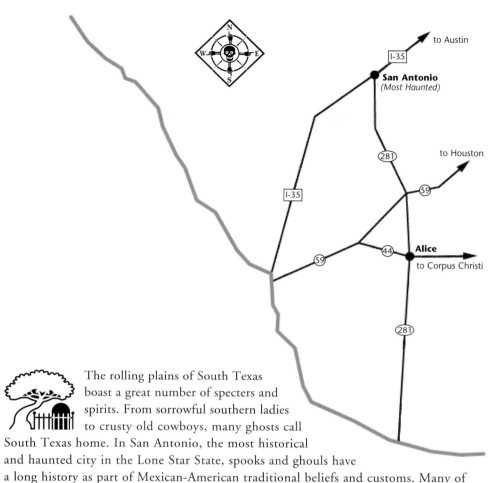

The rolling plains of South Texas boast a great number of specters and spirits. From sorrowful southern ladies to crusty old cowboys, many ghosts call South Texas home. In San Antonio, the most historical and haunted city in the Lone Star State, spooks and ghouls have a long history as part of Mexican-American traditional beliefs and customs. Many of the hair-raising tales from this region have been told and retold across generations and borders—a true oral narrative passed along from grandparents to grandchildren.

Whether you're entering the dark, cool sanctuary of an ancient mission or a grand suite in the state's oldest (and most haunted) hotel, known for almost 150 years as the Menger, remember that ghosts love the dim corners—those shadowed spaces where our eyes need time to adjust from the bright Texas sunshine outside. Don't be surprised to find you're not alone in an empty room here!

HAUNTED LOCATIONS

Alice's Lonely Shade

Alice was first established as a town in 1888, 31 miles west of Corpus Christi on Highway 44. Called Bandana, then Kleberg, the town was finally named Alice after the daughter of Captain Richard King (who haunts the Menger Hotel in San Antonio), the legendary rancher who established the famous King Ranch in South Texas.

As a result of the Texas-Mexican Railroad and the San Antonio-Aransas Pass Railroad intersecting at Alice, the community was the largest cattle-shipping point in the world from 1888 to 1893. Today, Alice is the county seat of Jim Wells County and serves as a hub for the petroleum industry.

GHOSTS OF THE GREAT OUTDOORS

Ghost of Leonora Rodriquez

Ghostly Visitations

A distraught woman in black stalks the section of Highway 281 at the Farm Road 141 underpass just south of Alice. She is believed to be Leonora Rodriquez, the wife of Don Raul Ramos, who lived in a hacienda in nearby Falfurrias in the 1700s.

An enraged Don Raul Ramos accused his wife of becoming pregnant by another man. He ordered his *vaqueros* to take his wife north along a dirt road leading away from their property and hang her. Dressed all in black, the sobbing, pregnant woman was hanged from a large oak tree along the road. "Leonora" haunts the site of her untimely death to this day. Numerous motorists have pulled off the highway to offer a ride to the forlorn woman in black, only to see her disappear before their very eyes.

Less Spooky Things To Do In Alice

The **South Texas Museum** was inspired by the architecture of the Alamo in San Antonio. The museum's exhibits focus on the history and traditions of South Texas and trace habitation from the Indians to twentieth-century agriculture, ranching, railroad, and oil industries. In 1994, the museum was designated as a Registered Texas Historical Site. Annual events in Alice include the **Fiesta Bandana** to celebrate *Cinco de Mayo* in May, the **Jim Wells County Fair** in October, and the **Alice in "Wonderland of Lights,"** which begins December 3 with a Christmas parade and lighting ceremony and runs through the holidays.

For more information on Alice, contact:
Alice Chamber of Commerce
612 E. Main St., Alice, TX 78332
361-664-3454

Specters of San Antonio

Most Haunted City in South Texas (and all of Texas)

San Antonio possesses a rich Mexican-American culture and a 300-year history that dates to before Texas gained its independence from Mexico. The city is located at the junction of Highways I-10 and I-35. Now the eighth largest city in the United States, San Antonio has retained its sense of history and tradition while carefully blending cosmopolitan progress. The city has always been a crossroads and a meeting place. Sounds and flavors of Indians, African-Americans, Germans, the Wild West, Old Mexico, and the Deep South mingle and merge. For history buffs, San Antonio is rich with historically significant buildings and museum exhibits. Close to seven million visitors a year delight in the discovery of San Antonio's charms.

Indians first lived along the San Antonio River and called the area *Yanaguana*, which means "refreshing waters." A band of Spanish explorers and missionaries came upon the river in 1691, and because it was the feast day of St. Anthony, they named the river *San Antonio*.

San Antonio is a ghost hunter's dream come true; invisible residents occupy dozens of public buildings throughout this beautiful, ancient settlement, making San Antonio the most haunted large city in Texas. Many researchers and psychics believe the existence of the numerous restless spirits in San Antonio is a direct consequence of the Battle of the Alamo. The fall of the Alamo in March 1836 resulted in the tragic deaths of 189 Alamo defenders and 1,600 Mexican troops, none of whom were given the benefit of a proper burial. The presence

San Antonio's Paseo Del River (Riverwalk) winds through the heart of the city.

of these lost souls is felt throughout buildings surrounding the Alamo Plaza downtown.

Five of the oldest hotels in San Antonio bear the distinction of being haunted. The Camberley Gunter, the Crockett, the Menger, the Ramada Emily Morgan, and the St. Anthony are all beautiful, comfortable, and extremely popular with visitors because of their rich, sometimes decadent histories.

Many of the haunted bed-and-breakfast inns of San Antonio are located in the King William Historic District, a 25-block neighborhood of Victorian mansions built by San Antonio's early German merchants. Developed in the 1850s, the King William District is the first and oldest historically designated neighborhood in Texas.

HAUNTED HOTELS

Camberly Gunter Hotel 😊😊😊😊

205 E. Houston St., San Antonio, TX 78205 • 210-227-3241

Description and History

The Camberly Gunter Hotel was built in 1909, on the site that is now the intersection of Houston and St. Mary's Streets. This is the same site where a previous hotel, the Settlement Inn, was built in 1837 following the Battle of the Alamo.

The Gunter has had its fair share of famous people stay the night. Will Rogers, Max and Buddy Baer, and Mae West were guests. John Wayne stayed here while filming *The Alamo*. When Harry S. Truman was president, he stayed in the 12th-floor presidential suite. Along with the elegance the hotel exudes lies a hint of intrigue. The Gunter was the location of the most unusual and bizarre crime in San Antonio history. This tragic event seems to be the source of some of the haunting activity in the elegant old hotel.

Accommodations include 312 rooms and 10 suites featuring traditional furnishings. The moderately priced Camberly Gunter Hotel is centrally located and offers a private lounge with complimentary breakfast, afternoon tea, and evening cordials (perhaps including the beautiful wine-loving ghost, Ingrid). Casual dining featuring regional specialties, a weight room, and an outdoor pool and whirlpool help make your stay in the Alamo City a time to remember.

Ghostly Visitations

In February 1965, a tall man in his late 30s checked into the hotel, requesting Room 636. Over the next few days, he was seen around the hotel in the

> **Most Haunted Areas:**
> *Rooms 635, 636, and 436*

company of an attractive blond. On February 8, a maid opened the room for cleaning and found the tall man standing over a blood-soaked bed holding a blood-soaked bundle in his hands. During the panic that ensued, he managed to flee with the bundle down the fire escape.

Police found two bullet holes in the bed and in a wall behind a chair, as well as evidence of a bloody butchery in the bathroom. Some officials believe the man shot and killed the blond woman, dismembered her in the bathroom, ran her body parts through a meat grinder, and flushed them down the toilet.

Investigators discovered the tall man had registered under an assumed name, which was traced to purchased items found in the hotel room, including a missing meat grinder! He was finally located at another haunted hotel, the St. Anthony, registered under his assumed name and staying in Room 536. (He had apparently requested Room 636, but it was occupied.) When officers entered the room to question him, the man shot himself in the head. The crime files have never been closed.

In a strange twist of fate, the hotel manager recently received a strange envelope in the mail. It was a post office envelope bearing no return address. The envelope was addressed to the Gunter (not the Camberly Gunter, as it is known today), and the ZIP code was the old one used back in 1965. Inside the envelope was an old room key—the key to Room 636. This was an old-fashioned key, similar to those the hotel used back then, not the credit-card-like plastic openers used today.

Many ghostly manifestations seem to center on Room 636, the scene of the heinous murder that remains unsolved to this day. After the murder scene cleanup, hotel management decided to split the large room into two smaller rooms and create a suite. A shared door connects Rooms 635 and 636, and 636 is outfitted with bunk beds perfect for guests with children (very brave children!). Sightings of a woman in ghostly garb have been reported by night watchmen walking the halls around Room 636 late at night. Guests have complained of loud banging noises where no source has been found.

The lobby of the Camberly Gunter Hotel.

Along with the woman seen near Room 636, several other ghostly visitors prowl the Camberly Gunter. In 1990, an apparition that materialized in a very dark room surprised a female employee of the hotel. The woman had entered the room to prepare for an important guest and discerned an old woman standing in the middle of the room, arms outstretched toward the startled staff member. The employee left quickly, slamming the door behind her. She claims she never recovered from the experience and still feels cold chills whenever she recalls the afternoon she surprised the woman in that dark room.

During a Christmas party given by a group of hotel employees in the ballroom, an uninvited ghost boldly posed for the camera. Other paranormal experiences include phantom voices and mysterious shadows that have been reported in the vicinity of Room 436.

Psychics who stayed overnight at the Gunter have identified two resident female spirits. One is named "Ingrid," a woman who died in the early twentieth century. Ingrid, rather avant-garde for her day, apparently loved wine and smoking. The Gunter was her favorite party headquarters. Many employees believe this is the dark-haired apparition in white who has been sighted all over the hotel, gliding silently down halls and in and out of rooms. The figure has long black hair, swept up on the sides and loose in the back. The other spirit is called "Peggy," and she's a flapper from the 1920s Prohibition era. According to the psychics, she and Ingrid do not get along. Perhaps a little ghostly jealousy over haunting the same hotel?

Crockett Holiday Inn 😀😀😀

320 Bonham, San Antonio, TX 78205 • 800-292-1050

Description and History

The Crockett Hotel is located on the bloody battlefield site of the March 6, 1836, Battle of the Alamo, directly behind the Alamo. During the night before the battle, hundreds of Mexican troops gathered in the area where the patio and hotel swimming pool are today, ready to attack the outnumbered Texans at dawn. The colorful Davy Crockett, for whom the hotel is named, defended the Alamo's southeast palisade.

In 1909, the original combination hotel and lodge hall was constructed. In 1982, San Antonio natives John and Jenne Blocker purchased the property and began extensive renovations. Today, the hotel has been completely restored with a new atrium and several new guest rooms. Maybe it was these renovations that stirred up a couple ghosts at the Crockett.

As a result of the careful restoration, the Crockett Hotel is listed on the National Register of Historic Structures. The Crockett is also designated as a historic Texas landmark, with 202 beautifully restored rooms. The hotel, moderately priced and centrally located behind Alamo Plaza, has a relaxed and inviting atmosphere to make your stay in San Antonio one filled with elegance, history, and possibly a ghost or two. For more information, call 800-292-1050 or 210-225-6500.

Ghostly Visitations

Several employees have spotted the figure of a man in the executive office section. This section is located in the modern two-story section of the

Most Haunted Area:
The executive office section

hotel that circles the patio and swimming pool. A witness saw a man wearing a dark blue jacket move into the small kitchen area adjoining the boardroom. A quick check of the kitchen revealed no one there. The sounds of people whispering are also perceived in this area. Other employees have watched in amazement while curtains ruffled in vacant rooms and electronic doors opened for disembodied footsteps.

Local historian and author Docia Williams conducted an investigation in 1996. With the help of two talented San Antonio psychics, Sam Nesmith and Robert Thiege, she detected two spirits inhabiting the Crockett. The man in blue is thought to be the type of spirit involved in a psychic photographic imprint, repeating something he did a long time ago. In the 1960s, a bar stood where the executive offices are located today. Maybe the man in blue is returning to his favorite watering hole. Sam believes this scene will continue to replay from time to time. The psychics also sensed the presence of a rather shy spirit. Both men believe that, eventually, the spirit will gain enough energy to materialize.

Menger Hotel ☺☺☺☺☺

204 Alamo Plaza, San Antonio, TX 78205 • 800-345-9285

Description and History

For San Antonio, the year 1859 was a time of trail rides, fast tempers, and quick triggers. It was also the year the Menger Hotel ushered in a new era of sophistication to the Texas frontier. Located on Alamo Plaza across the street from the Alamo, the Menger Hotel is the oldest hotel in San Antonio and the oldest hotel in America still operating in its original form. It is also the most haunted hotel in Texas.

Step back in time—and into a supernatural wonderland—in the Menger Hotel.

The Menger opened its doors to the public on February 2, 1859, just 20 years after the Battle of the Alamo. The hotel, built by German immigrant William Menger and his wife, Mary Guenther Menger, has long been the setting for glamorous balls and elegant dinner parties attended by San Antonio society.

Many famous people have visited the Menger over the years, including Captain Richard King, French actress Sarah Bernhardt, Beverly Sills, Buffalo Bill Cody, and Presidents Roosevelt, Grant, Taft, McKinley, Eisenhower, and Nixon. Oscar Wilde, in all his lace-frilled, black-velvet, and scarlet-stocking splendor, stopped here on his national lecture tour in 1882. Roy Rogers and Dale Evans were such frequent guests that the hotel named a suite for them.

The renegade Apache Geronimo was an unwilling guest at the Menger. He was imprisoned for a time in the basement of the hotel before being transported to a reservation. In addition, a number of suicides, murders, and other deaths have occurred at the Menger, creating an atmosphere ripe with supernatural visitations.

A centrally located hotel with a wonderful continental ambience, the Menger has a gracious staff, wonderful food, and a full-service spa. The hotel is just steps away from the Alamo, Rivercenter Mall, the Riverwalk, and the IMAX Theatre. With 320 beautifully restored guest rooms and moderate rates, the Menger promises to make your San Antonio vacation a memorable and possibly paranormal one. For more information on the Menger, call 800-345-9285 or 210-223-4361.

Ghostly Visitations

The most sighted specter wandering this grand old hotel is thought to be Sallie White, a chambermaid who worked at the Menger in 1876. She roams the long halls on the third floor of the original building,

Most Haunted Areas:
The second and third floor original side rooms, the King Ranch Suite, and the Menger Bar

regularly appearing dressed in a full-length skirt with a scarf or bandanna tied around her head, an apron, and a long necklace of beads.

Her life was cut short in March 1876 when she was shot by her jealous husband while she was working at the hotel. She died in one of the third-floor rooms in the original section of the hotel. In the lobby, you can see an interesting display of old hotel ledgers, one of which is opened to an entry by Frederick Hahn; in the "cash paid" column, he wrote, "To cash paid for coffin for Salie White, col'd chambermaid, deceased, murdered by her husband, shot March 28, died March 30, $25 for coffin and $7 for grave, total $32."

A man dressed somewhat like Colonel Sanders (of fried-chicken fame), wearing old-fashioned western-type clothing, a string tie, and a broad-brimmed black hat, has been seen pacing darkened hallways. He is thought to be Captain Richard King, a famous cattle baron who established the fabled million-acre King Ranch south of San Antonio in the 1840s. King often stayed at the hotel during his many visits to San Antonio.

King fell ill during his last visit and spent the final months of his life in his suite (now named the King Ranch suite, still furnished with the old four-poster bed in which he passed away). When he died in August 1865, his funeral was held in the original lobby of the hotel. His apparition has been observed entering the King Ranch suite, walking directly through the closed door.

Since 1996, activity in the old Menger bar has increased dramatically. In this bar, Teddy Roosevelt recruited many of his famous Rough Riders, volunteers for the first American Cavalry that fought in Cuba during the Spanish-American War. Local psychics believe the approaching 100th anniversary of the Rough Riders' recruitment may explain the heightened activity level concentrated in this area of the Menger Hotel. Teddy lured many a Texas cowboy into the Cavalry by buying him mugs of Menger's beer in this replica of the House of Lords Pub in London.

Some employees believe the military man seen in the bar is none other than Teddy Roosevelt having a mug of his favorite brew and continuing to look for recruits among the living. The spirit, dressed in an old-fashioned military uniform, appeared to a startled janitor late one night after closing. The military phantom beckoned to the young man, who turned to run out of the bar, only to find he had been locked in. While he frantically yelled to his coworkers to open the door, the military ghost sat quietly at the bar observing the custodian's panicked attempts to escape. The terrified young man did not return to his job at the Menger.

Another employee was in the bar after midnight when he happened to glance up at the balcony. Sitting on the side facing the Alamo was a man wearing a dark gray suit and a little hat. The employee ran to find a coworker to confirm the sighting, but when they returned a few minutes later, the enigmatic man in gray had disappeared.

The mysterious "Lady in Blue" is said to frequent a second-floor room in the old section of the hotel. Hotel personnel assigned to this room have experienced strange noises, flickering lights, and a general feeling of being watched. The most eerie incident occurred when a maid was cleaning the room and had the feeling she was not alone. She turned to see a beautiful woman in an old-fashioned blue dress sitting calmly in a chair a few feet away. The maid described the apparition as an attractive woman with shoulder-length blond hair worn in a style of the 1930s or 1940s. After just a few seconds, the figure disappeared.

Several years ago, a gentleman who had spent the night stopped by the front desk to question his bill. Several phone calls were charged to his room that he hadn't made during his stay. He noticed that they were all calls to his mother's old telephone number, but his mother had been dead for 10 years!

In the late fall of 1996, assistant manager Ernesto

The original lobby of the Menger Hotel.

Malacara observed a very solid apparition of an old woman—dressed in red, white, and blue and wearing a white sailor hat—sitting in the original lobby of the hotel. In fact, she looked so real that Malacara approached her to introduce himself as the assistant manager and ask if she was comfortable. The woman looked up from her knitting, assured Malacara she was "just fine," and returned to her work.

Nine months later, a visiting psychic touring the old lobby with Malacara saw this same woman sitting in the same chair reading a newspaper. She was not visible to Malacara, but then the psychic described her red, white, and blue dress and sailor hat to a tee. Malacara hadn't told anyone of his earlier experience because he didn't realize he'd seen—and talked to—a ghost.

Staying at the Menger Hotel while conducting research for this book, I had a brush with the paranormal. After an exhausting, ghost-filled day of interviewing witnesses, my friend Jill Pendleton and I retired to our room for the evening. We were asleep before our heads hit the pillow.

Sometime during the early morning hours, my friend woke to the sound of footsteps crossing the room. Thinking it was me walking to the bathroom, she rolled over only to find me sleeping soundly (and snoring softly) across the room. Jerking the covers over her head, she spent the next few hours trying to rationalize this strange experience and chose not to wake her famous ghost author friend (darn it all!).

Recalling the incident over morning coffee with Ernesto Malacara, Jill described the footsteps as sounding like a man in slippers. Malacara delightedly informed us that our room had been the scene of an apparition's appearance six weeks before our visit.

Is Geronimo haunting the Menger Hotel?

Photo courtesy of Glenn Welker

A maid had been cleaning the room when the figure of a tall Indian sporting a long black braid and wearing a white shirt and black pants suddenly materialized between the beds. An old hand at experiencing paranormal activity in the hotel, the maid stood quite calmly, then began screaming her head off—previous experience doesn't always build courage! The Indian vaporized instantly before her eyes.

Malacara believes the apparition may be Geronimo, the renegade Apache chief who had been an unwilling guest at the Menger. According to Malacara, Geronimo was imprisoned for a time in the basement of the hotel before being transported to a reservation. Was this famous Indian the one who visited our room that morning? Could Geronimo have returned to join Roosevelt and the collection of other ghostly guests who roam the Menger's hallways?

There have been multiple sightings in the dining room of "the maître d'," a man dressed in top hat and tails who appears to be working the room, silently chatting with unseen guests. Many of the waitresses who work in the early morning hours regularly see an old phantom they refer to as "Mr. Preston." He sits quietly on a patio bench, just outside the dining room.

Over the years, dozens of additional incidents of apparitions, dressed in the style of the late 1800s, have appeared to guests in hallways and elevators. As recently as July 1997, a guest came out of the bathroom and found a strange man dressed in an old-fashioned fringed buckskin suit holding a heated conversation with an unseen entity in the middle of his room. The young man watched in fascination for several seconds before the ghost vanished.

Employees have felt someone brush past them when no one was there. Glasses in the bar have rattled and moved, startling guests and employees. Doors do not stay closed even when locked and relocked. Musical notes, sounds of marching footsteps, and odd moans and groans are heard in various parts of the hotel. It seems as though the Menger is as popular with its ghosts as it is with its living guests.

As for the identity of the mysterious "Lady in Blue," the patriotic knitting ghost, "Mr. Preston," and the legions of others, your guess is as good as mine. Maybe you'll uncover some pieces of this paranormal puzzle during your stay at the Menger.

Ramada Emily Morgan Hotel 👣👣

705 E. Houston St., San Antonio, TX 78205 • 800-824-6674

Description and History

J.M. Nix built this historic neo-Gothic building in 1924; he later built the Nix Hospital and Majestic Theater in San Antonio. The hotel is located across the street and north of the Alamo at the intersection of East Houston Street and Avenue E. Once used as the Medical Arts Building, the hotel was named after the romantic Texas heroine Emily Morgan.

Known as the "Yellow Rose of Texas," Emily was a beautiful mulatto slave who caught the eye of Mexican General Antonio Lopez de Santa Anna. She sent messages from the unsuspecting general's tent to Texan troop leader General Sam Houston, prompting an attack. On April 21, 1836, Sam Houston's ragged troops surprised and defeated the far superior forces of Santa Anna along the banks of the San Jacinto River.

Just a short walk from the Alamo and the Riverwalk, the Ramada Emily Morgan offers at affordable prices in-room jacuzzi tubs, an exercise center, and a swimming pool. The hotel has 177 guest rooms and serves breakfast in the Yellow Rose Café and dinner in Emily's Oasis. Maybe you can spend some time with a few of its otherworldly guests during your stay. For more information, call 800-824-6674 or 210-225-8486, or visit the website at pwl.netcom.com/~ramadaem/index.html.

Ghostly Visitations

Apparition sightings, cold spots, and mysterious noises have centered on the lobby, the seventh floor, and the basement, which used to be the morgue when the structure was used as the Medical Arts Building.

> **Most Haunted Areas:**
> *The main lobby, the seventh floor, and the basement*

St. Anthony Hotel, Wyndham Heritage 😃😃😃😃😃

300 E. Travis St., San Antonio, TX 78205 • 210-227-4392

Description and History

Named after the city and a saint, San Antonio de Padua, the St. Anthony was built in 1909. It is located on Travis Street between Navarro and Jefferson Streets facing Travis Park. Designed to cater to rich cattlemen, elite travelers, and wealthy tourists, the hotel's furnishings are opulent, with fine antiques, crystal chandeliers, beautiful tapestries, and original oil paintings.

The St. Anthony Club, founded in 1959, was one of America's finest dinner clubs, known for a time as *the* nightclub of the Southwest. The big band sound was broadcast live nightly from its rooftop garden, where World War II soldiers and their dates swayed to the music underneath a star-filled Texas sky.

Doubtless, this romantic atmosphere created many fond memories for participants. Many proposals of marriage and tearful farewells between military men and their lovers must have been whispered here in the shadowed corners of the old garden. This may be the reason so many entities have chosen to return to this beautiful hotel.

With its rich heritage, the St. Anthony has been designated a Texas and National Historical Landmark. The moderately priced hotel is filled with beautiful French Empire antiques and original oils and watercolors by such noted artists as Remington, Cartier, and DeYoung. It also appears to be filled with its fair share of ghosts. For more information, visit the website at www.stanthonyhotel.com.

Ghostly Visitations

The general feeling among St. Anthony's employees is that they are never alone. Feelings of being followed down long hallways, glimpses of strange shadowy outlines, an

unseen whistler, doors opening and closing by themselves, and television sounds coming from unoccupied
rooms are just some of the manifestations. Various staff
members have reported hearing someone washing up in
the lavatory area, and the sound of water running from
the shower and faucets.

Guests have been known to check in at the front desk and return after just a few
minutes requesting to check out, claiming something spooked them in their assigned
rooms. One couple checked into the hotel late one night and was upset to find their
room occupied by a couple drinking cocktails. The front-desk manager went up to the
room to investigate and found no evidence of drinkers or glasses.

One strange apparition is that of a pair of legs clad in dark stockings and black old-
fashioned pumps. Several witnesses have seen this unusual sight in the first stall of the
mezzanine-level ladies' powder room. The owner of the legs never emerges from the stall
and eventually the legs just fade away. The smell of a sweet perfume sometimes lingers
here as well.

Local psychics Sam Nesmith and Robert Thiege staked out the hotel one night and
detected several entities. They believe the stockinged legs in the ladies' powder room
belong to an elderly woman named Claire or Clara who had a terrifying experience in
this bathroom. After she entered the first stall, she began having terrible chest pains and
thought she was going to die. She survived, only to die from a stroke shortly thereafter.
The psychics claim this was such a frightening and traumatic experience for the woman
that the energy remained as a psychic imprint and the scene periodically repeats itself.

A ride in the elevator sometimes reveals a ghostly lady in a red dress, and a tall man
clad in dark clothing who looks like Abraham Lincoln. A man in a tuxedo and a woman
in a white uniform are also part of the haunting crowd at the St. Anthony Hotel.

Nesmith and Thiege have made contact with the woman in the white uniform. She
is a Hispanic woman named Anita who used to work for the hotel in the 1950s. She loved
the hotel so much that she returns to visit (and clean?) periodically.

The sad little spirit of a woman in a white ballgown is thought to have lost her lover
in World War II. She and her soldier spent many lovely nights dancing in the garden and
she has come back to linger where she was once so happy. Phantom children have been
sighted in the roof garden as well. Authors of *The Haunted Alamo*, Robert and Anne Powell
Wlodarski, call this area of the hotel a hotbed of paranormal activity. Nesmith and Thiege
also determined that a honeymoon couple returns to the hotel where they spent such a
happy, romantic time. They cause a lot of the door slamming in a guest suite because
they want a little privacy.

Activity in the Anacacho Ballroom was reported by security staff member Al Langston,
who saw and heard a deadbolt lock slide into place. He also heard a kick against a closed
door and felt he was in the presence of something otherworldly.

At the Menger, the identities of the specters in residence are fairly well known, but
no one really knows who many of St. Anthony's spirits may be. Perhaps you'll meet a couple
on your visit to this lovely historic hotel.

BED & BREAKFASTS WITH A BOO!

The Bullis House Inn/International Hostel ☺☺☺

621 Pierce St., San Antonio, TX 78208 • 210-223-9426

Description and History

Construction on this beautiful white mansion began in 1906 and was completed in 1909 when the house's owner, Brigadier General John Lapham Bullis, moved in. The hotel is located on the corner of Grayson and Pierce Street, just across from Fort Sam Houston. Bullis lived in his home only two years before he died in 1911.

The front door of the house is noticeably wider than most doors because the general wanted to be sure it was wide enough to admit his coffin when he was brought home to lie in

Is Geronimo the Indian spirit seen in the Bullis House?

state. He did lie in state in the front parlor for a whole week following his death—this was a guy who liked to plan ahead.

General Bullis, a Union officer during the Civil War, ended up in Texas during the Reconstruction period. While serving at Fort Clark, he was rewarded for his valiant service during a raid on a hostile Indian band camped across the Mexican border. He later served as an Indian agent in New Mexico and Arkansas before he was transferred to Fort Sam Houston in San Antonio. During retirement, the general built the mansion across the street from the fort. After his death, family members lived here until 1949, when they sold it to another famous general, Jonathan Wainwright, who commanded Fort Sam Houston after his return from a Japanese prison camp during World War II.

Wainwright decided not to live in the house and leased it to a number of tenants, including various insurance companies. It was also used as a child care center in later years. In 1983, present owners Alma and Steve Cross purchased the house and converted it into a bed-and-breakfast inn. It has at least a couple of resident spirits hanging about.

This inexpensive and spacious inn is a Texas Historic Landmark. The owners guarantee you'll find "affordable elegance in the classic Southern style," with 14-foot ceilings and wood-burning fireplaces in many of the rooms. Although they cannot guarantee a ghost sighting, chances seem pretty good in this charming retreat.

Ghostly Visitations

One night during restoration, Alma and Steve heard loud men's voices having an extremely heated argument downstairs in the foyer area. Even though they searched the

entire house, the Crosses never found a source for the mysterious yelling.

Another night, while Alma was sleeping in a downstairs bedroom, the apparition of an Indian brave appeared at the foot of her bed at about 3 a.m. His long black hair was tied back from his face and he wore a bandanna, tied around his head. He disappeared as quickly as he came. Many Indian tribes lived in the area long ago, and Mrs. Cross believes the apparition was an Apache. General Bullis was instrumental in capturing the most notorious Apache of them all, Geronimo. Maybe the Indian spirit is that of Geronimo himself, visiting his enemy's home.

The Chabot-Reed House 👶👶

403 Madison, San Antonio, TX 78204 • 800-776-2424

Description and History

This lovely limestone home, built in 1876 by George Starks Chabot, is one of the most beautiful houses in the King William Historic District today. Chabot was born in England and came to San Antonio by way of Mexico, where he lived and worked for the British Foreign Service. After moving to San Antonio, he prospered as a merchant dealing in wool, cotton, and hides. Chabot's wife, Mary Van Derlip Chabot, was heavily involved in the community and well known in the art circles at the time.

The property remained in the hands of the Chabot family after George's death in 1902 and after Mary's death in 1929. In 1940, it was sold and turned into nine apartments; the entire home became a rental property in 1956. In 1975, Walter Mathis purchased the home and the 1917 apartment house next door, which he tore down to expose a beautiful carriage house that was once part of the Chabot property. The current owners, Sister and Peter Reed, bought the mansion in 1985 and completed the restoration of the main house and the adjacent carriage house, now used as a bed-and-breakfast inn.

The Chabot-Reed House is moderately priced and has several beautifully appointed rooms and lovely grounds. Sister likes to do special things for her guests like arranging for a horse-drawn carriage to pick them up for a romantic ride through historic downtown Sa...

Is there a perpetual party going on inside the Chabot-Reed House?

Antonio and having special bouquets of flowers and champagne waiting when they arrive. Who knows—maybe an otherworldly visitor will be greeting you as well. For more information, call 800-776-2424 or 210-223-8696, or visit the website at www.ivylane.com/chabot.

Ghostly Visitations

Most of the paranormal manifestations have centered on the first-floor library, located just to the left of the front entrance. One evening, Sister was

> **Most Haunted Areas:**
> *The library and staircase*

reading quietly when she detected faint strains of music playing. She described it as sounding like an old Victrola playing "speakeasy" music from the 1920s. Sister could also hear laughing and talking, sounding for all the world like a big party going on somewhere in the house. The sounds were detectable only from the library, and a source was never found. This has happened on more than one occasion. A presence felt on the stairs, footsteps, and odd sounds have been known to interrupt an evening spent watching television in the Chabot-Reed House.

This stately mansion has been home to many people over the years, including the Chabot family, subsequent owners, and quite a number of renters. It is not known who haunts the old house, but chances are there was once a glorious party that left its imprint on the old Victorian house, replaying the sounds of a bygone era from time to time. Maybe you'll receive an invitation during your stay.

 # The Ogé House: Inn on the Riverwalk

209 Washington St., San Antonio, TX 78204 • 800-242-2770

Description and History

Catherine Elder Mitchell and her husband, Newton A. Mitchell, are believed to have built this house sometime between 1857 and 1860, in what is now the King William Historic District. The house remained in the Mitchell family for several years, then was sold to a succession of owners. Louis Ogé purchased the house in 1881 for $7,000.

Among his many accomplishments, Louis Ogé was a member of the Texas Rangers and served under the famous Indian fighter and frontiersman Bigfoot Wallace. He was also a mail carrier and worked the route between San Antonio and El Paso. Ogé went on to work for the Butterfield Stage Company and later owned a ranch in Texas. He married Elizabeth Newton and they raised four children in the Washington Street house, where the family lived until 1942. At that time, the house was sold and converted into apartments; a succession of owners followed.

The grand old home is still called the Ogé House in honor of the colorful and interesting Louis Ogé. Patrick and Sharrie Magatagan, who purchased the Ogé House in 1991, have done a wonderful job of restoring this fine antebellum mansion to its former grandeur. In its original state, the house represented the pre–Civil War classical revival in residential architecture. It is one of the few buildings of its type dating to before the Civil War to be found in San Antonio.

As described by Docia Williams, a stay at the Ogé House is like "leaving the twentieth century outside the wide fanlighted doorway." From exquisite oriental carpet to the blending

How many spirits haunt the historic Ogé House?

of French and English Chippendale-style antique furnishings, the Magatagans have spared no expense in reviving the Ogé House to its former glory.

This moderately priced inn boasts five guest suites and five guest rooms, all with private baths and either a queen- or king-size bed. Most rooms have fireplaces and each floor has its own veranda complete with lovely views of the 1.5 acres of beautifully landscaped lawns and gardens surrounding the inn.

Located in the heart of San Antonio on the Riverwalk, it's a five-block stroll to other haunted San Antonio landmarks including the Alamo, La Villita, and Institute of Texan Cultures. It is registered as a Texas and State Historic Landmark.

The Ogé House accepts all major credit cards and is a nonsmoking establishment. The inn does not allow children or pets, but ghosts are apparently welcome. For more information, call 800-242-2770 or 210-223-2353, or visit the website at www.ogeinn.com.

Ghostly Visitations

During the restoration of the home, Sharrie Magatagan could sense a presence. She saw images appear on the dark tile of the kitchen floor and caught flashes of something or someone in her peripheral vision. The kitchen used to be

Most Haunted Areas:
The Mathis Room and the kitchen

Mrs. Ogé's bedroom, where she passed away. While cooking in the kitchen, Sharrie often saw the spices and herbs she was using blow away.

Although many visiting psychics describe a female presence, Sharrie firmly believes it is a male entity. She believes the spirit to be that of a former owner, perhaps Louis Ogé himself. The presence is felt to be benevolent and happy.

One psychic described the additional presence of a child's spirit, a 10- or 12-year-old girl who drowned in the nearby San Antonio River and comes to the house frequently. Sharrie has searched for historical evidence to back up the existence of the drowned child's presence and has not been able to substantiate it.

Most of the visitors who have sensed an otherworldly entity stayed in the Mathis Room. However, manifestations such as the lights turning on and off have recently slowed down. Maybe the spirits have gone on to greener pastures or maybe they're just on vacation.

The Riverwalk Inn ☺☺

329 Old Guilbeau, San Antonio, TX 78204 • 800-254-4440

Description and History

The inn is located on the beautiful Riverwalk downtown. San Antonio businessman Tracy Hammer and his wife traveled to Tennessee and Kentucky in search of old log cabins. Their intention was to buy log cabins for use in the construction of a bed-and-breakfast inn situated on the banks of the San Antonio River. The result is a glorious structure housing many antiques from the 1830s and 1840s, when most of the original cabins were built. The owners feel they have spirits still clinging to the old logs and to the many antiques filling the rustic inn.

A beautiful getaway right in the middle of downtown San Antonio, The Riverwalk Inn is a cozy, comfortable place to while away a lazy afternoon rocking on the shady porch overlooking the river or hunting for ghosts. Moderately priced, the inn is frequented by local storytellers, who make the expanded continental breakfast even more special with entertaining stories of the Alamo City. For more information, call 800-254-4440 or 210-212-8300, or visit the website at www.riverwalkinn.com.

Ghostly Visitations

The owners tell of the TV in the common room turning on and off by itself, doors closing by themselves, icy drafts, and footsteps on the stairs connecting the common room to

> **Most Haunted Area:**
> *The common room*

the bedrooms upstairs. Often, it feels as if someone is in the room when no one is there. The Hammers believe this presence is a woman.

During a wedding reception in the common room, a photograph of the bride and groom cutting the wedding cake included the image of a man in old-fashioned dress who was not visible at the time. Perhaps the male in the photo is Mr. Gilbo, the subject of a portrait hanging in the inn. The painting was bought from an antiques dealer without Mrs. Gilbo's companion portrait; the owners thought her portrait was too homely to hang in the inn. Maybe Mr. Gilbo is angry because his wife didn't make the journey with him to Texas.

The haunted Riverwalk Inn is constructed of materials from several Kentucky log cabins.

Royal Swan Guest Inn 🔑🔑🔑🔑
236 Madison St., San Antonio, TX 78204 • 800-368-3073

Description and History

One of the most haunted inns in San Antonio, the Royal Swan Inn is located in the King William District. San Antonio dentist Dr. Jabez Cain built the home in 1892 and it was his home until about 1900. His partner, Dr. James H. Graham, lived in the house for a short time as well. During World War II, the house was converted into apartments and fell into decline during the great move to the suburbs that followed the war.

In the 1970s, when the San Antonio Riverwalk was being developed, this wonderful neighborhood was rediscovered. Mr. and Mrs. Egon Jausch bought the Cain house and began renovations. A succession of owners followed and all continued the restoration process. In 1993, Doug and Donna West purchased the house and opened it as a bed-and-breakfast inn. In October 1995, present owners Curt and Helen Skredergard bought the house and continue to run the Royal Swan Inn as a bed-and-breakfast.

The Verandah Suite is the most haunted room in the Royal Swan Inn.

This inexpensive to moderately priced bed-and-breakfast inn has original stained glass in some of the windows, lovely fireplaces, and wood paneling of loblolly pine. Each guest room features a queen-size bed, private bath, cable TV, and a telephone with computer jack. Your stay includes a full breakfast served in the formal dining room or the sunny morning room. It may also include a visit from a lovely dark-haired señorita. For more information, call 800-368-3073 or 210-223-3776, or visit the website at www.royalswan.com.

Ghostly Visitations

Several paranormal manifestations have occurred in the Verandah Suite of the Royal Swan. From a violently shaking bed that convinced the occupants they were experiencing an

> **Most Haunted Area:**
> *The Verandah Suite*

earthquake to the feeling of someone sitting down on the edge of the bed, this room has been the scene of many an eventful night.

Most people believe this spirit is that of a woman. She often makes her presence known by turning faucets, radios, and ceiling fans on and off. Donna West, a former owner, told of a maid who went up to the Verandah Suite to clean and found a woman, who appeared to be of Hispanic origin, sitting in one of the rockers on the suite's veranda.

When the maid said, "Oh, pardon me," the young woman rose from the chair. The maid hurried downstairs and told Donna, "I am sorry, I didn't know we still had a guest upstairs in the Verandah Suite." Donna assured her they didn't and the two women went back upstairs to find a gently rocking chair, although there was no breeze that day.

This lovely apparition appeared to several guests staying in the suite, always making her appearance at 3 a.m. A drastic drop in temperature often accompanies her arrival. Generally, she appears to dark-haired women occupying the old iron bed in the larger of the two rooms that make up the Verandah Suite.

 ## Terrell Castle Inn ☺☺☺

950 E. Grayson St., San Antonio, TX 78208 • 210-271-9145

Description and History

Terrell Castle is a 32-room house complete with turrets and towers rising above East Grayson Street, facing Fort Sam Houston's Staff Post Road. The builder, Edwin Holland Terrell, was a lawyer and statesman who served as ambassador to Belgium under President Benjamin Harrison in the early 1890s. Terrell sent his architect to Belgium to duplicate the plans of a castle he loved. This mansion served as home for Terrell and his family for many years. Mother and daughter Katherine Poulis and Nancy Haley purchased the house in 1986 and started extensive revisions. Call the inn at 210-271-9145 to inquire about rates and to make reservations.

Ghostly Visitations

Haley often hears the sound of footsteps upstairs when she is sitting in the downstairs den alone in the house. She describes the footsteps as those of a woman wearing high-heeled shoes clicking rapidly across the hardwood floors. There is a tale of tragedy that took place in the building when it was used as apartments to house military families stationed at Fort Sam Houston during World War II. A soldier returned home early and caught his wife with another man. In a fit of jealous rage,

A jealous soldier killed his wife and her lover in the Terrell Castle Inn, setting the stage for a haunting.

he killed the man and then pushed his wife over the stair railing. She fell to her death three stories below. Is this the woman whose high heels click across the hardwoods?

Nancy tells of an unsubstantiated rumor that the original building contractor jumped off one of the upper balconies to avoid accusations of wrongdoing in his business. Is he the toilet-slamming ghost a visiting couple experienced while staying in the Alfred Giles Suite? During the night, at about 30-minute intervals, the couple heard a crash that sounded like the toilet seat slamming down. After several trips to the bathroom, they determined this wasn't the source of the noise.

After moving up to the fourth-floor Americana Room, the couple experienced a runaway ceiling fan that would spin rapidly and stop suddenly, even though the switch remained in the off position. They also watched in amazement as the TV in their room jumped off the table and landed upside down on the floor.

Housekeepers report glimpsing someone passing by in the hallways outside the upstairs rooms they are cleaning. Upon checking, the hallways are always empty—at least they appear to be empty.

RESTAURANT REVENANTS

Alamo Street Restaurant and Theatre ☺☺☺☺
1150 S. Alamo, San Antonio, TX 78210 • 210-271-7791

Description and History

The Alamo Street Restaurant and Theatre was constructed in 1912 in the popular Mission-style architecture of the day, near what is now the King William Historic District. The building, with its two identical bell towers and twin entrances at the front, served as a Methodist Church. Marcie and Bill Larsen bought the structure in 1976 after it sat empty for a number of years. The Larsens made major renovations, converting the bottom floor (where the Sunday School rooms were) into a restaurant, and the upper-floor sanctuary into a theater. The Alamo Street Restaurant and Theatre is the home of at least four otherworldly entities.

The Alamo Street Restaurant and Theatre is well known in San Antonio for its wonderful all-you-can-eat buffet-style lunches and dinners and the original plays the theater puts on every night. Owner Marcie Larsen writes many of the plays produced by the theater, which is a member of the San Antonio Theatre Coalition. She is compiling a cookbook of all the delicious recipes that make lunch and dinner at the Alamo Street Restaurant so memorable, including meatloaf, lasagna, chicken and dumplings, and fresh vegetables. And for ghost hunters with a sweet tooth, the restaurant is famous for its elaborate dessert table.

The restaurant, open for lunch Monday through Saturday from 11:30 a.m.-2 p.m. and for dinner from 6-10 p.m. on Friday and Saturday, is within walking distance of many of the haunted bed-and-breakfast inns in the King William Historic District. San Antonio author and historian Docia Williams begins her "Spirits of San Antonio" haunted tours at the Alamo Street Restaurant and Theatre, which is on the National Register of Historic Places. The restaurant accepts all major credit cards and reservations are a must.

Ghostly Visitations

For years, the presence of a beautiful young woman in Victorian dress has been felt and seen in the old choir loft of the theater. She is especially active during the rehearsals and the production of plays and has even been known to

> **Most Haunted Area:**
> *The choir loft in the upstairs theater*

watch performances, sitting with the audience in one of the long pews now used as theater seats. She is believed to be the spirit of Margaret Gething, who once lived on Guenther Street, just a block away from the old church. In life, she was a stage actress who often played in New York and Europe. The owners and employees call her "Miss Margaret" and she is a favorite among the ghosts here.

A visiting couple once photographed Miss Margaret floating above the exit sign beneath the choir loft. This photo is framed and displayed in the restaurant. Miss Margaret has been known to materialize above the actors on stage during performances and was even seen sitting next to the piano player during one play. Her appearances are often accompanied by a major drop in temperature—no small feat when you consider summertime temperatures can soar to over 100 degrees in this area of the building. Margaret Gething's home on Guenther Street acts as a museum and is open to the public during the week of San Antonio's Fiesta each April. A photograph in her home shows Miss Margaret dressed in the white high-

The Alamo Street Restaurant is one of the most active haunted locations in San Antonio.

Inside the Alamo Street Theatre.

collared Victorian dress she favored in life (and in death). This likeness is remarkably similar to the ghostly image in the Polaroid displayed in the Alamo Street Restaurant and to employees' descriptions of the theatrical spirit.

The youngest resident phantom is a boy called "Little Eddie." This small specter is responsible for most of the pranks that go on in the building. Eddie moved in when an old Victorian wheelchair was brought into the theater as a prop. Psychics claim Little Eddie was confined to the chair in life, but definitely has full use of all his limbs in death. During opening nights, when chaos reigns in the theater world, Eddie does his fair share to complicate matters further. He has been known to unplug the iron during costume pressing, hide costume changes during performances, and turn the stereo on and off.

A visiting psychic saw Eddie playing in the soup during the dinner buffet one night. The psychic approached the prankster and offered him a rubber ball in return for his good behavior. Little Eddie accepted; for the next three years, the rubber ball was found all over the old church, including locked offices and costume pockets. Eddie likes to spend time in the kitchen and loves to entertain diners by levitating serving spoons during the dinner and lunch buffets.

Local psychics have also picked up on the energy of an elderly lady named "Henrietta," who sits in the bell tower and waves to passersby. Several customers have come into the restaurant and mentioned "people" in the tower waving to the Alamo Street traffic. Henrietta is sometimes joined by an elderly man who is just "there." He is probably the figure that the artistic director, Deborah Latham, encountered one late night.

Shortly after 2 a.m., Latham was alone in the building working on an audiotape for an upcoming production. She left her office to cut through the dining room on her way to the bathroom. Sitting at one of the dining room tables was an elderly, graying man dressed in a three-piece suit. Startled, Latham asked him if she could be of any assistance. He promptly disappeared. She ran back to her office to retrieve her purse and noticed her desk chair hovering about a foot off the ground. Latham had the overwhelming feeling that she was not wanted there and exclaimed, "Okay, just let me get my purse and I'm outta here!" Latham says she's accustomed to the "ghost family" sharing her workplace and at one time or another has seen all the friendly spirits of the Alamo Street Restaurant and Theatre.

Café Camille 👧👦

517 E. Woodlawn Ave., San Antonio, TX 78212 • 210-735-2307

Description and History

This beautiful old house was once the property of a gentleman who is now more than 100 years old. It is now a delightful bistro called Café Camille, owned by Tracy Becker and Docia Williams. It is located in the old Monte Vista section on East Woodlawn at St. Mary's.

This relaxed dining room turns out imaginative French-influenced fusion cuisine. Specialties of the house include starters such as fried calamari in blue cornmeal and brown bread with tapenade and blue cheese to main courses of crab cakes with risotto and ancho-flavored mango sauce and herbed redfish with artichoke hearts and crabmeat. Beer and wine are available. Lunch is served Sunday and Tuesday through Friday 11 a.m.-2 p.m.; dinner is served Sunday and Tuesday through Thursday 5 p.m.-10 p.m., and Friday and Saturday 5 p.m.-11 p.m. This moderate-to-expensive bistro is closed Monday. All major credit cards are accepted. Although the dining room is wheelchair-accessible, the bathrooms are not, so call in advance so they can make accommodations.

Ghostly Visitations

The restaurant owners feel that the presence in the restaurant might be the deceased wife of the former owner. Manifestations include doors opening and closing

> **Most Haunted Area:**
> *The front of the building*

by themselves and an overwhelming sense of presence, especially in the front of the building. A large mirror and a hanging cupboard fell and shattered, even though they were firmly attached to the wall. Moreover, they didn't "fall" straight down, but were picked up and moved over before being dropped.

Enjoy a delicious meal and perhaps an invisible dinner guest at Café Camille.

Jesse's Bar and Restaurant 👻👻
212 S. Flores, San Antonio, TX 78204 • 210-223-5533

Description and History

The building that now houses Jesse's was constructed in 1870 and used as a general mercantile business by immigrant Herman Dietrich Stumberg and his son George. With farmers and ranchers from all over South Texas driving into town to buy supplies from the Stumbergs' store, their business flourished until it closed during the Great Depression in 1932.

The buildings were owned by a succession of people over the years, and in the 1980s, were renovated and restored in a redevelopment known as Stumberg Square. The project won the 1985 San Antonio Conservation Society Award for Excellence. In December 1991, the great-great-grandson of the German immigrant George Stumberg became the operating stockholder of the Cadillac Bar and Restaurant (now known as Jesse's) in San Antonio.

Jesse's Bar and Restaurant, open Monday through Friday for lunch from 11 a.m.-2 p.m. and for dinner on Saturday from 5 p.m.-2 a.m., serves terrific Mexican food and memorable margaritas, always a Texas favorite.

Ghostly Visitations

San Antonio author and historian Docia Williams brought in local psychic Sam Nesmith to investigate the ghostly goings-on at the former Cadillac Bar. Nesmith sensed the presence of at least two spirits

> **Most Haunted Areas:**
> *The back stairs and the upstairs party room*

haunting the old building. One is a slender old man with a white handlebar mustache who has been spotted climbing the back stairs leading from the kitchen to an upper-floor storage room. This ghost's name is either "Herman" or "Henry."

Former owner George Stumberg III recalls an ancestor named "Uncle Herman," who was considered the black sheep of the Stumberg family. Herman used to spend his time hanging around the mercantile business by day and the old Silver Dollar Saloon by night. Is Uncle Herman the specter seen climbing the back stairs of the bar?

Nesmith also sensed the spirit of a young woman named "Beatrice," who is the most-sighted ghost in residence. Beatrice is a rather sad, homely girl who frequents the upstairs party room. She is described as having stringy, dishwater-blond hair and protruding teeth. Many employees report feeling someone is staring at them when they are alone. Several employees have actually seen the wraith, dressed in white, standing at the top of the stairs or at the window looking out at them. She often appears to be angry and seems very unhappy. Who is she? We may never know.

Victoria's Black Swan Inn 👹👹👹👹👹

1006 Holbrook Rd., San Antonio, TX 78218 • 210-590-2507

Description and History

This elegant white plantation home sits atop a grassy knoll that overlooks the Salado River. Indians occupied this area more than 7,000 years ago. The same area was the site of a second invasion of the Mexican army in September 1842. A historical marker detailing this conflict sits just in front of the gates of the Black Swan Inn.

German immigrants Heinrich and Marie Biermann Mahler built this mansion in 1901. The Mahlers ran a dairy farm here until the mid-1930s, when they sold the house and surrounding land to two sisters and their husbands. Katherine and John Holbrook, along with Blanche and Claude Woods, conducted extensive remodeling and enlarged the mansion to accommodate the two families. They called the house White Gables.

The Holbrooks had no children, but the Woods had a beautiful daughter named Joline. Joline married an attorney, Hall Park Street II; the couple raised their two children, Joline and Hall Park Street III, at White Gables. Mrs. Woods lived in the large house with them after her husband and the Holbrooks passed away.

The Streets lived a luxurious life in the house until Joline died of cancer in her late 30s. Her daughter Joline was only 19 at the time. Years later, after Hall Park Street remarried, he allegedly committed suicide by strangulation. His second wife found him at her home on Northridge Drive with a belt looped around his neck and a bedpost. He was 55 years old.

Joline Woods and her family remained in White Gables with her grandmother until the old woman passed away in 1973. Mrs. Ingeborg Mehren then bought the house. The Mehren House was refurbished to hold large dinners, conferences, and receptions until it was sold again in 1984. The house had several more owners until it was sold to Jo Ann Andrews in 1991 and converted into a restaurant and party house, which she named Victoria's Black Swan Inn. Today, Jo Ann owns the property with her husband, Robert Rivera. No visit to San Antonio would be complete without a visit to this lovely, spirit-filled mansion on the hill.

Ghostly Visitations

After only a few nights in the house in April 1991, Mrs. Rivera was awakened at exactly 3 a.m. for about 10 nights straight. Her bedroom door would unlock, the hall light would turn on, and a man dressed in a white shirt and dark slacks would stand at the foot of her bed, hands on hips, and stare at her before disappearing. Jo Ann changed the positioning of her bed and the troubling visits stopped.

> **Most Haunted Areas:**
> *The upstairs bedroom to the left of the stairs, the small bedroom in the south wing, and the Possum Flats Haberdashers shop*

Jo Ann's daughter, Meredith, has witnessed a frightening sight on rainy nights. She has awakened to find an old, wrinkled, "evil-looking" man staring through her second-story bedroom window, which is inaccessible to *humans*.

Most people in the house have felt a benign female presence in an upstairs bedroom to the left of the stairs. She is described as very beautiful, wearing a 1920s-style dress and a beaded headband with a feather at the back over her dark hair. Psychics have identified her as Joline Woods Street, who died from cancer at such a young age. Former owner Ingeborg Mehren uncovered a photograph of Joline Street serving as a San Antonio representative at a gala ball in Washington, D.C. She's wearing a beaded headband with a feather at the back!

Because of the nature of some of the manifestations, such as dolls in a collection being moved around during the night, the owners believe one of the spirits is that of a small girl. Her mischievous presence has been felt most frequently in the Possum Flats Haberdashers shop located behind the Black Swan, which specializes in authentically constructed clothing of the Victorian and Edwardian eras.

Psychics have also identified the elderly Mrs. Woods ensconced in a small bedroom in the south wing. She spent several years confined here before she had to be placed in a nursing home. There is a feeling of sadness here.

Recent reports include a visitor who witnessed the arrival and sudden "departure" of two gentlemen who entered the room where she was sitting, gazed at her, and disappeared. Employees hear the sounds of a music box, piano, and strange hammerings on a regular basis. There is also the apparition of a beautiful dark-haired woman in a white dress who walks out of the front door of the restaurant, down the front sidewalk, and disappears behind the gazebo. Mrs. Rivera said this happens so frequently that the staff hardly bats an eye.

In December 1996, the Sci-Fi Channel's television program *Sightings* visited this mansion with a psychic consultant, Peter James. James confirmed that the Black Swan is literally crawling with otherworldly visitors—four to six entities in all. He found a woman on the stairs, another in the main reception rooms, two spirits in the south wing, and another in a hallway. He also saw a man looking into a window. James confirmed the existence of a little girl spirit named "Sarah," but always called "Suzie," who pulls pranks in the Possum Flats Haberdashers shop. James also communicated with former resident Hall Park Street, whom he believed was murdered in a south wing closet, then moved to another location, where the murderer made the death look like a suicide. James believes Street was killed because of a treasure he still guards in the south wing.

 # SPIRITED BUILDINGS AND HOUSES

Hertzberg Circus Museum ☺☺☺
210 W. Market St., San Antonio, TX 78205 • 210-207-7810

Description and History
The San Antonio Public Library's Hertzberg collection of old circus memorabilia is housed here today. The museum was once the site of a large mansion that a wealthy Irishman built for his family. John McMullen was an influential citizen and successful businessman living in San Antonio just after the Battle of the Alamo was fought. One night, he was murdered by a thief who slipped into his house, bound and gagged McMullen, and slit his throat. The case was never solved. McMullen's ghost is believed to haunt the halls of the Hertzberg Museum.

This unique museum showcases more than 20,000 items of Big Top memorabilia, including Tom Thumb's carriage. Weekend special events include jugglers, mimes, and magicians. It is open Monday through Saturday from 10 a.m.- 5 p.m., and Sunday from 1 p.m.- 5 p.m. Admission is $2.50 for adults, $2 for seniors, and $1 for children; every Tuesday is free admission for all. For more information, call 210-207-7819.

The tortured ghost of a murdered man is believed to walk the halls of the Hertzberg Museum.

Ghostly Visitations

Ghostly activities include an overwhelming sense of presence, footsteps, the sound of keys jangling, books falling, and a strange light that moves between the stacks of books in the library on the second floor. Two employees

> **Most Haunted Areas:**
> *The second floor library and elevator*

witnessed an odd incident on the fifth floor late one night. They were unloading some displays from the elevator to be put into storage when they heard a loud banging on the elevator door coming from the sixth floor. They looked up through the elevator shaft to see the sixth-floor elevator door shaking under the attack of someone banging hard on the door. When the two men went up to the sixth floor to investigate, they were unable to find a culprit. Is this the ghost of McMullen coming back to the site of his murder? Or is it the phantom of a circus strong man or bearded lady still lurking around their personal effects?

 # Institute of Texan Cultures
801 S. Bowie St., San Antonio, TX 78205 • 210-458-2330

Description and History

Built in 1968 and owned by the University of Texas, the Institute of Texan Cultures encourages you to study the many ethnic groups that built the Lone Star State. The museum is located in HemisFair Park at the foot of the Tower of Americas at the corner of Bowie and Durango Streets. It is a multipurpose museum with rotating exhibits, classrooms, and teaching docents who make the rich texture of Texas culture come to life.

The Institute of Texan Cultures is a museum for the interpretation and assimilation of Texas history and folk culture. Guided tours are available. The Institute is open Tuesday through Sunday from 9 a.m.-5 p.m. and is closed Monday, Thanksgiving, and Christmas. For rates on the tours, call 210-458-2330, or visit the website at www.texancultures.utsa.edu.

Ghostly Visitations

Several specters seem to walk the corridors of this museum. One is thought to be the first director of the Institute, the late Henderson Shuffler. Shuffler was a distinguished

gentleman who enjoyed his pipe while working
at the Institute. Sam Nesmith, local psychic and
historian, reports that when he worked as a
researcher at the Institute, he would often come in

on Sunday mornings when he could be alone to get more work done. More often than not,
he would smell pipe smoke wafting out of Shuffler's old office. Many employees believe
Shuffler is just hanging around, making sure his museum continues to run smoothly.

Reports of "Old John" have persisted for the last 20 years. He hangs out near the
audiovisual room, where his footsteps are heard, and also likes to spend time rearranging
books in the museum library. Many security guards refuse to patrol the downstairs
exhibits alone because of the pervasive "creepy" feeling they attribute to the presence
of Old John. There are also stories of a ghost in an orange work shirt, thought to be a
construction worker who committed suicide while working on the building.

Downstairs, the French exhibit area houses a haunted hearse dating from 1898.
Security guards claim the back doors of the hearse refuse to stay locked. They often close and
secure the doors, continue on their rounds, and return to find the doors wide open again.

Finally, there is the poignant story of Gerald, who worked as a grounds maintenance
man at the museum for many years. Gerald had a mild mental handicap and was much
loved by the staff. One Friday evening, Gerald suffered a heart attack and died. Several
staff members came to work as usual the next day, not aware of Gerald's death the night
before. Throughout the day, employees were surprised to see Gerald all dressed up in a
tan suit and pretty blue tie. Most were used to seeing him in the dark green uniform
worn by the groundskeepers. A couple of the employees actually talked to Gerald and
complimented him on his attire. Later in the day, they discovered that Gerald had died
the night before and his funeral was scheduled for that day. Employees who attended the
funeral said Gerald looked really spiffy in his new tan suit and pretty blue tie.

 # Jose Antonio Navarro State Historical Park ☻☻☻

228 S. Laredo, San Antonio, TX 78207 • 210-226-4801

Description and History

The restored homestead of Jose Antonio Navarro, an early San Antonio mayor and
Texas leader in revolutions against both Spain and Mexico, this "compound" of buildings
consists of a one-story house, a two-story corner building, and a small adobe and limestone three-room building. The park is located in downtown San Antonio, on South
Laredo and West Nuevo Streets. Documents and exhibits capture the life and times of
this notable patriot. The homestead is maintained by the Texas Parks and Wildlife
Department. Jose was one of two native Texans to sign the Texas Declaration of
Independence; he and his wife, Margarita, lived on this property until Jose's death
in 1871.

The Jose Navarro State Historical Park is open August through January from 1p.m.-
4 p.m. Wednesday and Thursday, and 10 a.m.-4 p.m. Friday and Saturday. From Februar
through July, the home is open daily from 10 a.m.-4 p.m.

Ghostly Visitations

Several spirits are said to reside in Jose Navarro's homestead. According to David Bowser, author of *Mysterious San Antonio*, the one-story house itself is the hub of the psychic disturbances. The many manifestations include footsteps, cold

> **Most Haunted Areas:**
> *The kitchen and office buildings*

spots, rearranged furniture, and a rocking chair that rocks when there is no wind or draft. A state employee working on the restoration of the house awakened one night with a feeling of extreme uneasiness and walked outside for some fresh air. When he glanced upstairs, he saw a face staring down at him through an attic dormer window. He didn't get much sleep that night.

Psychic Sam Nesmith visited the house and sensed the presence of a wounded man in the kitchen building. Nesmith said the man had bled to death in this room while waiting for help long ago. History tells us that Jose's brother Eugenio was the victim of a murder that took place on the property.

Additional sightings include a Confederate soldier, a bartender, and a prostitute who was murdered in the room over the main floor of the old corner office building during the time it served as a bar. There are also reports of a child who died in a fire on the second floor whose ghost is seen in this area of the office building.

Interestingly enough, none of the observed apparitions appears to be that of Jose Antonio Navarro. He must be resting peacefully, pleased with the way the Texas Parks and Wildlife Department is taking care of his house.

 # San Pedro Playhouse 👻👻
800 W. Ashby, San Antonio, TX 78201 • 210-733-7258

Description and History
The San Pedro Playhouse is the home of the San Antonio Little Theater.

Ghostly Visitations

According to local newspaper accounts, one of the ghosts haunting this theater is a stocky man of medium build, balding, and rather elderly. He wears a white shirt with the sleeves rolled up.

> **Most Haunted Area:**
> *On grids high above the stage*

Several of the actors and employees of the playhouse have also reported seeing a man dressed in military fatigues walking along the grids high above the stage. The identities of the soldier and the stocky man are unknown.

Spanish Governor's Palace 👶👶

105 Plaza de Armas, San Antonio, TX 78205 • 210-224-0601

Description and History

Completed in 1749, the Spanish Governor's Palace is one of the finest examples of Spanish Colonial residential architecture in the United States. Currently, the palace faces the *Plaza Del Armas* (Military Plaza). It's filled with antiques of the Spanish Colonial period as well as authentic fireplaces, room arrangements, and brick ovens, which literally transport you back to the eighteenth century, when this building was used as a house. Over the years, it has also been used as a secondhand clothing store, tailor's shop, bar, restaurant, and schoolhouse. One of the most prized antiques you'll see is the beautiful hand-carved secretary desk in the front bedchamber, once owned by the famous Alamo defender James Bowie. The Spanish Governor's Palace is one of the city's most visited landmarks and is operated by the Department of Parks and Recreation of the City of San Antonio.

The museum is open Monday through Saturday from 9 a.m.-5 p.m., and Sunday from 10 a.m.-5 p.m. Admission is $1 for adults, $.50 for children 7 and older, and free to children under 7.

Ghostly Visitations

Behind the house sits a 37-foot well that once provided drinking water to the occupants. Although it is now used by tourists as a wishing well, there is a terrible story attached to

> **Most Haunted Area:**
> *The haunted well*

it. Long ago, robbers broke into the house when the family was away, leaving only a servant girl to defend the family treasures. The thieves bound the girl and threw her into the well; she eventually drowned in the deep, dark hole. The present custodian tells of strange "gurgling" sounds that he hears emanating from the well as he locks up late at night. Employees report feeling someone is watching them while they are alone in the house and feeling cold spots throughout the building.

A grisly discovery was made during the 1930 restoration of the museum. In the front room to the right of the entryway, a tiny infant's skeleton lay buried in the wall. No one knows who this baby may have been or why the bones were buried here instead of a cemetery. The burial spot in the wall, behind a statue of a seventeenth-century virgin, is plainly visible.

Witte Memorial Museum of History and Science 👶👶

3801 Broadway, San Antonio, TX 78209 • 210-357-1900

Description and History

Opened in 1926, the Witte Museum was named for a stockbroker, Alfred G. Witte, who gave the city a large sum of money with instructions to build a museum for the people in Brackenridge Park. Ellen Schultz Quillin was the first director and the curator of the museum, which boasts several wonderfully eclectic collections, including its historic San Antonio Fiesta gowns, Texas wildlife dioramas, and dinosaur exhibit. Several old pioneer

The attic of the Witte Museum is the most paranormally active area.

homes have been reconstructed on the banks of the San Antonio River, which runs behind the museum.

This regional museum features history, science, the humanities, exciting hands-on exhibits of Texas history, natural science and anthropology, changing exhibits, and family programs. Permanent exhibits include "Texas Wild: Ecology Illustrated," focusing on the ecological diversity of the state's seven natural areas, and "Ancient Texans: Rock Art and Life Ways Along the Lower Pecos," focusing on the culture and cave paintings of a hunter-gatherer society that flourished in Texas 4,000 years ago. The museum also includes an EcoLab of live Texas animals, an outdoor Butterfly and Hummingbird Garden, and three restored historic homes.

The museum is open Monday, Wednesday, and Saturday from 10 a.m.-6 p.m., Tuesday 10 a.m.-9 p.m., and Sunday noon-5 p.m. It is open until 6 p.m. Memorial Day through Labor Day, and is closed Thanksgiving, Christmas Eve, and Christmas Day. General admission is $5.95 for adults, $4.95 for senior citizens, $3.95 for children 4-11; children 3 and under are admitted free of charge. Admission is free for everyone on Tuesday from 3 p.m.-9 p.m. For more information, visit the website at www.wittemuseum.org.

Ghostly Visitations

Most employees agree that the female apparition strolling the halls of the Witte is the first director of the museum, Ellen Schultz Quillin. Quillin came to San Antonio to teach

> **Most Haunted Area:**
> *The attic*

school in 1916. Through her efforts to raise money with her students, she succeeded in securing $75,000 from Alfred G. Witte to build the museum. Quillin served as acting director for 34 years before she died in 1970 at age 80.

She seems to be very fond of the attic, which was once used as the library. Research was her first love, and she spent many happy hours here. Furniture has been heard scraping across the attic floor, but no source is found. Footsteps on the stairs leading up to the attic have also been reported on numerous occasions. Cold spots have been felt and glimpses of a figure have been reported. One employee was in the attic alone one afternoon and claims to have felt a bony hand on his shoulder. Most believe Quillin is just keeping tabs on the museum's development—her dedication in life survived and persists in death.

Yturri-Edmunds Home 👁️👁️

128 Mission Rd., San Antonio, TX 78210 • 210-534-8237

Description and History

Manuel Yturri-Castillo obtained a land grant from the Mexican government and constructed this quaint three-room adobe house in 1824. The home is located across the San Antonio River from the grounds of the Lone Star Brewery at Mission Road and Yellowstone Street. When Yturri-Castillo died, he left the house to his daughter, Vicenta. Vicenta and her husband, Ernest Edmunds, added three more rooms to the structure and started a family. Edmunds died the day Vicenta gave birth to his third child, Ernestine. Vicenta was left with the new baby and two small children, Josephine and Edgar. Vicenta used her fluency in English, Spanish, and French to become a teacher at Mission Concepcion. She also held classes at her adobe home for the neighborhood children.

Ernestine followed in her mother's footsteps and embarked upon a teaching career that would span 50 years. "Miss Ernestine" never married and lived with her mother and spinster sister, Josephine, until their deaths in 1924. Ernestine continued to live in the house until she died in 1961 at the age of 87. She willed her property to the San Antonio Conservation Society, which operates a museum here today. The Yturri-Edmunds Home is open by appointment only. Call 210-534-8237 to arrange a tour.

Ghostly Visitations

Many Conservation Society members report feeling a presence in the house that could be any one of the three women who loved it so dearly in life. Since many of

Most Haunted Area:
Throughout the house

Ernestine's belongings are displayed throughout the house, members believe the phantom presence is Miss Ernestine. Cold spots are felt throughout the house, and docents have caught fleeting glimpses of someone or something in their peripheral vision. Many have described feeling sad and depressed when in the house, which has led employees to believe the ghost misses her mother and sister in death.

FRIGHTENING FORTS AND BATTLEGROUNDS

The Alamo 👁️👁️👁️👁️👁️

300 Alamo Plaza, San Antonio, TX 78205 • 210-225-1391

Description and History

The Alamo is the site of one of the most famous battles in American history, the valiant fight for Texas's independence from Mexico, and is also the state's most haunted mission/fort. Originally, the Alamo was built in 1718 as a Franciscan mission, known as *San Antonio De Valero*. The mission served as home to missionaries and their Indian converts for nearly 70 years. In 1724, construction began on the present site, which is now in the heart of downtown San Antonio.

More than a century later, in 1836, the spot was an outpost for a brave group of Texas defenders led by William B. Travis, Jim Bowie, and David Crockett—all determined to defeat the Mexican army, which outnumbered them nine to one. On March 6, after 13 days of siege, the Mexican forces, led by General Antonio Lopez de Santa Anna, overran the Alamo and

The Alamo, the most haunted mission/fort in Texas, is the focus of paranormal activity in San Antonio.

killed every armed defender at the outpost. Santa Anna ordered that all 184 bodies be dumped into a mass grave and left orders that the Alamo itself be torn down to the ground. Bodies smoldered for several days in two large funeral pyres erected on either side of the Alamo. The bodies of many Mexican soldiers were dumped into the San Antonio River.

There is no doubt what the battle has come to symbolize for Texans and others all over the world. People remember the Alamo as a heroic struggle against overwhelming odds. For this reason, the Alamo remains hallowed ground and the Shrine of Texas Liberty.

Many psychics believe the paranormal activity surrounding the Alamo in the heart of the city is due to the bloody battle fought here over 100 years ago. This fight for Texas Independence resulted in a tremendous loss of life, and thousands of dead soldiers were not given a proper burial. The land surrounding the Alamo is also the site of an ancient Indian burial ground. The Alamo grounds, both sacred and tragic, have produced an enormous amount of paranormal activity.

The Alamo is open Monday through Saturday from 9 a.m.-5:30 p.m., and Sunday from 10 a.m.-5:30 p.m.; during the summer months, it stays open until 6:30 p.m. The Alamo is closed December 24 and 25 and has restricted hours in March. A general admission fee, donated to the Daughters of the Republic of Texas, which maintains the Alamo, is appreciated. For more information, visit the website at http://thealamo.org.

Ghostly Visitations

Reports of ghostly sightings, disembodied voices, and an otherworldly presence have been experienced by so many for so many years that the Alamo reigns supreme as the most haunted site in San Antonio. The first tale of

Most Haunted Areas:
The Long Barracks and the Alamo Gift Shop

supernatural apparitions at the Alamo occurred just a few days after the famous battle for Texas independence. Ordered by Santa Anna to destroy the mission, Mexican engineers fled in fear after ghostly hands protruded from the walls to stop them. Some of the phantom hands held glowing "torches," and a thundering voice called out, promising a horrible death to anyone who desecrated the walls. The paranormal phenomena continue today.

A boy has been seen staring sadly from this window.

The most famous ghost in residence at the Alamo is believed to be none other than Hollywood legend John Wayne In the late 1950s, the "Duke" decided to direct a movie called *The Alamo*, which embodied his own life philosophy. He spent $1.5 million dollars re-creating the Alamo in Brackettville, just a few miles outside San Antonio.

During filming, Wayne became obsessed with the area, the history of the battle, and the heroic defenders he greatly admired. Many visiting psychics have described his presence in the mission. One even estimated that Wayne returns to the shrine about once a month to visit with the defenders' spirits who still reside here.

Another famous resident is frontiersman Davy Crockett, who has been observed carrying a rifle and strolling outside the Long Barracks dressed in buckskin clothing. He wears his traditional coonskin cap and moccasins. Crockett's portrait in the chapel has been found askew when rangers open the mission for the day. The painting hangs 10 feet up and cannot be reached by *human* hands.

One of the hottest areas for paranormal activity is the Long Barracks of the Alamo complex. It was here that the defenders made their last futile stand against Santa Anna's advancing army. Rangers have heard ghostly whispers and murmurs as well as emotional voices yelling, "No! Stop! Here they come! Fire! Dead!" and the most poignant, "It's too late!" Psychics have described the resident spirits as not only those of Texans but also several Mexican soldiers. Disembodied footsteps have followed guards as they make their late-night rounds through the barracks; one ranger reported he was kicked in the behind by an unseen force.

One of the most frightening encounters in the Long Barracks occurred after closing when a ranger entered a room to find a man dressed in buckskin leaning against a wall, bleeding from several bullet wounds. The phantom grimaced in pain as several Mexican soldiers materialized and began stabbing him with their bayonets. In the blink of an eye, the grisly scene vanished, leaving the guard extremely shaken and sad.

The informative book *Haunted Alamo,* by Robert and Anne Powell Wlodarski, cites the "wall of tears" as a particularly touching manifestation that occurred not long ago in the basement of the Alamo Gift Shop. On February 27 and 28, 1995, five employees were conducting an inventory in the basement of the gift shop. For two days the sound of a woman weeping accompanied their work. The sounds seemed to come from the surrounding walls. Two employees became so stricken with sadness that they could not remain in the basement. Others reported feeling watched and saw strange shadows creep across the walls Several woman and children were present in the Alamo during the bloody battle, and all lost loved ones. Does at least one woman remain still mourning her loss?

Another specter who frequents the gift shop is a small blond boy who stares despondently down from a window overlooking the courtyard. Many tourists and employees have seen the boy, who appears most often during the first few weeks of February. One psychic claimed the boy had been in charge of caring for the cattle at the Alamo and remained because of the enormous amount of guilt he carried regarding the outcome of the battle. The child believed he should have done something more to participate and contribute during the fighting.

The ghostly figure of a man gazing out of the window over the chapel doorway has been captured on film by a passing tourist. The specter has been spotted on several occasions by other tourists and rangers.

Numerous rangers have witnessed ghostly apparitions of men in 1800s homespun clothing walking from the chapel to various destinations on the grounds. The rangers always assumed them be trespassers, and are quick to approach the "intruders," only to have them disappear into thin air. Many believe these wraiths to be the spirits of the defenders of the Alamo. One could speculate just who the "real" intruders are here.

GHOSTLY MISSIONS AND CHURCHES

San Antonio Missions National Historical Park Visitor's Center

6701 San Jose Dr., San Antonio, TX 78214 • 210-932-1001

Park Hours and Admission

The National Park is home to three missions: Mission San Jose de San Miguel de Aguayo, Mission San Francisco de la Espada, and Mission San Juan de Capistrano. The missions are open Monday through Sunday from 9 a.m.-5 p.m. and are closed January 1, Thanksgiving Day, and Christmas Day. Admission is free but donations are accepted.

Mission San Jose de San Miguel de Aguayo 👁️👁️

Description and History

Founded in 1720, the Mission San Jose de San Miguel de Aguayo was named for Saint Joseph and the Marques de San Miguel de Aguayo, the governor of the Province of Coahuila and Texas at the time. The Mission San Jose offers visitors the finest example of the architecture of early Spanish colonial days through its meticulous restoration. Father Antonio Margil de Jesus, a very prominent Franciscan missionary in early Texas, founded the Mission San Jose. For more information, visit the website at www.nps.gov/saan/visit/missionsanjose.htm.

Ghostly Visitations

The Mission San Jose de San Miguel de Aguayo is haunted by the large headless figure of a monk or priest who walks the moonlit courtyard and the

Most Haunted Area:
The courtyard

inner confines of the mission. No one is sure who this monk is, but sightings of him have persisted for years.

There have also been reports of a huge black dog seen in the vicinity of the mission. Several people have been chased by the animal, which seems to grow bigger the longer it chases you.

Who is the headless figure in Mission San Jose?

 # Mission San Francisco de la Espada

Description and History

Founded in 1690, San Francisco de los Tejas was the first mission in Texas. In 1731, the mission was moved to its present location and renamed San Francisco de la Espada. For more information, visit the website at: www.nps.gov/saan/visit/missionespada.htm.

An Indian spirit has been seen at Mission San Francisco.

Ghostly Visitations

Believe it or not, a large, hairy, black dog or wolf with a broken chain dangling from its neck is said to frequent the grounds of this

Most Haunted Area:
The chapel

mission. Is it the same beast that patrols the Mission San Jose? The animal has been seen by numerous priests living at the mission. In addition, the apparition of an Indian clad in full ceremonial regalia has been sighted near the altar in the chapel.

Mission San Juan de Capistrano ☻

Description and History

Founded in March 1731, this lovely church was given the name of San Juan Capistrano in honor of a priest from Italy. This saint was famous as a chaplain of the Yugoslovian troops who were victorious over a Turkish invasion in the fifteenth-century. Ordinarily, chaplains did not wear armor but the little statue of San Juan on the altar at this mission wears a suit of armor over his priest's robe, and one of his feet rests on a decapitated head.

The small chapel seats about 100 people. For more information, visit the website at www.nps.gov/saan/visit/missionsanjuan.htm.

Ghostly Visitations

Late one afternoon in 1994, a couple touring the mission found themselves alone in the chapel.

Most Haunted Area:
The chapel

Suddenly, an Indian materialized, stood beside the altar, and watched them intently for a few seconds, then disappeared before their startled eyes.

Photo courtesy of the National Park Service, San Antonio

While at the Mission San Juan de Capistrano, look for a ghostly Indian in the chapel.

GHOSTS OF THE GREAT OUTDOORS

Villa Main Railroad Tracks 👹👹

Description and History

One of the most persistent ghost stories circulating around San Antonio is the haunting of the Villa Main railroad tracks south of town. The tracks are located far south of San Antonio at the railroad crossing at Villa Main Street on a small hill near the Stinson Airport; Villa Main Street turns into Shane Road on the other side of the tracks. The facts of the story are not supported by old newspaper reports, but the tale is so prevalent that there must be something to it.

The Villa Main railroad tracks are haunted by the spirits of 10 children.

As the story goes, late on a rainy autumn afternoon in the 1930s or 1940s, a school bus carrying 10 children (ranging from kindergartners to teenagers) stalled on the Villa Main tracks. A fast-moving train was unable to stop in time and hit the bus before it could be evacuated. All the children were killed.

As a memorial to the deceased, a small neighborhood just down Shane Road from the tracks named all the streets after the doomed children. Today, you can drive through streets with names such as Bobbie Allen, Richey Otis, Nancy Carole, Laura Lee Way, and Cindy Sue.

Ghostly Visitations

The ghosts of the dead children haunt this rural railroad crossing. It is said that the ghosts try to push cars across the tracks to safety. Motorists can stop their cars 50 yards from the tracks, put the car in neutral, remove pressure from the gas and brake, and the car will roll toward and over the tracks even though there is a slight incline. In 1995, hosts of a national television show sprinkled baby powder on a car parked at the tracks. In front of their cameras, a child's handprint appeared.

Residents of the nearby neighborhood report the sounds of crying and moaning coming from the general vicinity of the tracks on late afternoons. A general feeling of sadness pervades the area.

The following story appeared in the *San Antonio Express News* magazine section on November 26, 1989. Written by David A. Burnett, it details an eerie encounter he had while driving home from work on February 13, 1981. In Burnett's own words, "As I was driving along, I noticed a young girl who couldn't have been any older than 15 at the edge of old Mission Road. It was cold, and I'd always thought the area was kind of spooky, so I asked her if she needed a ride home. She said yes. She told me that her name was Cindy Sue and that she lived off Villa Main Road.

"I wondered what a girl her age was doing out so late. She was quiet to the point of giving me the creeps. She said nothing as we drove along, but I could see through the corner of my eye that she was looking at me.

"We approached some old railroad tracks. As we went across, Cindy Sue started squirming in her seat. I asked her what was wrong. She said 'nothing.' As we arrived at her house, she remained in the car. I quickly assumed she was having problems at home, so I told her I would talk to her parents.

"I rang the doorbell and an elderly man and woman answered the door. I expected her parents to be much younger. They both looked at me as if I was crazy when I said Cindy Sue was in my car. The elderly man became upset and told me to get off his property or he would call the police. As I walked back to the car, he yelled, 'Quit doing this to us. Let Cindy Sue rest in peace.'

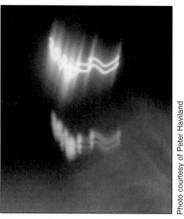

Photo of vortex taken near the Villa Main railroad tracks.

"When I got back to the car, Cindy Sue was gone. I never heard the car door open or shut; she just vanished. I remember that when she got into the car, she locked the door and fastened her seat belt. To my disbelief, the door was still locked and the seat belt still fastened."

SPOOKY SIDELINES

Hauntings History Tours

The walking tours through downtown San Antonio take you to some of the most haunted locations in town. The tour is about a mile long and lasts for an hour and a half. Tours start nightly at 8:30 p.m. at the Alamo defenders monument (the Cenotaph) in front of the Alamo. The cost is $10 per person. Groups of 10 or more should call for special rates and tour times. Prices and tour times are subject to change without notice; call 210-436-5417 for more information.

Spirits of San Antonio

The ghost tours are hosted by Docia Williams, a local historian and author of six books on the supernatural, including *Spirits of San Antonio and South Texas* and *When Darkness Falls*. These bus tours must be reserved in advance for groups of 30 or more. The cost per person is $36. The tour departs from a local haunt, the Alamo Street Restaurant and Theatre. Inquire at the restaurant (see page 218).

Less Spooky Things To Do In San Antonio

The **Paseo Del Rio (Riverwalk)** winds through the city, its foliage lining the banks of this historic river. Cobblestone walkways lead visitors past retail shops, restaurants, and nightclubs. Theme parks such as **Sea World** and **Six Flags Fiesta Texas** tempt entire families to the bustling city. The **Tower of the Americas** offers a panoramic view of San Antonio and the surrounding area through glass-walled elevators that ascend to the restaurant and observation level. Art lovers can't miss a walk around **La Villita**, an arts and crafts community with shops, restaurants, and a post office. This landscaped historic district offers shopping and dining options.

For more information on San Antonio, contact:
San Antonio Convention and Visitors Bureau
121 Alamo Plaza at Commerce, P.O. Box 2277
San Antonio, TX 78298
800-447-3372
www.sanantoniocvb.com

Elusive Boos of South Texas

Your trip to South Texas will include many of the oldest and most historically significant towns and battlefields in the state. Hopefully, you'll also see a ghost or two along the way!

Chamade Jewelry Store, La Villita

504 Villita St., San Antonio, TX 78205 • 210-224-7753

We talked to some employees who reported mysterious noises and cold spots in this historic building.

Courthouse in Gonzales

This spot is haunted by the spirit of a condemned man who was hanged on the gallows behind this old courthouse.

Grey Moss Inn, Helotes

19010 Scenic Loop Rd., Helotes, TX 78023 • 210-695-8301

Three spirits—Mary Howell, an Indian maiden, and an unidentified man—are all said to haunt the restaurant. The Grey Moss Inn is the oldest continuously operating restaurant in South Texas.

Ghost Clubs of South Texas

 With all of the ghosts that the most haunted city in Texas "possesses," it is a good thing that there are two active ghost organizations operating in the San Antonio area.

Alamo City Paranormal

302 Surrels Ave., San Antonio, TX 78228 • 210-436-5417

Alamo City Paranormal, headed by Martin Leal, is based in San Antonio. Leal is an invaluable resource for our group, the Capital City Ghost Research Society, and has come to Austin for several investigations and activities. He is an expert in the use of ghost-hunting equipment such as electromagnetic field meters and thermoscanners. Leal also gives haunted walking tours of downtown San Antonio. Their website is at www.webspawner.com/users/mleal.

San Antonio Paranormal

San Antonio Paranormal has photographs and investigation details posted on the website at www.saparanormal.com.

Appendix I

Ghost Investigative Report *page 1*

 Before you embark upon your haunted vacation, make copies of this report and take them with you. Upon completion of an investigation, send a copy of your report to the author (e-mail: ghostlyguide@austinrr.com) and your local ghost club. Or, if you don't have a ghost club in your area, why not start your own?

Date: _____ *Time*: _____

Exact location (Include location within building, or outdoor location, city, and state.):

_____

_____

Weather conditions (dry, rainy, foggy, clear, windy, calm, etc.):

_____

_____

Temperature: _____

Moon phase (Circle one.):   FULL   HALF   QUARTER   NEW

Duration of sighting: _____

Electromagnetic field (EMF) measurement: _____

Were there other people who witnessed the paranormal event? _____
If so, how many and who? (Each witness should complete a separate report.)

_____

_____

_____

_____

Were there other people present who didn't witness the paranormal event?
If so, how many and who?

_____

Ghost Investigative Report page 2

Describe your experience with the following:

1. Background location information (historical data you may obtain at a later date):

_____

_____

_____

_____

_____

2. Describe your reaction to the ghost (Include physical reactions, such as feeling chilled, nauseous, dizzy, agitated, etc., as well as mental/emotional reactions.):

_____

_____

_____

_____

_____

3. Describe the ghost (visible or invisible; audible or silent; orb, vortex, mist, or apparition; opaque or transparent; entirely or partially visible; discernible facial and clothing features, etc.):

_____

_____

_____

_____

_____

_____

_____

_____

Ghost Investigative Report *page 3*

4. *Circle/describe the emotional characteristics or personality of the ghost* (These may also manifest as feelings that wash over you during the experience.):

ACTIVE	FRIENDLY	NOISY
AFFECTIONATE	GENTLE	PATIENT
ALERT	GREEDY	QUIET
ANGRY	HAPPY	SAD
ANXIOUS	HELPFUL	SHY
BITTER	HUMOROUS	STRONG
CALM	IMPATIENT	TOLERANT
COLD	INDEPENDENT	TRUSTING
COMPLAINING	IRRITABLE	WARM
CONFUSED	MISCHIEVOUS	WEAK
FEARFUL	MOODY	

Describe: _____

_____

_____

_____

_____

5. *Describe the ghost's activity* (Circle all that apply.):

STANDING STILL	COMING TOWARD YOU	MOVING IN CIRCLE
FLOATING	MOVING AWAY FROM YOU	PACING
FLYING	WANDERING AIMLESSLY	DANCING
TURNING A CORNER	LOOKING OUT A WINDOW	RUNNING
WALKING	LOOKING FOR SOMETHING	GLIDING
SITTING	TRYING TO COMMUNICATE	LYING DOWN

Other: _____

Ghost Investigative Report page 4

6. Was there communication between you and the ghost? (verbal, telepathic, visual cues, writing, etc.)

_____

_____

_____

_____

_____

_____

_____

7. Was there more than one ghost? _____

_____

_____

_____

_____

8. How did the ghost leave or the experience end? _____

_____

_____

_____

_____

_____

_____

_____

Appendix II

Bibliography and Reading List

 The following list includes books and articles used as source materials for this book, as well as some great ghostly reads. Dig into them before, or bring them along on, your haunted vacation.

Books

Buckner, Sharry. *The Great Stays of Texas: The Official Guide to Texas Finest Historic Bed & Breakfasts, Country Inns, Hotels, and Guest Houses*. Fredericksburg, Texas: Historic Accommodations of Texas, Inc., 1998.

Drago, Gail; Marjie Mugno Acheson; and Lyn Dunsavage. *Texas Bed and Breakfasts*. Houston, Texas: Lone Star Books, 1999.

Fowler, Zinita. *Ghost Stories of Old Texas, II*. Austin, Texas: Eakin Press, 1992.

Hauck, Dennis William. *The National Directory of Haunted Places: Ghostly Abodes, Sacred Sites, UFO Landings, and Other Supernatural Locations*. New York: Penguin Books, 1996.

Holzer, Hans. *Life Beyond: Compelling Evidence for Past Lives and Existence After Death*. Chicago: Contemporary Books, 1994.

Rodriguez, June Naylor. *Off the Beaten Path*. Old Saybrook, Connecticut: The Globe Pequot Press, 1997.

Syers, Ed. *Ghost Stories of Texas*. Waco, Texas: Texian Press, 1981.

Texas State Travel Guide. Austin, Texas: State Department of Highways and Public Transportation, n.d.

Turner, Allan and Richard Stewart. *Transparent Tales: An Attic Full of Texas Ghosts*. Lufkin, Texas: Best of East Texas Publishers, 1998.

Williams, Docia Schultz. *Best Tales of Texas Ghosts*. Plano, Texas: Republic of Texas Press, 1998.

Williams, Docia Schultz. *Ghosts Along the Texas Coast*. Plano, Texas: Wordware Publishing, Inc., 1995.

Williams, Docia Schultz. *Phantoms of the Plains: Tales of West Texas Ghosts*. Plano, Texas: Republic of Texas Press, 1996.

Williams, Docia Schultz and Reneta Byrne. *Spirits of San Antonio and South Texas*. Plano, Texas: Republic of Texas Press, 1993.

Williams, Docia Schultz. *When Darkness Falls: Tales of San Antonio Ghosts and Hauntings*. Plano, Texas: Republic of Texas Press, 1997.

Wlodarski, Robert and Anne Powell. *The Haunted Alamo: A History of the Mission and Guide to Paranormal Activity*. Calabasas, California: G-HOST PUBLISHING, 1996.

Newspaper and Magazine Articles

Bigony, Mary Love. "In the Spirit: State Park Ghosts Wish You a Happy Halloween." *Texas State Parks and Wildlife Magazine* (October 1988).

Burnett, David A. *San Antonio Express News* (November 26, 1989).

Bustin, John. "The Paramount Theater Was Once Majestic." *Austin American-Statesman* (December 1971).

Cuellar, Catherine. "Favorite Haunts." *Dallas Morning News* (October 31, 1999).

Free and Easy, vol. 1, no. 6 (1974).

Grieser, Andy. "The Haunting of Thistle Hill." *Fort Worth Star Telegram* (October 23, 1997).

Kooris, Eli. "The Grimes Ghost Project: Things That Go Bump." *Austin Chronicle* (October 29, 1999).

Matsumoto, Lisa; Roberto Rivera; and Kelly West. "Ghost Stories Abound in the Capital City and Give a Spooky Twist to Texas History." *Daily Texan* (October 29, 1999).

San Antonio Monthly Magazine (October 1981).

Society of Architectural Historians, Texas Chapter, vol. 2, no. 1 (Fall 1991).

Syers, Ed. *San Antonio Express News* (September 24, 1981).

Tewes, David. *Victoria Advocate* (November 8, 1992).

Waco Semi-Weekly Tribune (July 16, 1916).

"With Students or Exes—Old Seville is Tops." *Daily Texan* (March 12, 1944).

"Witte's Ghost." *San Antonio Express News* (July 3, 1988).

Wolff, Henry. "Ghost Hunters Tap Into Spirits in Goliad." *Victoria Advocate* (February 12, 2000).

Appendix III

Ghostly Websites

Fortunately for ghost lovers, many information-rich websites are available for browsing on a stormy night. The following listings include my own website, a few of my favorites, and sites of Texas ghost clubs.

Alamo City Paranormal
www.webspawner.com/users/mleal

Alamo City Paranormal, based in San Antonio, is headed by Martin Leal. He has been an invaluable resource for our group, the Capital City Ghost Research Society, coming to Austin for several investigations and activities. Martin is an expert in the use of ghost hunting equipment such as electromagnetic field meters and thermoscanners. He also gives haunted walking tours of downtown San Antonio.

ARK-LA-TEX Ghost Hunters
http://mypage.goplay.com/arklatexghosts

As its name suggests, this club lists on its website hauntings in Arkansas, Louisiana, and Texas (eastern region).

El Paso Ghost Research
http://members.delphi.com/epgr/index.html

As the only active group of ghost hunters in West Texas, members of the El Paso Ghost Research team have their work cut out for them. Edward Weissbard and Heidi Crabtree were very helpful in providing information on haunted El Paso for this book, and they conduct regular investigations in and around the El Paso area.

Fort Bend County (FBC) Paranormal
www.angelfire.com/tx2/hauntedsugarland

Nichole Dobrowolski's group, Fort Bend County Paranormal, is based in Sugar Land and conducts paranormal investigations in Fort Bend County, Brazoria County, Harris County, and the Houston area. The club's website includes some interesting photographs of ghostly mists, orbs, and vortexes captured at various haunted locations in this part of Texas. Nichole encourages paranormal buffs to correspond with FBC Paranormal regarding supernatural encounters and is happy to answer questions about the paranormal.

Ghost Hunters Inc.
www.angelfire.com/tx3/ghosthtml

A central Texas-based group, Ghost Hunters Inc. is dedicated to discovering scientific proof that ghosts exist, while at the same time enjoying the hunt!

Ghost Stalkers
www.ghoststalkers.com

The two founders of this group have a combined 12 years of experience in hunting ghosts. Both have backgrounds in photographic and film production, making spirit photography and filming a specialty. Ghost hunts have taken this Fort Worth-based team all over the world.

Ghostly Guide/Capital City Ghost Research Society
www.ghostlyguide.com

Through Ghostly Guide, the website for my series of haunted travel guides, I would like to hear about your paranormal experiences. Log on to my website to send me an e-mail about your encounter and to get comprehensive ghostly activity updates for the public places listed in *Haunted Texas Vacations: The Complete Ghostly Guide*. You will find links to all of my favorite ghost websites, as well as the stories behind haunted places I've visited all over the world while researching the Ghostly Guide series of haunted travel guides.

Ghostly Guide contains a link to information about my ghost club, the Capital City Ghost Research Society, based in Austin, Texas. The mission of the CCGRS is to provide a forum for people who are interested in ghosts, supernatural activity, and hauntings to meet and discuss Austin-area hauntings, plan and participate in investigations, and provide information to the public about these haunted places. The CCGRS meets once every month at a haunted Austin locale to discuss upcoming activities and share a spirit or two!

Ghosts of the Prairie/American Ghost Society
www.prairieghosts.com

Troy Taylor's Ghosts of the Prairie website is home base for the American Ghost Society. Troy has a library of books on ghosts and hauntings available to purchase via the Web, plus a wealth of information about hauntings all over the United States.

Ghostweb/International Ghost Hunters Society
www.ghostweb.com/index.html

For ghost researchers, ghost hunters, and ghost believers, the International Ghost Hunters Society has created Ghostweb. This website contains everything there is to know about ghosts and how to hunt them. Hundreds of anomalous photographs are posted, and ghost-hunting equipment is available to purchase.

Haunted Places
www.haunted-places.com

The author of *The National Directory of Haunted Places*, Dennis William Hauck, has created a wonderful site called Haunted Places. It's packed with information about all things ghostly. Included are case reports of paranormal activity currently occurring all over the country, plus a list of international haunted places.

Invisible Ink
www.invink.com

Invisible Ink is a one-of-a-kind online catalog offering ghost fans a huge selection of mostly nonfiction books on ghosts and hauntings from all over the world. Shoppers also can locate and buy hard-to-find videos and audiotapes.

Lone Star Spirits Paranormal Investigations
www.lonestarspirits.org

Lone Star Spirits researchers have conducted several investigations in and around Houston. They've captured some remarkable anomalies on film in several of the haunted buildings located in Spring, known as the most haunted town along the Texas coast. The website is highly informative, with lists of haunted locations, ghostly tales, and a networking area where you can find other ghost hunters in your corner of Texas. The Lone Star Spirits website is one of the most comprehensive of the Texas ghost club sites on the Internet today.

Otherworld Investigations
http://home.flash.net/~brockam/paranorm.html

Affiliated with the Philadelphia Ghost Hunters Alliance, members of Otherworld Investigations describe themselves as "intrepid freelance investigators in the field of parapsychology."

Paranormal Research Society of North Texas
www.geocities.com/ladellpepper

I really like the acronym this group uses—SPOOKS, or Supernatural Phenomenon Organization of Kindred Spirits. SPOOKS is especially interested in Texas urban legends and their origins.

San Antonio Paranormal
www.saparanormal.com

Photographs and investigation details are posted on the San Antonio Paranormal website.

The Shadowlands: Ghosts and Hauntings
theshadowlands.net/ghost/

The Shadowlands website features more than 1,500 ghostly experiences as submitted by visitors, free photo and sound (EVP) gallery, ghost-hunting training information, thousands of local haunted places listed by state, and a moderated message board.

Index

Note: Citations followed by the letter "m" denote maps; citations followed by the letter "p" denote photos. Specific haunted places do not appear on maps, only the towns they are located in.